W9-ACY-657

To Isabel and Edith

Islam and Pakistan

Mosque in Islamabad, capital of Pakistan. The dome of this mosque is a modern expression of the traditional forms to be found in the domes of the Star Mosque, the Pearl Mosque, and the seventeenth-century Badshahi Mosque. (Courtesy of the *Pakistan Quarterly*.)

Islam and Pakistan

By FREELAND ABBOTT

BP
63
.P2
A62

BP63.P2A62   ST. JOSEPH'S UNIVERSITY   STX

Cornell University Press

ITHACA, NEW YORK

98144

Copyright © 1968 by Cornell University

All rights reserved. Except for brief quotations in a review, this book, or parts thereof, must not be reproduced
in any form without permission in writing from the pub-
lisher. For information address Cornell University Press,
124 Roberts Place, Ithaca, New York 14850.

First published 1968

Library of Congress Catalog Card Number: 67–23757

PRINTED IN THE UNITED STATES OF AMERICA
BY THE COLONIAL PRESS INC.

Preface

The founder of Pakistan, Mohamed Ali Jinnah, frequently said that the Muslims of India could not hope for security until they had achieved their own sovereign government. The Muslims were doomed to be a minority in a Hindu-dominated India; their only recourse was to get out. It was not long before this initial appeal for a state for Muslims became voiced as an appeal for an "Islamic state." But there were nearly as many definitions of the "Islamic state" as there were individuals defining it.

Whatever an Islamic state was, its creation obviously depended upon an understanding of the nature of Islam, the religion of the Muslims. In Pakistan the search for such an understanding has produced some of the new nation's gravest problems, as evidenced in 1953 in the extensive riots known as the Punjab Disturbances, or in the continuing dispute over the Muslim Family Laws Ordinance of 1952. It is a search that reflects the reawakening of Islam after long centuries of political decline, and that has inspired the questions Muslims everywhere are asking themselves as to why they did decline and what must be done to promote new strength. The answers to these questions necessarily involve some assessment of the faith, an assessment that every Muslim state has made in its own way.

This study is a historically oriented investigation of the religious reassessment in one particular Muslim area—Pakistan, and the Indian subcontinent before partition. It does not pretend to be exhaustive, and might appropriately be thought of as an introduction. The first chapter treats Islam, the religion, in terms of its "flesh and blood," to indicate something of how an individual Muslim might feel toward his faith. The second chapter briefly surveys Islam as it developed in India, and as it appeared during the height of the Mughul dynasty; we cannot know what Islam *is* if we have no idea of what Islam *was*. The third chapter considers the initial, largely negative responses of the Indian Muslims to their fall from power. The fourth and fifth chapters depict the development of various positive responses that provide the poles of conflicting thought; and the final chapter is concerned with the effort in Pakistan not only to assert its Islamic heritage—variously interpreted, to be sure—but also to define its role in the contemporary world.

One might argue that in many ways Pakistan is not a typical example for such a study of a Muslim nation, not so much because it is not an Arab country, for most Muslims are not Arabs, but because it has been formed by so many influences (which may be a reason why Islamic feeling is so high there). There are strong Arabic influences in both geographic wings of Pakistan, but for centuries the dominant political power on the subcontinent was Persian or Turk or Afghan in origin— the Mughul emperors, essentially Persian in culture, ruled with varying degrees of power for over four hundred years before they finally succumbed to Sikh, Mahratta, and western powers, as well as to their own debilities. But the Muslims who pushed into India confronted a great religion already established there—Hinduism. As almost invariably happens under similar circumstances, the Muslims, although always remaining loyal to the fundamentals of Islam, assimilated much of Hinduism to themselves. That is a subject, however, with which this book is not directly concerned. With the arrival of the western powers in the seventeenth century, and especially after the West had firmly established itself on the subcontinent late in the eighteenth century, the influence of western civilization began to permeate the area. East Pakistan, in fact, was under effective British control for 250 years before independence, and West Pakistan for about a hundred years. All these elements have had their influence upon Islam in the area that is now Pakistan. In addition, the influence of the sufis, the Muslim mystics, has been strong throughout the subcontinent and remains so today; indeed, it may be the strongest single influence upon Islam in the subcontinent. It is also one means by which Islam and Hinduism mutually influenced each other —a kind of common ground whose boundaries extend from the simple devotional movement of Kabir, the weaver's son, to the activity of the Mughul prince, Dara Shikoh. Some Buddhist influence, although of a minor nature, can also be detected.

With the opening of an independent state to many Muslims of the subcontinent, the necessity to reassess their faith became more pressing. It is one thing to preach theory when there is little likelihood it will ever be practiced; it is another to be forced to apply accepted theory. Once the British were removed as a scapegoat, the Muslims of Pakistan had to begin to act for themselves and to assume responsibility for their actions. This has involved, sometimes openly but more often in a quiet manner, a new questioning of Islamic ideas and practices. It would, perhaps, be unfair to describe this somewhat inchoate movement as one of modern trends in Islam; more properly one might say of modern emphases in Islam. Theoretically, Islam is always one and the same: men read it differently. But it is being read today with modern eyes.

I have written this study to invite some sort of understanding of Islam the religion as it has been understood and accepted by many of its adherents, particularly those whose interpretations vary from what is generally considered traditional, and to provide a sketch of the changing emphases that have been accepted within Islam through the years by Muslims of India and Pakistan. Because it has been my experience that many westerners find it difficult to think of Islam except in categorical terms—"that religion of the desert," "those fanatics for holy war," and so on—I have occasionally offered analogies which I hope will suggest to the reader that many problems the Muslims have had to face do not really differ in kind from many problems that Christians have also faced. An analogy, however, can only be rough at best.

The book is, then, an explanation, an account, and a description. In its descriptive aspect it offers some suggestions leading toward a fertile field of study for students of comparative religion or any other aspect of comparative culture. There are very few great religious movements about which much substantiated information exists. One is the movement in European Christianity, from the fourteenth or fifteenth century, as a result of which the medieval church in the West was divided into Protestantism and Catholicism; another is the movement in Islam, begun in the eighteenth or nineteenth century, which challenges many of the traditional interpretations of that great religion. A fruitful study of the nature of religious movements, and perhaps of the nature of religion itself, might be made by reviewing one of these movements in the light of the other. Some day perhaps someone will do this. My book, however, is not so much a study of the theology or of the philosophy of Islam as an analysis of the practical attitude of those adherents who have tried to influence it in certain directions.

Any study of religious reassessments by Muslims involves one in the perplexing problem of the use of adequate descriptive terms relating to religious attitudes. I have tried to avoid the words "orthodox" and "fundamentalist" as applied to Muslims in preference for the term "traditionalist," referring to the follower of the Sunni tradition. In fact, none of these three terms truly applies, but there is some virtue in consistency, and I have tried to be consistent.

I have relied entirely on English sources and on translations into English; the translation has always been indicated. I have not hesitated to write Arabic words, where necessary, with an English plural. The Arabic plural of *madrassah* is *madarsi*, but I have unabashedly written *madrassahs*. For names, I have sought forms that seemed most likely to be recognized by western readers. So far as contemporary names are concerned, I have preferred to use the forms most frequently used by the individuals, but variant spellings used in publications have been retained in the footnotes.

Some parts of this study have previously appeared in print. In somewhat modified form parts of Chapter One have appeared in *The Christian Century* and *The Unitarian Register*. Chapter Two has appeared in *Studies in Islam*, the quarterly journal of the Indian Institute of Islamic Studies; Chapter Three as several articles in *The Muslim World*; and part of Chapter Five in *The Light Weekly of Lahore*, an Ahmadiya publication.

I am, of course, deeply indebted both to many people and to several institutions. Without a research grant from the Ford

Foundation, 1953–1955, and a Fulbright research grant from the United States Educational Foundation, 1959–1960, as well as the cooperation shown by Tufts University, this study would not have been made. Naturally, none of these institutions is responsible for what is said here, but I am grateful to them for giving me the opportunity to say it. My good friends in Pakistan are far too numerous to mention, but I shall always remember their warm reception, and I take this opportunity to extend my thanks for their patience once again. My thanks, too, to Mrs. Carolyn MacVicar, who typed the manuscript, reading strange names written in a stranger hand; to my wife, whose editorial skill is responsible for whatever initial clarity of expression may be found here; and to the staff of Cornell University Press, who improved the efforts of everyone.

F. A.

Medford, Massachusetts
April 1967

Contents

Illustrations

Maps

Islam and Pakistan

Chapter One

Is Change Possible
in Islam?

In western Europe medievalism was toppled during the two or three centuries summed up in the phrase "the Renaissance and the Reformation." Refined by the warfare of the seventeenth century and the rationalism of the eighteenth, the new social emphases that had emerged by the end of the eighteenth century made their way during the nineteenth and twentieth centuries to every corner of the earth. Wherever these emphases appeared they challenged the existing intellectual and social orders; wherever they appeared they were partially adapted and partially rejected.

This whole process, known by historians as "the Europeanization of the world," was—and is—something more than that. It is the demise of a set of attitudes that can fairly be characterized as medieval: the unquestioning acceptance of authority, the belief that every man is born into his place in the social order and must remain in it, and that life consists in making do with the present to ensure the achievement of a true reward after death. With the weakening of these attitudes also came the weakening of the social beliefs and structures built upon them—a process noted a century ago by John Stuart Mill when he wrote, "The first of the leading peculiarities of the present age is, that it is an age of transition. Mankind have outgrown old institutions and old doctrines and have not yet acquired new ones." A far better term than "Europeanization" would be "modernization."

The institutions and doctrines of the new age will be forged out of the institutions and doctrines of the old, either by a procedure of extreme adaptation to the old, or by a violent rejection of it. This is not a problem of how to adopt western ways, for there is much about the West, such as its loosening family relationships, that is not appealing to people in other parts of the world. It is a problem of selection and experimentation based not only on undeniably western ideas, but also on incorporating intellectual and social attitudes already present in the society. It is an adjustment that cannot be made without strain and effort, for it involves a reconstruction of the social, and often religious, structure of the society. But one must be careful in trying to forecast the turn a society might take in terms of its previous values. One frequently hears, for example, that Islam so intensely emphasizes the existence of God that there is little danger of the acceptance of communism by any Muslim people. It may be true that for a Muslim to accept communism requires some straining, but for many young Muslims today it requires far less straining than the wholesale acceptance of what we may call medieval Islam.

This is one reason why so many state leaders have worked so hard to encourage new thinking about Islam. Habib Bourguiba of Tunisia has most prominently set himself up as a spokesman for those who favor interpretations other than the traditional ones. But he is not alone. Gamal Abdel Nasser of Egypt has defended his concept of "Arab socialism" as being compatible with Islam, although the traditional religious leaders of Egypt have denied that it is. President Ayub Khan of Pakistan, in addition to promoting new thinking within his country, has toured the Arab countries of the Middle East to urge a reformist revival in Islam.

Such leaders all recognize that religion is the strongest force opposing widespread change in their countries. They recognize, too, that it is not a force that can be supplanted or ignored. Each of them has experienced civil revolt centering around religious issues. For fifty years the French *colon* in Algeria promoted European social and intellectual attitudes, yet in that time he could not prevent a Muslim awakening.[1] For a hundred years missionaries have been trying, with great heroism and notable individual successes, to woo Muslims to Christianity. Their over-all success has not been very great, except as they may have led Muslims to rethink their own faith. The Communist approach—to deny the reality of religious faith and ignore the genuineness of religious feeling— is even less of a solution than conversion. Islam is unlikely to be abandoned, either for another religion or for no religion: social changes must be Islamic, or else they will not be. If the social order of the Muslim world is to be reconstructed, then one of the world's great religions will have to undergo something like a "reformation." Is such a reformation possible?

Juridically speaking, at least, there has been practically no change within Islam for a thousand years. The major theological debate as to the meaning of the Qur'an ended at the close of the eleventh century; since then Muslim scholars have been applying glosses on the glosses and commentaries

[1] Joan Gillespie, *Algeria, Rebellion and Revolution* (New York, 1960), p. 173.

on the commentaries, but contributing nothing new. Does this
mean that Islam today is incapable of change? Might it not,
through new interpretations, adapt itself to new conditions
and insights? Change has, after all, occurred within Christianity. The potent hell-fire-filled sermons of Jonathan Edwards which caused his eighteenth-century audiences to
writhe in torment would elicit little more from believers
today than amused smirks. More and more the Old Testament
Lord of Justice has given room to the God of Love of the
New Testament. This change in emphasis is the result of far-
reaching reinterpretation of the meaning and spirit of Christianity. Is Islam equally capable of reinterpretation?

These are questions with which Muslims themselves must
wrestle. A westerner cannot tell them what their faith teaches
or what is good or bad by Islamic standards; the most he can
do is try to understand the problems involved. Basically they
boil down to interpreting the words of the Qur'an, but this
is not all. Differing interpretations of the Qur'an have always
existed, and so independent is the character of this faith (and
so minor most of these interpretative differences) that no one
has been especially perturbed: for the most part Sunnis and
Shi'as both read it the same way. After all, God's word is not
changed because man misreads it, and it remains God's word
even when improperly used. This is an argument, incidentally, used by both the traditionalist and the modernist. What
is called for today is not merely a new interpretation, but a
revolutionary departure from the traditional interpretations.
Western society faced a similar situation in respect to the
Bible—was it to be understood literally, word for word, or in
terms of the spirit behind the words? This was the argument
over which Martin Luther and Ulrich Zwingli came to an
impasse in 1529 and went their separate ways.

Christian analogies, however, possess only limited validity

so far as Islam is concerned. While all religions must face certain similar problems, the answers each arrives at reflect a particular social organization, intellectual heritage, and a host of other differentiating conditions. Thus whereas both Luther and Zwingli headed organizations and were recognized as religious leaders ordained for that role, nowhere in Islam is there anything even remotely resembling their situation. Muhammad was adamant in his opposition to an organized priesthood because he was intent on emphasizing the direct relationship between the individual and God and because he wanted to avoid the dangers of spiritual monopoly he felt such a priesthood entailed. Any attempt today to create an organization within Islam would be certain to meet strenuous objections from Muslims. It is interesting that the most highly organized Islamic group, the Ahmadiya, has aroused the strongest opposition, partly because of its organized character. Many unifying elements may be found in Islam—for instance, the annual pilgrimage to Mecca, the daily prayers said while facing toward Mecca, the influence of such theological schools as Al-Azhar in Egypt and Deoband in India; but there is no organizational structure as known in Christianity. How can a reformation develop under such conditions?

Islam's lack of organization gives rise to further problems. While there is much to be said for the absence of an organized priesthood, it does lead to difficulties and dangers. Islam pays its tribute to leadership: the best man in the congregation —"best" in knowledge and character—is chosen to lead the prayers. But his leadership is temporary, lasting only as long as the service. Again, lack of organization means lack of religious instruction. It is fair to say that in Pakistan, for instance, a child receives practically no formal religious training. He learns the forms of prayer by imitating his elders; and he learns some simple prayers and hears the Qur'an read in

Arabic, a language he may not understand. From time to time
individuals in his village will tell him stories of a moral character or stories that depict some of the basic attitudes of Islam.
Nothing, however, corresponds to the Protestant Sunday
school; direct religious instruction as we think of it in the
West is seldom to be found. In Pakistan an attempt has been
made to improve this situation by having religious or semireligious instruction offered in the public schools. Results of
this instruction, however, are limited by the small percentage
of Pakistani children attending school. How can a reformation be effected in the absence of some kind of religious education?

More important, perhaps, is the question: What is there to
reform? Is it not true that to the Muslim the Qur'an represents God's word, unchanged and unchangeable? The traditional interpretation of the Qur'an represents the combined
efforts of the best theological minds produced by Islam over
centuries. Muslim scholars have pored over the Qur'an as
Christian scholars have over the Bible. Almost every possible
interpretation has been probed, and by a process of sifting
and comparison an accepted interpretation has been evolved
which, except in a few minor points, has been standardized
for a long period of time. If the Qur'an is unchanging, and if
it has been thoroughly and fully interpreted, how can it serve
as the basis for a reformation?

Let us look at the whole problem from another angle—
from the point of view of history. To be sure, history offers
few examples of great religious change, and historians have
uncovered relatively little exact information about most of
them. Some striking parallels do exist, however, between the
sixteenth-century religious movement in Europe and movements in the world of Islam today. By comparing these two
events, not in terms of theological doctrine but as social

phenomena, we may get an idea of the possibility of the emergence of an Islamic reformation.

Three elements seem to have cooperated to secure the success of the Protestant Reformation: a developing national spirit, exemplified by Frederick the Wise of Saxony and his protection of Luther, despite the demands of pope and emperor; a developing secular interest, marked by an increased self-confidence in the layman as to his ability to understand religious problems; and the invention of the printing press, a means whereby new ideas could be quickly and accurately disseminated. Basic to the success of such attitudes and technological innovations, of course, were the genuine religious feeling of large numbers of people and their genuine interest in religious issues.

The Protestant Reformation was in fact characterized by so much nationalistic fervor that some historians have belittled its religious aspects and emphasized its political side. So with the Islamic world today: it is marked by nationalistic fervor, and again as in Europe, neither everywhere to the same degree nor everywhere at the same time. Nevertheless, hardly a day passes but that our newspapers report some happening prompted by nationalist sentiment among Muslims, whether in Morocco or Egypt, Iran or Turkey. Without doubt much of the current rethinking of Islam has its roots in nationalistic feeling—even though the concept of nationalism is foreign to traditional Islamic thought, as it was foreign to medieval Christian thought.

Like the European Reformation, this Islamic movement also concerns the abandonment of certain social ideas. Both the medieval church and medieval Islam banned usury, essentially for the same reason: because there was little occasion for moneylending in the economic system of the day (and, in the case of Islam, because of a qur'anic passage variously inter-

preted by the Companions of the Prophet). The pressures of
a developing new economic system led to a gradual softening
of the church's position in regard to interest. The same softening can be found in Islam now. Some leaders of the traditional
school, for instance, maintain that there is nothing un-Islamic
about an interest rate of 1.5 per cent. If this is allowed, then
the problem becomes one of determining the degree of interest that can be charged—of differentiating between usury
and interest. What catches our attention here is not the problem of usury as such but the character of the modification.

Again, just as sixteenth-century Europe saw increased emphasis on the *spirit* of the law rather than on the letter, so
today Muslims are trying to decide when the spirit takes
precedence over the letter. It is not without significance that
one of the most influential books Muslims are reading is *The
Spirit of Islam.*

Finally, the Reformation in Europe did not catch fire until
people everywhere—lay people, as distinguished from the
clergy, people who spoke in the vernacular rather than in
Latin—began to talk and read and ponder. It was the layman
who prompted new interpretations, at the very least by opening the eyes of the theologians to the changed world in which
they were living. It should not be forgotten that both Luther
and Calvin began their careers with the study of the law.
The development and dissemination of their ideas and interpretations were made possible by the printing press. In a real
sense the Protestant Reformation is the child of that invention.

Interestingly enough, educated people throughout Islam,
perhaps reflecting the secular spirit of our times, have begun
to ask questions about their faith, so much so that warnings
from the theologians are now a matter of course. "To understand Islam," such a warning might run, "requires a lifetime
of study. No one should attach any weight to the opinion of

a person who has not studied Islam exclusively throughout his life." Nevertheless, the number of educated people who do attach weight to the opinions of nonspecialists seems to be increasing. More than one Muslim has agreed with the pamphleteer who said that commentators on the Qur'an do little except create misconceptions.[2] This cynical remark does not seem to have affected the commentators, but it does suggest the individual's independent attitude toward some theological approaches. A list of the leading students of Islam today would include the names of many men who never attended any strictly Muslim religious school. In Pakistan perhaps most religious writing stems from what we may term lay sources: individuals, that is, who have not attended any of the institutions, such as Deoband or Bareilly, devoted to qur'anic study.

At this point our comparison breaks down. The printing press has been available in Muslim countries for hundreds of years, and no reformation has occurred. Mass understanding and support of change have been lacking. Sixteenth-century Europe had a far greater degree of literacy than the Muslim world has now. In Pakistan, for instance, only about 15 per cent of the country's hundred million inhabitants are officially literate, and perhaps half of the 15 per cent can read. Consequently, serious thinking about Islam reaches very few people.

If there is to be a general reinterpretation of Islam or of the Qur'an, it must wait on widespread literacy. And because literacy is a necessity for the modern state, it may very well be that development of a political order that spreads literacy will go hand in hand with a reformation in Islamic thought—

[2] Hunaif, *Does the Quran Need a Commentary?* (Karachi, [c. 1954]). Its author maintains that because the Qur'an stipulates (3:5) that it is composed of two kinds of verses—those that are clear (and in these lies its essence), and those that are ambiguous (and no one knows the explanation of these except God)—no need for commentators exists.

not, it must be emphasized, because of literacy alone, but, as in sixteenth-century Europe, because of literacy combined with far-reaching social change.

The broad social elements that seem to inspire massive religious change, so far as we can judge from the specific example of the Protestant Reformation, are present in the Islamic world today and have been for a generation. But other elements are also present—elements not found in Luther's Europe. The role of foreign powers, the tremendous gap between the economics of western and of Islamic countries, the influence of communism, and the tendency among Muslims to avoid religious organization in the western sense—these are a few of the differences that will ensure that an Islamic reformation will follow a course of its own.

Two other points should be mentioned in this connection. First, there is no way of measuring the time required to bring any broad social movement to fruition. The Protestant Reformation took about a century to establish itself—roughly from the date Luther tacked his theses to the church door in Wittenberg to the beginning of the Thirty Years' War—and debate is still continuing. But there is no reason to conclude that a similar length of time would be required for a reformation of Islam: it could take more or less time.

Second, should a reformation be developing within Islam, it is extremely unlikely that any basically new ideas will emerge from it. Over the centuries, Muslims have evolved as many religious concepts as anyone else. There were as many heresies in medieval Islam as in medieval Christianity, and the acceptance of new positions—as Luther discovered during the Leipzig debate—often involves the acceptance of old heresies. Whatever the change that may be developing in Islam, it will not be of such a nature as to force Muslims to seek or invent a new rationale. "Out of the old day the new day is born," wrote Thomas Carlyle; and just as Luther and Calvin searched the past for substantiation of their ideas, so will Muslims search as they face the need for change. They will build on the rich intellectual heritage of their faith.

The direction that will be followed as a result of the pressures for social readjustment, of course, depend upon the character of Islam itself. Something of the essence of Islam can be seen if we read the qur'anic account of Adam and Eve in the Garden and consider their mistakes as portrayed in the Qur'an in terms of the biblical story. If nothing else, this will show us how the strictly unitarian Qur'an—a long composition continually playing variations on the theme of the First Commandment—may be open to a variety of meanings, and, above all, how rich these meanings can be.

The story of Adam and Eve does not occur at any one place in the Qur'an. It is told in bits and patches, as fragments used to emphasize particular thoughts in some places and to point up a particular moral elsewhere. Stories, as such, did not interest Muhammad; he was much more concerned with the lesson that might be derived from them.

If we bring all the pieces together, the qur'anic story of Adam and Eve begins with God's decision to create man as his representative on earth. To that decision the angels object; they are afraid such action will disrupt the fundamental harmonies. Whereupon God teaches Adam the names of all things and then asks the angels if they know these names. When they acknowledge their ignorance, God has Adam tell the names, thus convincing the angels that man is smarter than they. Man begins, then, a little superior to the angels.

One angel refuses to bow down before Adam. That is Iblis. "Why should I?" he asks. "I saw you make man of clay—of black mud. But I was created out of fire, and I am better than he." Only Iblis does not believe in the ideality of man; he is

the typical materialist, the devil. God warns Adam about
Iblis: "Don't let him drive you out of the Garden, lest you
become miserable." But the wiles of the devil prove too great,
both for Adam and for Eve. "You can trust me," Iblis says
to them. "I give you good counsel, believe me." Adam and
Eve are taken in, and they both eat of the tree.

The Qur'an does not say what the tree is, but it is not the
tree of the knowledge of good and evil; Muslims believe that
knowledge would absolve man, not lead to his fall.

Thus, Satan (Iblis) makes those in the Garden slip from
their privileged state. Adam and Eve are tempted, and they
fail, but do not fall. They are thrown out of the Garden, and
Satan with them. "Get ye down, all ye people," says God,
"with enmity between yourselves. On earth will be your
dwelling place and your means of livelihood for a time." But
God first teaches Adam how to ask for forgiveness, and then
He forgives him. "He is the Relenting, the Merciful." Thus,
with the expulsion comes forgiveness and the promise that for
all who follow His guidance there shall be neither fear nor
grief—the qur'anic expression of salvation.

The variations in this account from that of the Bible are
interesting. Man is made of dust, but there is no mention of
Adam's losing a rib that Eve might be. Although there is a
tree, there is no serpent; although there is a woman, she does
not tempt the man; and, although there is an exile from the
Garden, it is not really presented as a punishment. Travail is
no punishment for the woman, nor is field labor punishment
for the man. And finally, man's expulsion from the Garden
meant no lowering of status, for he had been forgiven. It is,
indeed, a rise in status, for he can now act as God's representative—what God intended all along.

Most likely, Muhammad had heard the story from several

sources, but much of the new twist he supplied himself. He told the story in such a way that he could believe in it.

However we choose to assess Muhammad, of one thing there can be no doubt: he was no theologian. Theological intricacies seem to have held no interest for him, and his approach to religion was very simple. The heart and soul of Islam is the submission of the individual to the One God. Indeed, one of the remarkable aspects of Islam is that it emphasizes the lack of a priesthood or organized church in the western sense—an emphasis designed to avoid the monopolistic dangers of a priestly caste. Muhammad may best be described as a religious genius, untouched by theological conceits. His mission was to reveal a simple, personal, and direct faith in God to a people deep in idolatry and superstition, although not unacquainted with monotheism. It became his purpose to demonstrate a faith whose practicality would appeal to the Arab, and in that he was eminently successful.

Islam, someone has said, is a great practical religion, while Christianity is a great idealistic religion. There is much truth in that observation, for the faith of the Muslims tends to offer guidance for particular situations. Matters of form and behavior loomed large in the eyes of seventh-century Arabs, including those of Muhammad. His genius, however, is demonstrated by his ability to break away from a too-narrow viewpoint. "Do not put to me too many unnecessary questions," he is reported as having once said to a group of insistent followers. "Whoever does it is an enemy of the Muslims because the answers given would become binding on them and thereby their liberty of action would be curtailed." Nevertheless, much in the Qur'an lends itself to the most idealistic interpretation. Indeed, it is true of the story of Adam and Eve, relating not the fall but the rise of man.

Two points must continually be borne in mind if one is to avoid specious criticism of Muhammad's retelling of biblical stories. In the first place, he was interested not in the story itself but in the point which the story could illustrate and emphasize. This attitude is closely akin to that of Protestant modernists today who, for example, argue that the importance of the Eden legend does not lie in the events related, but in the religious truths expressed. In the second place, Muhammad's stories were based on the traditions and writings of his day, current primarily among the Jews and perhaps Christians of northern Arabia. How he told a story, then, is related to the nature of the traditions maintained by the advocates of Judaism and Christianity at what may be considered only a remote outpost of the two faiths.

Much speculation and analysis has been devoted to an effort to discover the source of Muhammad's revelations, and thus explain away his claim to Prophethood. The results have not been conclusive. Some say Muhammad had a Jewish tutor, which may be true; some think he was acquainted with, and impressed by, Syrian Christian monks, which may be true; others think the trading society in which he lived offered in itself a kaleidoscopic picture of different religions, which may also be true. What is fundamental, of course, is that Muhammad did not lay claim to originality for his religion. Time and again he announced that his revelation was only a confirmation of previous revelations. To be sure, Muhammad was so convinced of the divine inspiration of his revelations that he felt they abrogated any of God's previous revelations which might conflict with them. Nevertheless, tracing the sources of qur'anic passages to Jewish or other traditions, while interesting and revealing to scholars, has no effect upon the Muslim's faith. To the Muslim, this kind of analysis seems inconsequential, and perhaps the absence in Islam of anything corresponding to the "higher criticism" of Christian scholars today is partly dependent upon this attitude. It is, of course, more dependent upon the unquestioned belief that the Qur'an is God's word—and why should one try to criticize what God has said? It is one thing to investigate meanings and interpretations; it is another to investigate sources and origins. Muslims generally do not admit of any genuine relationship between the two so far as the Qur'an is concerned.

Muhammad's genuine religious feeling is preserved in the Qur'an, especially in those passages which are not attempts to defend himself or to castigate his enemies. "Do you want to know what Muhammad was like?" Aisha, his favorite wife, is reported to have asked. "Then read the Qur'an, for that *is* Muhammad." In order to understand Islam, Westerners must read the Qur'an, not for explanations or accounts of specific points of doctrine, but for a realization of Muhammad's religious outlook. For it is that which has gained and kept adherents for Islam.

The nature of the religious truth seen by Muhammad is fundamentally important. Great religions are not built on fine technical points, but on simple concepts of God and man—though, to be sure, every religion produces its theologians to add technical obscurities to it. Muhammad's basic belief is that all of nature is ordered; there is no chaos in it. The entire universe is run according to purposive laws, both physical and moral. The Qur'an purports to be a guide toward achievement of the moral order. At the peak of that moral order, higher than the angels, stands man, created not in God's own image but as His representative on earth.

To ensure that man would be the best possible representative, God began by giving him knowledge, thus allowing him to triumph over the angels, who (except for Iblis) bowed down before him. Knowledge, in fact, is one of the attributes

of God, and it is part of man's duty, as His representative, to
acquire knowledge, for without knowledge man could not be
responsible for moral decisions, and consequently could not
be God's representative. "After God and me," Muhammad is
reported to have said, "the most beneficent is the man who
acquires knowledge and spreads it." Throughout the Qur'an
the emphasis on knowledge and learning is great. Man constantly is urged to study nature, to investigate things, to find
out for himself the order with which God has created the
universe. In the course of time, Muslims have substituted for
that wider study the more constricting study of the Qur'an
alone, forgetting, apparently, that the Qur'an was only *part*
of God's revelation.

The qur'anic Eve demonstrates another notable attitude of
Muhammad. In the temptation of the tree, Adam and Eve are
together in their weakness, and blame falls equally on man
and woman. Muhammad seems to have recognized that in
matters of faith the sexes are equal, for he presses the point
in other parts of the Qur'an. That is far removed from Paul's
injunction for women to keep silence in churches. It is another of this world's paradoxes that in Islam silence eventually
was imposed on women, and that in Christianity women have
approached more closely to equality of status.

Neither man nor woman is to blame for the incident in the
Garden: that was the work of Satan, and it is he who makes
them slip from the state they are in. What is that state?
A condition of sexual innocence? A condition of amity, the
absence of war and hatred among humans? Or merely an
animal state, in which moral sense is lacking? It is impossible
to be sure of Muhammad's meaning, and commentators have
made many guesses. The Muslim poet Sir Muhammad Iqbal
thought the state of Adam and Eve in the Garden was animal.
The result of Satan's wiles, then, was the development of a

moral sense in man, marking him off from the animals. But with moral sense came violation of the law. How could man be God's representative on earth if he had no moral sense? Did God, then, want to have Adam and Eve out of the Garden? Was not the concept of moral law, the violation of it, and the sense of violation necessary for man's ultimate rise?

At least three contributions to the story seem to be Muhammad's. One is that failure to accuse woman of leading good, strong men from bliss. Another is the detail in which Adam and Eve are forgiven before they leave the Garden— God teaches Adam how to ask for forgiveness in order that He may forgive him! The merciful, forgiving nature of God is emphasized again and again throughout the Qur'an; the doctrine of original sin, as it was developed in Christian theology, is a concept totally alien to Muhammad's mind. Muhammad's third contribution lies in the promise of salvation God extends to the wrongdoers departing from the Garden— provided they follow His guidance. Muslim opinion is divided about whether Adam refers to just one individual and Eve another or whether they are merely symbols representing mankind. It is agreed, however, that what is important is not how the world began, but how man should live in it. Man, having been given moral responsibility, sins through his own error, and God forgives. But man must try to follow the revelations—the guidance—God chooses to bestow.

The difficulty facing every religion is to determine the nature of God's guidance. The particular difficulty facing Islam is that it has received that guidance in black and white. Perhaps Muhammad thought he was giving to the Arabs what the "people of the Book" had already received, but the character of the revelation in the Qur'an is not to be compared with that in the Bible. The Qur'an is a synthesis of the world's culture as received through one man, which has been

preserved more or less intact by his followers. The revelation
of the Bible was received through many writers. Because of
its multiple authorship the Bible lends itself more to critical
analysis than does the Qur'an.

Differing interpretations of the Qur'an are to be found
throughout the history of Islam, although, on the whole, an
amazing homogeneity of interpretation has been effected. On
particular points, a variety of interpretations can be held
without exciting much attention. Thus Iqbal's contention
that man's state before he left the Garden was animal, while
not generally accepted, is not in any way unacceptable. It
does show how a modern philosopher can find a basis for his
Bergsonian principles in the Qur'an without straining. Similarly, the question as to whether the Garden was on this earth
or in paradise may be debated. The Qur'an seems unclear
about it, although it does say that paradise itself is without
limits: its breadth is as the heavens and the earth, a passage,
that for some, renders such a question purely academic. Indeed, some mystics of Islam claim that even Muhammad was
not always able to interpret his revelations, citing his reported
remark, "O God, I haven't recognized Thee as Thou ought
to be recognized," in support of their position.

The elements that make reinterpretation possible exist
within the Qur'an. The great problem facing modern Islam is
to reconcile the revelations of Muhammad as recorded in the
Qur'an with new concepts, with a broader understanding.
The Qur'an must be read with post-medieval eyes, and the
reading should be in the spirit of a "back to Muhammad!"
movement. Desire to return to the original purity of the
church is the stuff of every religious reform, and it is the way
some modern Muslims are now approaching the task. In general, reforming Muslims argue that the permanent basis of
Islam is the spirit of the Qur'an, not the specific words aimed

for a seventh-century audience. Traditionalists, on the other hand, hew to the absolute letter; they place form and ritual first, maintaining that without them the spirit cannot be approached.

The reformation is not emanating from those trained in Islamic disciplines in Muslim seminaries so much as from those who have had no formal Islamic training. In Pakistan, where the phrase *Islamic state* is used more frequently than anywhere else, none of the leading commentators on Islam has had a theological background. Among them have been, and are, retired government servants, newspaper editors, and schoolteachers.

Indeed, to look among religious scholars, the *ulama,* for the initial signs of modification is to misunderstand the nature of religious change. The *mullah* is subject increasingly to ridicule because pressures for change from the laity, representing a society with which he is not especially familiar, are being resisted by him. In this respect, the mullah plays a probably necessary, however unenviable, role in the shifting of emphases within Islam. He acts as a brake and a block to those who urgently desire something different, but who do not know just what it is. The mullah is the one to ensure, at least in the non-Arabic Middle East, that changing emphases within Islam are of the nature of reformation rather than of catastrophe. But he is not able to still the swelling urge toward a questioning of the validity of the old interpretations. Islam is as subject to change as any other great religion. It is inconceivable that its central chord can ever be other than the strictest monotheism; but on the basis of those notes innumerable tunes may be played.

If the Qur'an can be interpreted in several ways, it follows that measures would be taken to ensure as uniform an interpretation as possible. In the Christian world such uniformity was achieved through the powers and efforts of the Church hierarchy, whether Greek or Latin. But there was no such spiritual hierarchy in Islam. Muhammad had vigorously insisted that the relationship between God and man is an individual matter, subject to the intercession of no one. (Prayer in Islam is a group matter because it serves to unite the faithful into a community, not because God can hear several voices more clearly than one.) Though it lacks the Christian church hierarchy, Islam does have a strong juridical aspect which is largely absent from Christianity.

Jesus never founded a community; he seems to have been content to serve as a wandering teacher. Indeed, historically, the opportunity to establish a community of his own may never have occurred. For Muhammad the opportunity did occur. The fears and jealousies of the Meccan tribesmen led to his migration from Mecca to Medina, some two hundred miles north. There he did establish a civil community, and he did endow it with laws. These laws became part of the faith, and the judges who later appeared to rule on the legal aspects of Islam had to interpret and apply them. Thus the judges played a role as promoters of uniformity within Islam. Muslims argue that because Islam includes such a practical example of how a civil community should be organized it is closer to completeness and hence to perfection than Christianity or any other religion.

One could argue just as well, however, that the great weakness of Islam has rested in this claim of completeness. The decline of Islam from its glorious days is certainly related in part to the feeling of Muslims that they, because of their religion, were self-sufficient unto themselves. This has always been a fatal assumption, as the experiences of other religions indicate. The Muslim invasion of India was successful in part because the Hindus had weakened themselves through self-imposed isolation and aloofness. The greatest service of the European Reformation was to neutralize such a self-sufficient attitude by splitting western Christianity into two camps. Modern European progress began when Europeans developed an intellectual spirit enabling them to learn from others without feeling inferior about it.

Islam became a religion of law and commandments, with primary emphasis on the civil side; the judges of the law and the commentators on the law were in their own way as influential as the Christian clergy. The extraordinary development of the mystics, the *sufis*, in Islam is a reaction to this emphasis on the legal, the "practical," which often seems to a westerner so particularized as to be impractical. It may be that Muhammad partially realized this himself, for he constantly advised his followers that God wanted them to have an easy religion not to be complicated with their unnecessary questions.

In addition to limitations imposed by answers to questions asked of Muhammad, other bounds were set by an extensive analysis of Muhammad's life. Islam was to be a faith of precept and law, one great code of conduct, and "code" was meant literally. God would not entrust his revelation to any except the most perfect of men, and it followed that one could only gain by emulating so perfect a human example. Muhammad himself taught, according to a *hadith*, or anecdote about him, that the message of the Qur'an should be interpreted in terms of his own actions. He is reported to have said that the people were to learn from the Qur'an "and from the example of the Prophet."

The practice of following the traditional pattern of life of one's forefathers was considered a virtue among the Arabs. What Muhammad did was to offer his religious teachings and his own life as the exemplar over that of previous Arab tradition. The Arabs referred to such traditional patterns of life as *sunna,* an idea reflected by Longfellow in his lines:

> Lives of great men all remind us,
> We can make our lives sublime.

But Longfellow did not identify specific great men. Very early, Islamic theologians established the principle that the sunna referred only to Muhammad.[3] And whereas Longfellow spoke of an example, the Muslim sunna became a rule of conduct. Indeed, it is the practice of having rules rather than examples, of having precepts that guide the spirit, that lead Muslims to refer to Islam as the great practical religion.

In time the hadith—vast collections of anecdotes about Muhammad and sayings of Muhammad—were collected. They were sifted for accuracy with great care, yet apocryphal stories crept in. Many Muslims seemed to feel no compunction about telling a story they felt *could* be true, or *should* be true, whether it was to glorify Muhammad or to improve their own position. Thus the hadith can readily be divided into three broad groups: those depicting a general view of Muhammad's life; those which are questionable because they are not consistent with Muhammad's sayings (stories of Muhammad's miracles, despite the qur'anic denial, are included here); and those dealing with prophetic revelation. Stories of Muhammad's miracles are legion, as are stories supporting one Muslim sect against another. In modern times attacks on the traditionalist approach to Islam have centered on these stories; such attacks, however, are not new in Islam.

[3] This was a contribution of al-Shafi'i (767–820); he maintained that only traditions from the Prophet should have the force of law, and that the model behavior of the Muslim community should be the model behavior of Muhammad.

Particular stories in the hadith literature have always been under attack, even though they are contained in the most highly regarded collections.

During the first years after the death of Muhammad in 632 little theological or legal speculation as such arose. Conquest, the politics of conquest, and the enjoyment of conquest occupied most of the attention of Muslims. Eventually, though, it became necessary to find some answer to the many questions arising from the Qur'an, and formal doctrines such as those that cloak every religion began to appear in Islam. This development undoubtedly was stimulated by new ideas reaching the Arabs as a result of their geographical expansion. Islam had to defend itself as never before against un-Islamic ideas. Those who looked upon themselves as the defenders and preservers of Islam from foreign interests might properly be called traditionalists, for their central position was an absolute acceptance of all that was in the Qur'an and sunna. So uncompromising was their attitude, and so zealously did they support it, that one result of their efforts was to limit the scope of received revelation by limiting the interpretations that might be held concerning it. To insist that the Qur'an and sunna could be read in only one particular way, however, seemed necessary if the institution of Islam were to be preserved. The Qur'an, after all, was God's word, and Muhammad was a man selected by God to spread the word, exemplifying it in his personal life. Tampering could not be condoned, because if it were permitted, the principle of revelation would be weakened and the Arabs, whom God had selected to put the one true religion on the right path, would fail.

The traditionalists of Islam, like their fellow scholastics in the medieval Christian church, believed in the primacy of revelation over reason. This belief was exemplified by

Anselm, the Archbishop of Canterbury, who argued that one should not try to understand in order to believe, but should believe in order to understand. Such a view led Islamic traditionalists into conflict with other Muslims. The first struggle was with those who had absorbed some elements of Hellenistic thought and insisted upon understanding as the first step. This theological school was known as the Mu'tazila. Revelation, they maintained, must harmonize with reason and be constantly tested by it. Once a rational explanation of the Qur'an had been achieved, the Mu'tazila used every means possible to enforce its acceptance. They won the support of the 'Abbasid caliph of Baghdad and used it to persecute the traditionalist theologians. By the middle of the tenth century, however, the traditionalists had turned the tables and saved the purity of Islam by preventing the faith from being defiled by Greek thought. The struggle was won, it is interesting to note, by the simple expedient of converting the ruler to their traditionalist view against the rationalists, who were then politically persecuted out of existence. In short, tyranny was a partner to both sides.

The defeat of the Mu'tazila in the ninth century marks the first great victory of Islam's preoccupation with itself, and the beginning of the decline of Islamic civilization. But the Mu'tazila represented only one means by which foreign ideas, and a rationalist approach to religion, might attack Islam. Philosophy, as distinct from dogma, was another enemy.

In the traditionalists' struggle against such philosophers, the reaction against Greek learning reached its peak. Muslim philosophers had sought at first to produce a philosophy that was simultaneously Muslim, Aristotelian, and neo-Platonic. Such a synthesis was later abandoned and the Aristotelian viewpoint generally accepted, as was the hope that philosophy and religion could be kept separate. This hope, however, was in vain. The philosophers, for all the pious (and conventional) remarks by which they prefaced their writings, sought to deal with their intellectual problems quite apart from the religious world. The nature of revelation, or, indeed, its existence, was not a problem that particularly concerned them, and they were frequently done with it once the proper pious remarks had been uttered. Consciously or not, they were promoting dualism in a unitarian world. To the traditionalists the position of the philosophers was anathema. Al-Ghazali, who lived from the mid-eleventh to the early twelfth centuries, attacked the philosophers as being incoherent. He took his stand on revelation, simple trust in God's own words as recorded in the Qur'an. So thorough was his attack and so complete his victory that no great Muslim philosopher succeeded the famous Averroës of the twelfth century.[4] Islam was building still stronger barriers to isolate itself from new ideas and thus constructing more surely the elements of its decline.

The development of Islamic traditionalism, so briefly sketched here, has broad similarities to intellectual development in the western Christian world, but a reformation such as that which occurred with almost staggering suddenness in the West, has developed only slowly in the Muslim East. Some changes have occurred, however, and one example is worth mentioning.

Abu Bakr Rhazes was a ninth-century Persian philosopher and physician. He was the first to give accurate clinical accounts of smallpox and measles, and he also made extensive studies of the human eye. His reputation as a physician was deservedly great during his lifetime but, like many other

[4] This statement is true for the Sunni, but it may not apply to the Shi'a.

Muslim scientists, Rhazes made little impact upon his world. To the Muslim community, deeply influenced by traditionalist thought, his discoveries seemed irrelevant and unnecessary. The community held that the important thing in life was not to improve one's well-being but to get to heaven when one's earthly life was over. And the road to heaven was charted as a clear path. That path, preserved and sharply defined by the traditionalists, included prayers and creed, but it did not include so living as to avoid measles or small-pox. The attitude was not so much one of fatalism—it was an attitude found in medieval Christianity, too—as it was one of simple indifference. Rhazes' discoveries were nonessentials so far as the purpose of life was concerned, and this being so, they were ignored, or even attacked.

Present-day Muslims, however, point to Rhazes when they claim that the basis of modern science can be found in Islamic civilization. (Both the Chinese and the Indians could enter similar claims, since modern science did not begin until Europe rose out of itself and began to borrow ideas and concepts from every hand, just as Islamic science died—and Islamic civilization waned—when the Muslim world turned in on itself and acted on the assumption that what it had was sufficient.) In any case, both traditionalist and modernist Muslims have now brought Rhazes back into the fold. Over the centuries he has been transformed from heretic to hero.

A final challenge to the traditionalists of Islam, and one that remains today, was the development of sufism (mysticism). Traditionalists have always read the Qur'an more or less in their own image, deriving a picture of an absolute God most remarkable for his absoluteness—in the manner of an Arab chieftain. They viewed God somewhat as an all-powerful ruler who did what he pleased because he pleased to do it, but who fortunately did not please to do everything. Other Muslims chose to think of God not as a distant ruler but as a close friend. These individuals sought their satisfactions in direct religious experiences rather than through indirect revelation. The Qur'an, it must be emphasized, lends support to the views of both traditionalists and sufis.

The lines of division between the traditionalist position and that of the mystics became clear very early. The traditionalists believed the way to salvation was blind obedience to religious rituals, for had they not been prescribed by God in the Qur'an? The sufis held that God may be reached only through love. The traditionalists maintained that good deeds were themselves a sign of a pure heart, but the sufis held that without a pure heart a person's good deeds had no value. Sufism served for much of Islam somewhat the purpose that the Marian cult and the Resurrection has for Christianity, by making the sense of God's closeness more real to the masses. Although the first word to describe God in the Qur'an is *rahim* (mercy), the traditionalist approach does not seem to have emphasized this. It was the sufis, many of whom commanded large personal followings, who stressed the divine qualities of love and mercy.

Although sufism could not be annihilated, it could be restrained, indeed, from the traditionalist point of view, it had to be restrained. Not only were some individuals moved to excesses in their mystical search for closeness with God, but others portrayed Islam as simply one among God's religions. Shah Abdul Latif, an eighteenth-century mystic of Sind in what is now West Pakistan, said, "When the truth is one and the beloved is the same, why should men fight over the means?" And when he was asked what religion he followed, he replied, "Between the two," meaning all or none. The broadmindedness reflected here was a little too strong for the literal-minded traditionalists, whose sunna could not be so inclusive.[5]

Sufism needed to be restrained, too, because it led Islamic unitarianism into what seemed strange fields to the traditionalists. The mystic seeks a personal union with God; he seeks to identify himself with God. This can lead to pantheism, to the idea that all existence is one, including God. Everything that is, is either a manifestation of or an emanation from God. Thus the mystic, from his soul-searching introspection, could reason that when he knew himself well, he would know himself to be God. The West accepts the proverb that there's a spark of divinity in every man; the Muslim mystic felt that by contemplating this spark he could fan it into a flame. To traditionalists, wedded to the idea that God was whole and separate, such a notion was anathema. Traditionalists could accept sufism so long as mystical intuition was used to support revelation (this was al-Ghazali's position), but if this were to be the case such intuition had always to be under the control of trained reason. Although traditionalist Islam could not accept the idea of unification with God himself, it had less objection to the idea of unification with the spirit of Muhammad. This kind of "practical" mysticism became proper and was sanctioned by traditionalists. The traditionalist victory here lay not in preventing the mystic from flying, but in charting his course; they never achieved a complete victory, however, over the sufis. Muslim religious thought continually has been affected by sufistic thinking.

Islam has been customarily presented to the West as a "static religion"—one that has not changed for centuries and that is perhaps incapable of change. This charge bears validity

[5] A. M. A. Shushtery, *Outlines of Islamic Culture* (Bangalore, 1938), II, 479.

if we look at its juristic side. It would be foolhardy to say there has been less change, or fewer forces for change, in Islam than existed in Christianity up to the sixteenth-century Reformation. To compare Christianity after its medieval period with an Islam still largely medieval is obviously unfair—even though Muslims like to maintain that Islam has not changed and, being but the reflection of God's word, cannot change. Men change; what men understand as Islam and how men read the revelation on which Islam is based, these too change. Since Babar in the sixteenth century moved from Kabul through the Khyber Pass and onto the Punjab plain, to establish the great Mughul dynasty, the currents of change have been constant. Perhaps through a study of them we can obtain insight into the nature of Islam today, into the stresses and strains that affect it, and into the character of the social reconstruction that is taking place, at least in the Islamic Republic of Pakistan. The undercurrents of Muslim thought that existed during the more than three centuries of Mughul rule in India have their modern counterparts in Pakistan today, and the emphases developing in Pakistan are in many respects representative of the contemporary Islamic world.

Chapter Two

Islam in India
to the Eighteenth Century

Muslims had been on the Indian subcontinent at least eight centuries before Babar put in his appearance in 1526. They had come first as traders, then as plunderers; in the eleventh century the Turkish warrior Mahmud, whose capital was at Ghazni in modern Afghanistan, annexed part of the Punjab to his kingdom. Mahmud's successors were able to hold it for about a century and a half before succumbing to the attacks of another Turkish tribe, the Ghurids. For the next three centuries, or until Babar's appearance, northern India was under the control of Turkish or Afghan Muslim rulers who constantly pressed east and south with their armies. By 1327 Hindu rule even in south India was ended; Bengal, in the east, had already been under Muslim rule for more than a hundred years.

On the whole, the Muslim rulers behaved very much as did their medieval counterparts in Europe—they were the Lion-Hearteds and the Barbarossas of their time and place. Balanced precariously in a position of power, completely de-

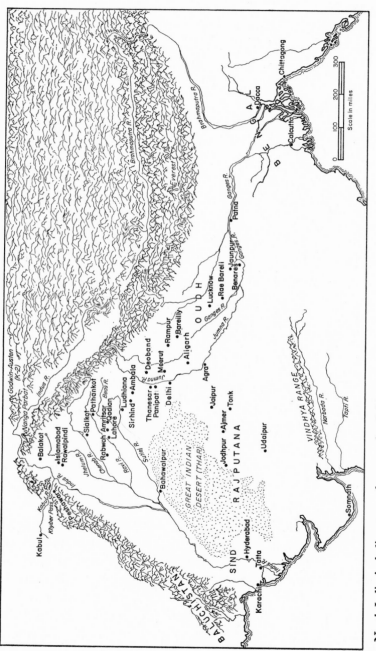

North India, including most of present-day Pakistan.

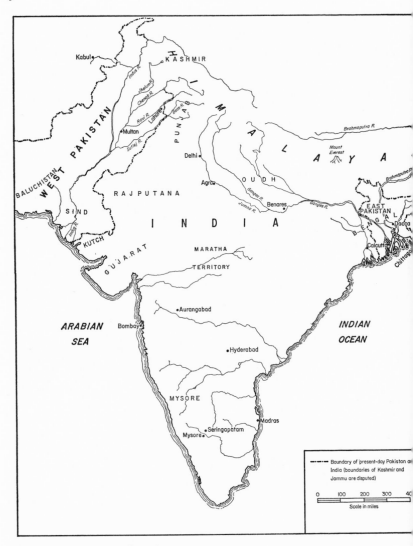

The Indo-Pakistan subcontinent.

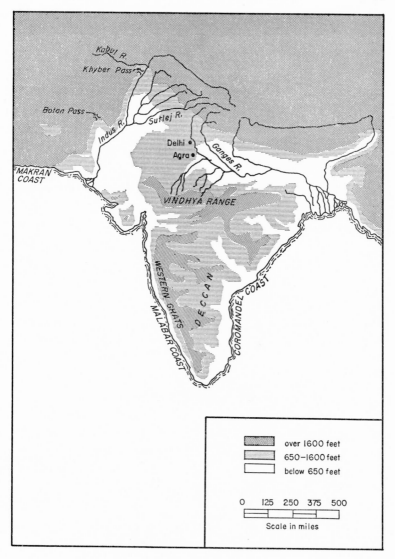

Principal relief on the Indo-Pakistan subcontinent.

pendent upon the loyalty of their troops and the support of
their nobles, they lived in a world in which military prowess
was the measure of a man's character, and in which the
personality of the ruler determined the strength and the
nature of the government. No ruler, if he wanted to preserve
his power, could afford to be a despotic tyrant for long nor
could he afford to be lax in the business of governing. No
ruler could afford to lose the support of his army or to take
action that would lead to conspiracies in his court. Ideally,
at least, he was a benevolent despot, and India is filled with
the marks of such benevolence in the form of caravanserais,
wells, and canals. That these often gifted warriors, sometimes extremely pious according to the lights of their time,
do not seem to have been marked by any great degree of
consistency in their actions, is undoubtedly true. Mahmud
of Ghazni, perhaps one of the ablest generals of all time,
attacked the great Hindu temple at Somnath on the most
famous of his many expeditions into India, partly because
he felt that the destruction of this idol was the surest way to
show the Hindus the futility of idolatry. The usually accepted picture of Mahmud was presented by his secretary
who, not without a touch of braggadocio, wrote of his Indian
campaigns that "Islam or death was the alternative Mahmud
placed before the people." [1] Mahmud, however, did not
hesitate to employ Indian troops, and in one section of his
Afghan capital at Ghazni he permitted Hindus freedom of
worship.[2] Mahmud was a stern unitarian, opposed both to
deviations from his traditionalist creed and to idolatry, yet
one cannot escape the impression that his movements were at

[1] S. R. Sharma, *Studies in Medieval History*, quoted in R. C. Ma-
jumdar, ed., *The History and Culture of the Indian People*, V (Bombay, 1957), 499.
[2] Pakistan Historical Society, *A Short History of Hind-Pakistan*
(Karachi, 1955), p. 110.

least as strongly tempered by sheer avariciousness as were those of the Anglo-Norman kings of England.

The same characteristics also describe some of the other Turkish rulers. Ibn Battuta, the famous Muslim traveler who in the fourteenth century visited the Delhi of Muhammad ibn Tughluq, wrote that "Muhammad above all men delights most in giving presents and shedding blood. At his door is seen always some pauper on the way to wealth or some corpse that has been executed. Stories are rife among the people of his generosity and courage, and of his cruelty and severity." [3] A Muslim historian has described Muhammad ibn Tughluq as "a mixture of opposites," a term that is applicable to many of these rulers. The inconsistency may be exaggerated by Muslim chroniclers who sometimes felt that rulers should be contradictory by nature, if only as an aid to inscrutability, and bore this in mind as they wrote their chronicles. [4]

Certainly religious toleration of the Hindus was not considered by the Muslim theologians of fourteenth-century India to be a requirement of the faith. Sultan 'Ala' al-din Khalji in 1300 drew up a set of laws specifically designed to reduce Hindu landowners to poverty. When, apparently stirred by doubts, he asked the opinion of his religious adviser as to the legality of these laws in terms of Islam, he was told that not only were they lawful, but that they were actually more lenient than they need be! The judge who rendered this decision evidently reasoned that inasmuch as the Hindus could not properly be called "people of the Book"—that is, recipients of God's revelation—they could not properly be held to deserve the tolerant treatment the

[3] H. G. Rawlinson, *India, A Short Cultural History* (London, 1952), p. 230.

[4] P. Hardy, *Historians of Medieval India* (London, 1960), pp. 124–125.

Qur'an stipulates for people designated as such.[5] The traditionalist Muslim read his Qur'an very literally: God has fires
in hell waiting for infidels, and the Hindus were certainly
infidels. If God was not going to show them any mercy, why
should anyone else? This is the spirit, one need only note,
that also appeared among the New England Puritans who
persuaded themselves that the Indians had no souls, and
among the California zealots who argued that the Chinese
had no souls, or, if they did, that their souls were not worth
saving. It is not unlike the medieval Christian attitude toward
heretics.

When Muhammad bin Qasim, the Arab conqueror of Sind
in the eighth century, was faced with this same question, he
adopted a more liberal response. The Hindus and Buddhists
of Sind were given the status of protected persons, as though
they were "people of the Book," perhaps because Muhammad
bin Qasim did not have sufficient troops at his disposal to risk
stirring up unnecessary discontent. The pattern of treatment
he set was generally followed by subsequent rulers. Sultan
'Ala' al-din Khalji's action, and the decision of his religious
adviser, represent an attempt to overthrow what had become
established practice. Whether 'Ala' al-din Khalji's request for
legal advice represented something more than a moment of
pique is hard to say, but it does not seem to have stemmed
from any great desire to secure the supremacy and welfare
of Islam as those elements were viewed by the theologians of
his time.[6]

His action seems to have been taken initially for civil rather
than religious reasons. "Be assured," he is reported to have

[5] Ziau-d Din Barni, *Tarikh-i-Firoz Shahi*, in Henry M. Elliot and
John Dowson, *The History of India As Told By Its Own Historians*,
III (London, 1871), 184.
[6] Hardy, pp. 32–34.

said, "that the Hindus will never become submissive and obedient until they are reduced to poverty. I have therefore given orders that just enough shall be left them of corn, milk, and curds, from year to year, but that they must not accumulate hoards and property. . . ." [7] He consulted his religious judge only to be sure that he was not overstepping the bounds of Islam. Despite the favorable ruling, however, this seems to be one of the few instances in which the Muslims designed legislation specifically aimed against the Hindus. Ghiyath al-din Tughluq, a successor of Sultan 'Ala' al-din, also subjected the Hindus to repressive legislation and apparently for the same reason. He decreed that while the Hindus could live in comfort they could not acquire so much wealth as to become ambitious. But Ghiyath al-din came to the throne by overthrowing a Hindu convert who had tried to organize a Hindu reaction against Islam and the sultanate. The problems of government forced rulers not to irritate the Hindus too greatly, and it is clear that enforcement of even thoroughly Islamic strictures was considerably lax. One reason advanced by Timur the Lame (Tamurlaine) in support of his invasion of India in 1398 was that the Muslim rulers were not harsh enough on the Hindus.[8]

The head tax, called *jizya*, and levied by qur'anic injunction on all non-Muslims, was by the early fifteenth century not regularly assessed from the Brahman class, a favor apparently won for them by Hindu officials who served in the Muslim court. It is reported by the Muslim historian Ziya al-din Barni that the pious fourteenth-century Sultan, Firuz Shah Tughluq, insisted on adherence to the qur'anic rule, and that the Brahmans in turn insisted on their prescriptive

[7] Rawlinson, pp. 228–229.

[8] Sharafu-d Din Yazdi, *Zafar-Nama*, in Elliot and Dowson, III (London, 1871), 480.

right to exemption from this tax. Sultan Firuz Shah remained
unmoved by their threats of suicide and starvation, and in the
end the Brahmans arranged for lower-caste Hindus to pay
not only their own tax but that of the Brahmans as well.[9]

The only conclusion one can safely make concerning the
treatment of the Hindus by these Muslim rulers is that it was
uneven, as was the treatment of the Muslims themselves, for
all the expressed piety. For the most part the rulers seem to
have been content with collecting the head tax, at least from
the middle of the fifteenth century.

One must question how deeply some of the Sultans of
Delhi understood Islam. 'Ala' al-din Khalji at one time considered establishing "a new system of religion, that, like
Mahommed, he might be held in veneration by poster-
ity." [10]

Muhammad ibn Tughluq was most strict about the observance of prayer: in one day he executed nine people for
neglecting it. "He compelled the people to master the ordinances for ablutions, prayers, and the principles of Islam," [11]
ibn Battuta remarks, and then he subjected them to an examination, punishing those who were ignorant. He insisted on
receiving no favors for himself from the courts of law, and
would not permit the judge to rise when he entered the
courtroom, emulating the action of the caliph 'Umar in an
earlier day. He was extremely sensitive to all the formal details of the faith, but he does not seem to have felt the absolute necessity of applying Islamic law to public affairs—a
matter his personal friend and historian, Ziya al-din Barni,

[9] *Cambridge History of India*, III (New York, 1928), 188.

[10] A. Dow, *The History of Hindoostan*, translated from the Persian of Muhammad Ferishta of Delhi (London, 1768), p. 264. See
also Ziau-d Din Barni, *Tarikh-i Firoz Shahi*, in Elliot and Dowson,
III, 169.

[11] Quoted in Rawlinson, p. 231.

finds difficult to explain.[12] Muhammad ibn Tughluq insisted, despite the arguments of the traditionalist theologians, that human reason was to be preferred to divine revelation in ordinary matters. Yet he was absolutely servile in his veneration for the temporal as well as the spiritual powers of the caliphate, even though the caliphate had, since the Mongols sacked Baghdad in 1258, been a rather sorry institution, and had been for several centuries even before that date. For all this, Muhammad ibn Tughluq must be acknowledged as one of the most learned and accomplished scholars of his time.

The Turkish Muslim governments were all imperialist in nature. Expeditions and sieges, plans for them, and schemes to support them took up almost all of their time. Despite some administrative niceties introduced at times, these governments remained essentially military and were led, as they had to be, by fighting men. Indeed, the nature of medieval society, the necessity of preventing any unification among the Hindus, the constant pressure from tribes to the north —especially the dreaded Mongols—and the ever present urge to expand and to secure the rewards of expansion forbade alternatives to military rule.

Despite the aloofness of the Hindus and their heroic, although isolated, struggles against the Muslim invaders, and despite the elementary and puritanical religious fervor that marked many of the alien ruling class, the Hindus were in general left alone, if only for reasons of expediency. Nevertheless, the governments existed only for the Muslims. Akbar, the great Mughul emperor who conscientiously tried to integrate the diverse elements of his empire, had to put down at least one rebellion, that of the Uzbegs, which arose in opposition to his liberal treatment of the Hindus.[13] It is unfair,

---

[12] Cf. *Cambridge History of India*, III, 137.

[13] Rawlinson, p. 301.

however, to accuse the Muslims of lacking tolerance in an age when no one showed it. The Brahman's tolerance extended only to Brahmans, and the record of medieval Christians in Europe against Jews was even less enviable than that of the Muslims of India against the Hindus. In Europe the Jews were so few that they could safely be used as scapegoats; far too many Hindus were in India for that.

Even if the Muslim rulers had thoroughly understood Islam and had genuinely desired to defend the purity of Islam throughout India, it is doubtful that they could have defended it, any more than the 'Umayyad caliphs of Damascus, who ruled a vast Arab empire, could have maintained the simple organization of Muhammad. In addition to being a minority, the Muslims were split among themselves. And if at one time it may have seemed possible to work out some kind of social assimilation between Muslims and Hindus that would compromise the religion of neither, the influx of Muslim refugees into India in the thirteenth century, fleeing the Mongol invasions, undid whatever assimilative development may have taken place. Because the sultans of Delhi especially welcomed sunni scholars, the cause of traditionalism in India was greatly strengthened, the more so because these scholars were thoroughly conversant with the defeat of the Mu'tazila, the silencing of the philosophers, and the channelizing of mysticism. Once settled in India, they became the guardians of Islamic purity, and at the same time advisers to sultans and teachers in the Muslim schools, and very frequently the chroniclers of medieval India as well.

Despite the influx of scholars, the Muslims had to make use of Hindus in government. Except for these strict Muslim theologians, the upper strata of Muslim society seems to have been very latitudinarian. It had to be, for it had almost daily contact with Hindu nobles. The Muslims were always in a minority—in 1890 no more than 10 per cent in the Delhi region—and in many areas the Hindu chiefs were left undisturbed if they submitted to the Muslim conquerors. Administrative positions, except those of an executive nature, were usually manned by Hindus. To enforce the stricter dicta of Islam throughout the sultanate would have created problems of the first order. So long as the sultans remained aliens ruling over a foreign empire the laxity did not lead to any complications; but with the appearance of rulers who hoped to strengthen the government so as to reduce civil disturbances by bringing increasingly more Hindus into high positions, the situation was altered.

The problem of asserting the purity of Islam throughout India was additionally complicated by the Hindu converts to Islam. Some had been converted by force, and others voluntarily, in order to improve their social position. Most, however, were won over by Muslim missionaries who entered India with the invading armies and remained to evangelize. They had the greatest success with the lower and depressed classes. The simplicity of the creed won some converts; others were attracted to Islam's egalitarian character, so different from the Hindu concept of caste; simple and credulous farmers were won by the marvelous qualities of the missionaries. Imam Shah of Pirana is said to have once converted a number of Hindu farmers by causing rain to fall after two years of drought.[14] Many of the converts accepted the major tenets of Islam while still retaining traditional Hindu beliefs. In effect they can be considered another kind of Muslim group in India.

The Shi'as and the Sunnis represent the two main divisions (each of which is divided into various sects) within Islam. Shi'ism originated in the days of 'Ali, son-in-law of Muham-

[14] T. Arnold, *The Preaching of Islam* (Lahore, n.d.), p. 277.

mad and fourth caliph. The initial cause of the split between Shi'as and Sunnis was political, but with the death in battle of 'Ali's younger son Hussain, Shi'ism found a martyr. An extensive theology began to develop in which Hussain appeared as a mediator between man and God, and it was charged that sunni scholars had suppressed some qur'anic passages relating to the inheritance of the house of 'Ali.

In part, the success of Shi'ism is to be found in Persian nationalism; the movement found its primary strength in Persia (where it remains dominant to this day). Naturally enough, it was little short of anathema to the sunni traditionalists. In present-day Pakistan Shi'as make up perhaps 10 per cent of the population; that they have not, as a movement, played any significant role in the changing emphases in Islam is probably a result of their tightly woven theology. Individual Shi'as have, however, regularly been in the forefront of change, among them Ameer Ali, the author of *The Spirit of Islam*; the Agha Khan; and Mohamed Ali Jinnah, the leader of the Pakistan movement and the nation's first Governor-General.

To these groups we must add the sufis, for sufism exerted an influence in India greater than in any other Muslim country. In large part the story of Islamic development in India is the story, on the one hand, of the efforts of the sunni traditionalists to restrain and control the sufis, and on the other hand, of the persuasive penetration into Indian thought —both Muslim and Hindu—of sufi ideas. There has been no great Muslim theologian of India who has not been greatly influenced by the mystics of Islam. The overriding need of Muslims in India has been to effect an understanding and compromise between the harsh, legalistic approach of the sunni traditionalist and the softer, more devotional approach of the true sufi. In one sense this struggle resulted from the attempt to prevent Islam from succumbing to its Indian environment.

The first sufis to enter India seem to have been evangelists, but later, attracted by the mystical elements in Hinduism, they began to make studies in comparative religion. On a popular level a similar current is evidenced in the devotional movement (*bhakti*) of Kabir in the fifteenth century.

Kabir, the son of a Muslim weaver of Benares, became the disciple of a Hindu teacher in revolt against every narrow orthodoxy. Kabir began himself to preach nonsectarianism and the hollowness of institutional religion. "God is One," said Kabir, "whether we worship him as Allah or as Rama." [15] "Be truthful, be natural. Truth alone is natural . . . there is no truth in the external religious symbols and observances. . . . Truth resides in the heart and is revealed in love, in strength, in compassion. Conquer hatred, and extend your love to all mankind, for God resides in all." [16] Kabir's teachings represent a blending of the devotional doctrine of sufi and Hindu; he was theistic and opposed both idolatry and caste. In India and Pakistan today Kabir is claimed as a coreligionist by both Muslims and Hindus.

Undoubtedly one of the greatest religious figures in Indian history, Kabir represented a syncretism that alarmed the orthodox, Muslim and Hindu. In fact, Muslims complained to Sikander Lodi, the sultan of Delhi, about Kabir's teaching, but the ruler took no action.[17] Less fortunate was the Brahman who, when abused by a Muslim for his idolatry, replied that everyone worshiped the same God, and that, therefore, he "believed the Mahomedan and Hindoo religions to be equally good." The Muslim considered this an impious answer

[15] Rawlinson, p. 245.
[16] *Cambridge History of India*, IV, 382.
[17] Rawlinson, p. 246.

and hailed the Hindu before a judge. The case aroused such public interest that Sultan Sikander Lodi called together all the learned Muslim scholars to decide it. The Brahman, they said, should either "be forced to turn Mahomedan, or be put to death." Despite his insistence on parity among religions, the Brahman refused to accept Islam and accordingly was killed.[18] The decision of the Muslim scholars was completely in line with traditionalist theology as it had developed from the time of the Mu'tazila defeat. The scholars' position was far more uncompromising than that of Muhammad bin Qasim, whose lenient treatment in the Sind just eighty years after Muhammad's death reflected Islam before a rigid theology had been framed. The learned doctors of Sikander Lodi, casting their mature reflections on the moderate reply of Budhan the Brahman, portray the closed mind that marked the beginning of isolation in Islam and foretold its decline. Total victory was not to be theirs, however, for almost two centuries; meanwhile the sides were forming.

The period of the Tughluqs (1320–1388) marks the beginning of the division between the traditionalist Muslims, with their essentially legal approach, and the mystics, who refused to be fettered in any way. During the time of Firuz Shah, the third ruler of the Tughluq dynasty, clear and definite declarations were made to the effect that individual interpretation of Islamic laws was no longer permitted, and that no one was to go beyond those scholars who had established the primary schools of Islamic law, such as Abu Hanifa, who died in 767, or al-Shafi'i, who died in 820. Once, when a speaker backed up his point by referring to a tradition of Muhammad, the Muslim theologians were not satisfied—they

[18] A. Halim, "Justice of Sikander Lodi," *Journal of the Pakistan Historical Society*, II (Oct., 1954), 272–279. See also Dow, pp. 66–67.

insisted that approval be found in Abu Hanifa! [19] By the end of the fourteenth century all the essentials of the traditionalist position had been firmly established in India. The law of Islam—the *shari'a*—had become fixed and static in an environment which called for some kind of dynamism. At the same time, while rigidity was developing among the traditionalists of India, the pantheistic philosophy of ibn Arabi was attracting increasing attention among the sufis of India.

The syncretist and devotional thought that is seen in Kabir was to prove of tremendous influence on sufis, some Shi'as, non-Brahman Hindus, and the illiterate in general throughout India. But Kabir's thought—and that of those who carried on in his tradition—made very little headway among either the traditionalist Muslims or the Brahmans. So far as the Brahmans were concerned it abjured caste, and so far as the Muslims were concerned it denied the true faith, or certainly the true theology which had developed from God's own word and the sunna of God's own prophet.

Something of the strength of this syncretic movement must be reflected in the efforts of the advisers of Timur the Lame to persuade him not to invade India. If you do, they said, and if you permanently settle there, "Our race will degenerate and our children will become like the natives of those regions . . . ," [20] a cynical assessment of the purity of the faith in the land south of the Indus. Assuring them that he meant only to raid and plunder, not to settle, Timur convinced them that he would not be tempted by the allure of infidel India. Babar, a direct descendant of Timur, however, did

[19] K. A. Nizam, "Some Religious and Cultural Trends of the Tughluq Period," *Journal of the Pakistan Historical Society*, I (July, 1953), 234–243.

[20] *Autobiography of Timur*, p. 10, in Elliot and Dowson, III, 307. The authenticity of this work may be doubted, but there is no reason to question the accuracy of this passage.

move into India to settle 125 years later. He found, when he became Emperor of Delhi in 1526, that some Indian Muslims were even then like "the natives of those regions." Before two centuries had elapsed a powerful movement, which proved generally successful, had arisen among the traditionalists to restore Islam in India to a purer form and to preserve the Muslim culture.

Muslim India reached both its peak and its nadir under the Mughuls. Babar established the kingdom through his victory over the Afghan Lodi dynasty at Panipat in 1526; his son Humayun (1530-1556) desperately held on to it. Akbar (1556-1605), grandson of Babar, overextended it to the south, but gave it organization and tried to make it national rather than semireligious. Jahangir (1605-1627) was an aesthete given to excessive drinking, but he fell in love with a woman who was able to run his kingdom for him. Under Shah Jahan (1628-1666) the Mughul fortunes reached their peak, but he is chiefly remembered for building the Taj Mahal in memory of his empress, Mumtaz. The last of the great Mughuls was Aurangzeb (1659-1707), son of Shah Jahan. After his death in 1707 the fortunes of the dynasty rapidly declined. A hundred and fifty years later, after enduring a line of steadily weakening rulers and steadily constricting borders, the Mughul empire expired. The final coup was administered by the British, but effective life had, by 1857, long since departed.

Babar, who had won and lost several kingdoms before he set out for India, determined to win land he claimed as his only because Timur had held it for two years during an extended raid. The empire Babar established, and the empire his sons and grandsons held, always remained an empire of personal rule. As in the days of the Delhi sultanate, the measure of efficiency remained the character and the energy of

the emperor, and of those the emperor elected to have speak
for him. Babar had been invited to India by discontented
nobles who were outsmarted by their own cleverness. They
had assumed he would return to the hills of Afghanistan
after overthrowing the Afghan dynasty that ruled northern
India, leaving them to fill the vacuum. But Babar stayed.
His son Humayun was driven from India not by the Rajputs
but by the Muslim Afghans his father had overthrown—a
fact that helped convince Akbar that the dynasty could not
depend on Muslim support alone, but must also woo the only
other power in India, that of the Rajputs. Humayun fled to
Persia, gathered support, and finally marched back to victory
in 1555, bringing a strong Persian (and Shi'a) element to the
Mughul court. One year later he died, leaving his newly
regained throne to his son Akbar.

True to his belief that the government needed a broader
base for its support than just the Muslims, Akbar set about
winning the confidence and cooperation of every element of
the population he possibly could. This required, of course,
the cultivation of tolerance so far as religion was concerned,
and his innovations to achieve this end really belong in a class
by themselves. They are the product of an extremely rational
mind, yet one that was inherently religious and not untinged
with mysticism—a broad, compassionate, and above all intensely political mind. In one sense Akbar represents all of
the intellectual currents of his age. The influence of Kabir
and his followers—the bhakti movement of Hinduism; the
soul-searching of sufism; the acclimatization of the invading
foreigners to India; the intense practicality of the Turks; the
stern unitarianism of Islam—these are all reflected in the person of Akbar. But the net result remains Akbar. "My sole
object, oh wise Mullas," he said, "is to ascertain truth, to
find out and disclose the principles of genuine religion, and

to trace it to its divine origin." [21] This attitude, illustrated here in relation to religious knowledge, was reflected by Akbar in other matters, too. "Truly," he is reported to have said to his court physician when tobacco was first introduced into India, "we must not reject a thing that has been adopted by the wise men of other nations merely because we cannot find it in our books; or how shall we progress?" [22]

The rational, compassionate, and political approach of Akbar was manifested very early in his reign. He came to the throne at the age of fourteen, enduring first the rule of regent, and then of queen-mother. Seven years later, ruler in his own name at last, he prohibited the enslavement of prisoners taken in war in an edict that referred particularly to the women and children of the combatants. "For if the husband pursues an evil course . . . how can the children be blamed?" [23] The following year he remitted the special tax imposed on pilgrims at holy shrines. Such pilgrimages are superstitious, he said like a good traditionalist, but, he added like a good sufi, it is the method these people have of worshiping the Almighty, "and the throwing of a stumbling-block and obstacle in their way could never be acceptable in the sight of God." [24] The next year Akbar went even farther and decreed the remission of the poll tax (jizya) paid by the Hindus.[25] He also decreed that no Hindu widow could be forced against her will to commit *sati* (being burned alive on the pyre of one's dead husband)—a practice that was anathema to all Muslims. Once when he heard of such a case he hurried to the place himself, fearful that sending an agent might take too long. He was

[21] Shaikh Nuru-l Hakk, *Zubdatu-t Tawarikh*, in Elliot and Dowson, VI (London, 1875), 190.

[22] *Wikaya'-i Asad Beg*, in Elliot and Dowson, VI, 167.

[23] Abu-l Fazl, *Akbar-Nama*, in Elliot and Dowson, VI, 25.

[24] *Ibid.*, p. 29.

[25] *Ibid.*, pp. 29–30.

successful in this instance. Those relatives who were trying to force the widow to the burning pyre were confined, but Akbar later accepted their assurance of repentance.[26]

In his own way Akbar was proffering to the Muslim community just what Rhazes had offered at a much earlier date. Whereas Rhazes had argued that medicine and science should be studied in order that people might be made healthy, and that helplessness against disease was not part of God's order, Akbar argued that people's beliefs should be respected because it made for good government, and because God didn't really care how He was worshiped so long as honor and sincerity were present. Both Akbar and Rhazes had a concern, whatever its source, to improve the condition of mankind on earth. Looked at from one narrow point of view, and this was the viewpoint of the traditionalists, these were both extraneous positions. Man existed on earth only to submit himself to God—not to challenge Him by combating God's disease or by admitting other forms of worship than those presented in God's Revelation. The world was a place where man earned everlasting bliss or everlasting damnation—it was a heaven-sent opportunity to achieve the former by serving God. And the service of God was, even by the time of Rhazes, well spelled out. Being God's representative on earth did not necessarily involve making efforts to improve the material establishment. No profound feeling opposed it; it was just so unnecessary. Akbar, of course, moved not much farther along this line than had Rhazes, but in a different sphere.[27]

To the traditionalists Akbar was threatening the faith by

[26] *Ibid.*, p. 69.

[27] His son, Jahangir, upon his accession to the throne in 1605, ordered hospitals to be built in large cities and doctors to be appointed to attend the sick; this was all to be financed from the royal treasury. *Memoirs of Jahangir,* in Elliot and Dowson, VI, 286.

denying its exclusiveness. Akbar did not believe he was chal-
lenging Islam, but only the conception of Islam that had
become standardized by the traditionalists (his position was
not unlike that of many advocates of a modern Islamic state
in Pakistan). Akbar's position was predicated upon the idea
that God acknowledged all worship of Him, no matter the
method, an idea that probably reflects both sufi and bhakti
influences on Akbar.

"To repeat the words of the Creed," he said, "to perform
circumcision, or to lie prostrate on the ground from dread of
kingly power, can avail nothing in the sight of God:

> *Obedience is not in prostration on the earth:*
> *Practice sincerity, for righteousness is not borne*
> *upon the brow.*" [28]

Although traditionalists did not disagree with this, they did
insist that without the creed, without circumcision, no genuine sincerity could be achieved. God has provided a way,
clearly presented in the Qur'an and the sunna; since it is un-
thinkable that God would require that which is not necessary,
then clearly the forms must be necessary—without them truly
sincere worship must be lacking. But Akbar was primarily a
politician; his first duty was to run a government. He knew
that his subjects were to be trusted, not on the basis of how
they bowed and scraped, but on the basis of their loyalty,
upon how sincerely they supported him. Was God's position
any different? To Akbar the problem seemed to be one of
the evidence of loyalty, whether to God or to the sultan.
He thought of this problem in terms he understood; the traditionalists maintained that no one can understand God's
position, except God: the truly religious man recognizes this,

[28] Abu-l Fazl, *Akbar-Nama*, in Elliot and Dowson, VI, 60–61.

and accepts God's revelation. Both Akbar and the traditionalist theologians of Islam considered sincerity of worship of
prime import, but they disagreed, among other things, on
what really was necessary to establish sincerity.

The point was a delicate one, for royalty was always likely
to be the subject of attack. Akbar knew that the Hindus were
too numerous to be effectively subdued by military means
alone, nor did he think 'Ala' al-din Khalji's repressive policy
could be maintained. He could do little except to bring the
Hindus to cooperate with him. He utilized Hindus in governmental positions on a larger scale than before, although
Hindus still occupied only about 10 per cent of the higher
ranks.[29] Akbar believed that the Hindus could be reconciled,
and he believed on religious grounds that they should be
reconciled, for God could not worry about the method by
which He was worshiped. This thinking of Akbar's had to
lead to an entirely new concept of the Muslim state; to the
traditionalists it was not Islam, it was heresy, and they labeled
Akbar an atheist.

But Akbar, like his European contemporaries, was not sure
that several different faiths *could* exist equitably side by side.
At least it would be much simpler if everyone would adopt
the same faith. And as it was obvious that the Hindus would
never become Muslims, nor the Muslims Hindus, why not
combine the best elements of all faiths, and so satisfy everyone? Why not have a court faith which, while not trans-
gressing one's own beliefs, would serve to emphasize the essential unity of all faiths? Akbar, like the Roman Empire's
Julian, tried to manufacture a religion by taking bits and
pieces from every other. His Divine Faith was indebted to
Zoroastrianism, Hinduism, Buddhism, Christianity, and Islam.
But this attempt to create a faith pleasing to all proved pleas-

[29] G. Dunbar, *A History of India* (London, 1939), p. 200.

ing to none. Akbar does not seem to have concerned himself
very much with the philosophical side of religion, but he did
appreciate the importance of symbols. It is not unfair to say
that his Divine Faith was little more than a combination of
symbols of all the religions of which he knew. Actually, very
little is known of either the Divine Faith itself or of Akbar's
purpose in advancing it. Perhaps he looked upon it primarily
as a device to emphasize to men that they were all worshiping
the same God, call Him what they will, and bend to Him
how they will. He does not seem to have considered it a
substitute for other religions—he, himself, apparently never
abandoned Islam, and he does not appear to have tried to
persuade others to do so. Nevertheless, religious instruction
emanating from the Emperor was nothing to be treated
lightly, and an implied threat was always present; in this case
his religious sensibilities seem to have dominated his political
insight, for although both Muslims and Hindus vigorously
protested against the Divine Faith, Akbar never abandoned it.

It is an amazing and somehow warming picture this great
sovereign presents, sitting night after night in the building he
had especially constructed for the purpose, listening to "*Sufis*,
doctors, preachers, lawyers, *Sunnis*, *Shi'as*, Brahmans, Jains,
Buddhists, Char-baks, Christians, Jews, Zoroastrians, and
learned men of every belief" [30] argue their theological positions, sorting and sifting in his own mind those points that
struck him as particularly valid, searching for something in
common that would unite all. Many of the discussions were
intemperate, and the level of argument was not always very
high. The Portuguese missionary Padre Rodolpho Aquaviva,
for instance, advanced this apparently clinching argument to
win his point with the traditionalist Muslim teachers: "If
these men have such an opinion of our Book, and if they

[30] Abu-l Fazl, *Akbar-Nama*, in Elliot and Dowson, VI, 59.

believe the Qur'an to be the true word of God, then let a furnace be lighted, and let me with the Gospel in my hand, and the 'ulama with their holy book in their hands, walk into that testing place of truth, and the right will be manifest." The Muslim scholars shrank back from this challenge, as did Savonarola in another place and time under somewhat similar conditions. Akbar was impressed by the sincerity of the Christian missionary, and he took the occasion to deliver a few remarks to the Muslims. "Man's outward profession and the mere letter of Muhammadanism, without a heartfelt conviction, can avail nothing. I have forced many Brahmans, by fear of my power, to adopt the religion of my ancestors; but now that my mind has been enlightened with beams of truth, I have become convinced that the dark clouds of conceit and the mist of self-opinion have gathered round you, and that not a step can be made in advance without the truth of proof. That course only can be beneficial which we select with clear judgment." [31] Here is the rationale of Akbar's Divine Faith.

Akbar's eclectic approach to religion, of course, aroused bitter feeling among traditionalist theologians. But while they could rant and rave and lead little riots against the emperor, or support such invaders as Akbar's half-brother Mirza Muhammad Hakim of Kabul,[32] making "the pleasant land of India full of the dust of opposition," they were able neither to incite the mass of Muslims to take action against the emperor's policies nor to persuade the emperor that his policies were wrong. Indeed, the pointless theological wrangling of the traditionalists in Akbar's House of Religion had in itself done much to convince him of the necessity for his approach. His Divine Faith died with him, however, and ever since the

[31] *Ibid.*, p. 60.

[32] Quoted in M. Yasin, *A Social History of Islamic India* (Lucknow, 1958), p. 143.

Muslims of India and Pakistan have been divided as to whether
or not Akbar had remained a true Muslim in advancing it.
Whatever the answer might be, he was certainly a true representative of that strong syncretic current which on a different level produced Kabir.

The future of Muslim traditionalism in India depended
upon finding a sultan who adhered to its interpretation, and
who was willing to enforce it steadfastly as part of his public
policy. Traditionalist theologians emphasized this point. The
ruler, it was argued by Shaykh Ahmad of Sirhind, as by
medieval Christian theorists, is the soul and the people are the
body; if the soul is pure so, too, will be the body.[33] A sultan
was required who could be amenable to the traditionalist
position without weakening his hold upon the throne, and
who was himself deeply and genuinely religious. Consciously
or not, the tactics that had led to the demise of the Mu'tazila
were to be used again!

Both Babar and Humayun were ostensibly traditionalists,
but each decided in effect that "Paris is worth a Mass," and
outwardly adopted Shi'ism to gain Persian military support.
Humayun's conversion resulted in a steady stream of Shi'as
from Persia into India and into court circles. Akbar was too
much of a freethinker to lend assistance to the traditionalists
in their struggle against all deviation from sunni interpretation. His son Jahangir was a religiously credulous man who
bent with the wind, and Nur Jahan, the lovely and talented
lady of whom he was enamored, was a Shi'a. Many of her
relatives, all Shi'as, were given high positions at court; the
command of the government that was so necessary for the
traditionalist triumph was just not possible during Jahangir's
reign. Shah Jahan was more of a traditionalist than any of his
Mughul predecessors. His policy. in fact, was the reverse of

[33] *Ibid.,* p. 151.

Akbar's, but he was never strong enough to effect it fully. Akbar hoped to create a united India; Shah Jahan hoped to create a Muslim India, and he could point to indications that Akbar's tolerant policies would not be successful in creating a united India. A Hindu revival movement was in progress which in some places assumed an aggressive attitude—as when a mosque and tomb were razed at Thanesar, and a temple was constructed in their place.[34] Nevertheless, although Shah Jahan did impose restrictions on temple building, he did not try to re-establish the poll tax on Hindus, or to establish the practice of sacrificing cows as Shaykh Ahmad of Sirhind urged. Dara Shikoh, Shah Jahan's eldest son, was a liberal sufi interested in the unity of all religions, yet he remained his father's favorite. Dara said of his brother Aurangzeb, "There is only one of my brothers I fear, the Prayer-monger."[35] In the race for the throne, even before the death of Shah Jahan, it was Aurangzeb, the sunni traditionalist, who was victorious.

Thus up through the time of Akbar, Islam was developing in India along lines peculiar to the subcontinent. Shi'as formed an important part of the Muslim population and were frequently influential in court circles. Sufism was extremely popular, and of a form that seemed to invite comparisons between religions, for Muslim sufis like Dara Shikoh found much in common between their beliefs and those of the mystics of Hindu Vaishavism. Most of the Muslims on the subcontinent were converted Hindus who often retained many of their old Hindu customs; on the other hand, Muslims moving into India frequently adopted Hindu customs, and a general laxity seems to have crept in among Muslims in general. It is re-

[34] S. M. Ikram, *Rūd-i-Kawthar*, trans. by S. W. Zaman (Lahore, n.d.), p. 280.
[35] Rawlinson, p. 333.

ported of Makhdum-ul-Mulk that in order to avoid payment
of his religious tax—the annual tax on his wealth, and one of
the so-called five "pillars" of Islam—he would transfer all of
his property to his wife just before the time for the payment,
then transfer it back to his name when the time for payment
had passed.[36] The long, hairsplitting arguments of the traditionalists and the bitter personal quarrels that resulted from
them strongly influenced Akbar toward his liberal course.
Finally, because the Muslims were a minority, and yet in
political control, they could not afford to become weak
through division or through indifference. Thus the traditionalist Muslim's reaction to Akbar's wooing of the Rajputs
was not that a strong, harmonious government might be
formed, but that a truly Islamic government would be denied.
Only Muslims may share in an Islamic government as envisaged by the traditionalist; followers of other religions
might be placed in a protected status in return for the payment of a tax. But Akbar had even abolished the collection
of this tax. Akbar and his liberalism became objects of intense
vituperation on the part of the traditionalists, who devoted
every effort to restoring Islam to its purity as they conceived it.

For Akbar was not following the distinct path God had
revealed to the Muslims; instead, he affirmed the validity of
alternative paths. Mankind, the traditionalists insisted, was
created for submission to God—does not Islam itself mean
"submission"? What, then, constitutes submission except following the shari'a—God's clear path—and bending all one's
thoughts to God as He has expressed Himself in the Qur'an?
Ideally, no knowledge should be taught except that based
upon the affirmations, "God has said," and "The Prophet has

[36] B. A. Faruqi, *The Mujaddidd's Conception of Tawhid* (Lahore,
1943), p. 10.

said." [37] When Akbar said that nothing must be rejected merely because it cannot be found in Islamic books he was treading the way of heresy so far as the traditionalists of his day were concerned.

The religious question at issue between Akbar and his Muslim opponents, although often obscured, was essentially the same religious question as that at issue in Pakistan today, although it, too, is often obscured: what constitutes submission to God? The question of the nature of submission involves defining the nature of God, of God's world, and of man himself. That the qur'anic story of the Garden is open to various interpretations is evidence that Islam offers a variety of definitions of these basic elements and of their relation. The story of medieval Islam—like that of medieval Christianity—is of the triumph of one particular and finite interpretation.

This problem of interpretation has been, of course, one of the perennial questions of Islam, whether in India or not. It had made its appearance several times during the Delhi sultanate, but too much Muslim heterodoxy existed then for it to be crucial. Under Akbar, who moved farther than any of his predecessors toward establishing a government based on religious toleration, however, the traditionalist revival was spurred to greater efforts. Traditionalists were able to respond so energetically to the challenge of Akbar for two reasons. As the Mughul government established itself schools were founded which became centers for traditionalist Sunni teaching, and during the reign of Jahangir a remarkable leader emerged, Shaykh Ahmad of Sirhind, one of the two greatest Muslim theologians produced on the subcontinent. Shaykh Ahmad, a traditionalist Muslim, was a traditionalist mystic as

[37] Ziah al-din Barni, *Fatawa-yi Jahandari*, in W. T. deBary, ed., *Sources of Indian Tradition* (New York, 1958), p. 481.

well. His theological position today would generate little excitement among the youth of Pakistan who, while they might decry Akbar in imitation of their elders, seem to be far closer in spirit to him than to Shaykh Ahmad. The practical sciences for Shaykh Ahmad were those relating directly to the Qur'an, the sunna, and the shari'a. He agreed with al-Ghazali that what the philosophers had produced—such as mathematics—was of little practical value.[38] The young Muslim in Pakistan today often accepts the idea that religion is a personal and a voluntary matter, but Shaykh Ahmad believed that the strength of Islam lay in the community— a community made up of Muslims who believed as he did. In today's Pakistan, the good Shaykh would be permitted to have his thoughts, but not encouraged to express them.

The Shaykh's influence was unquestionably tremendous, but whether it ultimately worked for the strengthening or the weakening of Islam on the subcontinent is unknowable, for such a question involves an understanding of both Islam and Hinduism. Through preaching, conversations, and letters Shaykh Ahmad sought to convince the Muslim nobility of the importance of abandoning the many innovations that had been introduced into Islam in India in order to return to the true faith. He took a strong stand against the pantheistic thinking that was so much a part of sufism. There is no unity of existence, he argued, but rather a duality: God, the Creator, and that which is created. The two must never be confused. The mystic who reaches the stage at which he can, like the tenth-century al-Hallaj, say, "I am God," has not reached the final stage of mysticism, because to identify himself with God is still to be aware of himself. God is as incomprehensible through intuition as he is through reason: He is known only

[38] Yasin, p. 158.

through His revelation. The unknown, he argued, can be perceived only through the known. To know God, then, one studies revelation and the sciences based on revelation; "there is no purpose in seeking anything beyond the Shari'a." [39] Obviously the design of Shaykh Ahmad's mysticism was not the same as that of other mystics, and in this lies the primary difference between his Nakshbandi order and the other sufi orders in India (although Shaykh Ahmad had himself been initiated into two other sufi orders).

The Nakshbandi order originated in central Asia. Its founder came from near Bukhara, and it reflected the simple, unshaded perspective that seems to have marked these early Turks. It was a strict order; its mysticism seems to have been of the austere quality of Loyola's Jesuits. The Nakshbandi order emphasized conforming to the shari'a and was about as puritanical as mysticism could be. Only by following the shari'a could one truly come to know God, and, indeed, the most successful could (like Shaykh Ahmad) do no better than reach the stage beneath that which Muhammad himself had attained. Muhammad was only a man, however perfect; there was no question of identification with God on his part. Consequently, to the Nakshbandi, those mystics who identified themselves with the Creator were grievously wrong and thoroughly un-Islamic.

The Nakshbandi order, as it was developed in India by Shaykh Ahmad, grew rapidly—faster than the three other principal sufi orders in India. In the area of Sind it became almost the largest single order. And in India, where sufism had such a strong attraction that it became almost identified with Islam, the triumph of the Nakshbandi meant a real triumph for the traditionalist school; it was assurance that the

[39] Shaykh Ahmad Sirhindi, *Maktubat*, in deBary, p. 451.

sufis of India would never wander far from traditionalist interpretation, and the temptations emanating from the bhakti movement were largely stilled.

Shaykh Ahmad's role extended beyond his arguments against pantheism and his development of the Nakshbandi order. Indeed, his success in these areas was dependent upon his interpretation of the Muslim law. Basic to Shaykh Ahmad's thought, and to that of all traditionalist sunni Muslims, is the idea that the present is to be controlled by the laws of Islam; the laws of Islam are not to be altered by changing circumstances. The traditionalist juridical interpretation was thus advanced as the only interpretation, and for all times; except on slight variations no other interpretation was permitted. The Shi'as, of course, did not concur, but their minority position in the country, once their position at the Court was challenged, render them a group apart. Much of the controversy concerning Islam in Pakistan today revolves around this same question. But there was no room for controversy in Shaykh Ahmad's mind. He insisted, too, that the laws of Islam and the observance of those laws could not be separated. If one did not outwardly observe, then he could not inwardly believe.

Shaykh Ahmad illustrates the type of mind that urged Islam into intellectual isolation, and thus encouraged its decline. His insistence on absolute obedience to the shari'a prevented him from realizing that many customs, even from other religions, might not clash with the shari'a itself. Shaykh Ahmad's attitude was in many ways similar to that maintained by the Roman Catholic Church during the famous Rites Controversies of the seventeenth century, when the Jesuits hoped to secure a firm place for Christianity in China by acknowledging certain Chinese adaptations as essentially Christian. The Church's decision was that Chinese practices could not be adapted as part of Christian rites, which must be zealously guarded from external variations as well as propagated. Similarly, the law of Islam was to be jealously guarded, and Shaykh Ahmad was afraid the slightest contact with infidels would shake the whole structure.

The westerner can only look at this argument from his own particular background: Shaykh Ahmad reflected a society whose background included neither the Reformation—the sudden overthrow of scholastic thought—nor the humanitarian developments of the eighteenth century which grew out of the Reformation and may even be considered a part of it. He reflected, as many Muslims do, a belief that the conditions of Muhammad's seventh-century Arabia represented the prevailing conditions of men of all times—this is why God selected Arabia as the place for His last revelation, and why Islamic law must be considered universal. Consequently, accusations in the Qur'an seemingly addressed to the non-Muslims of Muhammad's Arabia were accepted by Shaykh Ahmad as addressed to all non-Muslims at any time and anywhere. Shaykh Ahmad of Sirhind, thus, could be extremely bitter against the Hindus, and yet be extremely Muslim. His attitude actually required less rationalization than does that of Christians who support apartheid or other forms of race prejudice.

In spite of the prevalence of his views, with surprisingly few exceptions Indian Muslim religious figures had not urged that harsh treatment be meted out to non-Muslims. Some rulers, such as 'Ala' al-din Khalji and Muhammad ibn Tughluq, practiced repression, but the sufis did not, as a whole, display any particular intolerance against the non-Muslims. Indeed, as missionaries many sufis had to maintain a close contact with non-Muslims if they were to be successful in their conversion. Shaykh Ahmad, however, belonged to a different school.

He took great umbrage at the slightest offense Hindus
might levy on Muslims. To him India *was* a Muslim state.
It pained him that Hindus should openly observe their rights
and customs, or that they could cook and sell food during
Ramadan, the Muslim month of fasting. "Islam's honor lies,"
he wrote in a letter, "in the ill-treatment of infidelity and
infidels." In another letter he said of the poll tax imposed by
the Qur'an on all non-Muslims: "The poll tax aims at dis-
gracing and insulting the nonbelievers." This is what the
Hindus had maintained all along, and it was why Akbar
abolished the tax. Shaykh Ahmad vigorously advocated restoring the tax—partly because he felt vindictive toward the
Hindus, partly because the tax was part of the shari'a. "To
the extent that nonbelievers are honored," he wrote, "Islam
is insulted. . . . Most people have lost sight of this and have
destroyed the faith." [40] Shaykh Ahmad dearly wanted to see
not only the poll tax reimposed, but all restrictions placed on
the sacrifice of cows by Muslims removed. Interestingly
enough, Shaykh Ahmad always described the Hindus as "infidels," although nowhere in the Qur'an is there any stipula-
tion that the poll tax should be collected from infidels—it
was a protective tax limited to the "people of the Book."

Hinduism, of course, was far from being a dormant religion, and several revival movements were operating. Perhaps Shaykh Ahmad felt that it was all-or-nothing, so far as
the relations between Hinduism and Islam were concerned.
At any rate, he could brook no tolerance for the Hindus,
since God Himself had urged warfare on the polytheists and
the infidels. He did not intend the reimposition of the poll
tax to be in any sense an act of toleration, but rather the
opposite. In this case Shaykh Ahmad seems to have been
using the poll tax in a manner not sanctioned by the Qur'an,

[40] Ikram, p. 272.

and was letting his personal animosities and fears determine his reading of the Qur'an.

The teaching of Shaykh Ahmad was spread by hundreds of his students. The emperor Aurangzeb became a follower of one of his sons, and intellectuals all over Mughul India became associated with Shaykh Ahmad's teachings, and, indeed, with his Nakshbandi order as well. Nevertheless, Shaykh Ahmad was not successful in effecting a wholesale conversion of Indian Muslims to his views of the nature of Islam. He did not win over Jahangir, and Shah Jahan, who certainly had traditionalist leanings, did not agree so completely as to let them override political considerations. That became the role of Aurangzeb, who fell into the peculiar position of finding that political considerations as well as his own convictions led him to accept wholeheartedly the teachings of Shaykh Ahmad and, as sultan, to try to put them into practice.

Shaykh Ahmad's uncompromising belief and the success with which his followers indoctrinated Indian Muslims with this belief, served to divide the Shi'as and the Sunnis in India more sharply than ever. Pakistan is still trying to arrive at some compromise between these two great Muslim sects. Shaykh Ahmad's attempt to promote orthodoxy among the mystics met with some success, although it may be argued that the net effect was to divide the sufis as well—a separation that remains reflected in the division between the Muslim theological schools at Deoband and at Bareilly, in India, to this day. The vehemence with which he approached the question of Hinduism served to incite both the Muslims and the Hindus. There can be no doubt that Shaykh Ahmad was a great divisive factor on the Indian scene, but the traditionalists could not have been strongly revived in India without creating divisions. One party can thus praise the Shaykh for bringing Indian Islam back to the true path, while another can assail him for starting procedures which hastened the collapse of the Mughul state.

His teaching certainly played a prominent role in bringing out into the open an ideological conflict among the Muslims of India. His strict traditionalism met the heterodoxy of Indian Muslim ways head on. In the last years of Shah Jahan's rule, this struggle centered around the figures of his oldest and youngest sons, Dara Shikoh, the liberal sufi, and Aurangzeb, the follower of Shaykh Ahmad.

Although favored by his father, Dara Shikoh lost out to Aurangzeb in the mad scramble for the throne that was so much a part of the Turkish and Mughul political scenes. In this particular race, the two contestants did not even wait for the death of Shah Jahan—he died after eight years of "kindly captivity" in the hands of Aurangzeb. The failure of Dara Shikoh had many facets, but probably more important than his religious views was the fact that the Rajputs, on whom Akbar had depended, failed Dara; in the realm of intrigue he was no match for Aurangzeb. And while the victory of Aurangzeb assured the application of traditionalist concepts, it was a victory based as much on Dara Shikoh's incompetence as on anything.

Aurangzeb, too, had Hindu backing in his struggle for the throne, but he made the traditionalist concept of Islam the basis of all of his policies—and the traditionalist view envisaged only one kind of state: Muslim-dominated, the infidels repressed, and the "people of the Book" protected. Dara Shikoh had maintained that the Hindus, too, were "people of the Book," and that the Upanishads were a revelation from God far older than the Qur'an.[41] No traditionalist Muslim of the time entertained, or was willing to entertain, this view.

[41] deBary, pp. 446–448

Some might have held that the original Upanishads were God's revelation, but they would have insisted that the existing Upanishads were corrupted, and could by no stretch of the imagination be ranked with the revealed word of God.

Aurangzeb was sure that what was just was Islamic; this, indeed, was his definition of justice, just as it was the definition of Shaykh Ahmad. The emperor could not in honor, then, contemplate any religious compromise with non-Muslims. He was like Charles V of the Holy Roman Empire a century earlier: too positive of his own religious belief to think of compromise, his court too divided to give him true support however he decided the issue. Aurangzeb might more fairly be compared with Louis IX of France—St. Louis—except that where conditions favored Louis' success as king, they did not favor Aurangzeb at all. Aurangzeb was a tragic figure in many ways; he was the inheritor of all the problems created by the Mughuls, of all their faults and most of their virtues. Unhappily, in the realm of nation-building, it was the fault that dominated. But Aurangzeb wanted to build only one kind of nation—the Muslim state envisaged by the traditionalist theologians, a benevolent despotism run by and for the Muslims.

The kind of state that the Muslim traditionalists required, however, had always been a chimera so far as India was concerned, especially at this period. On the other hand, if the religious compromise that Akbar had dreamed of, and had so crudely tried to achieve, had been incorporated by Aurangzeb as part of his policy it is questionable—to say the least—how successful he might have been. The evidence for success is admittedly slight. The Brahmans were just as set in their views as were the Muslim traditionalists. It can be said for Akbar's compromise, however, that it did not require one to abandon his faith, only to recognize the validity of others.

One of Aurangzeb's feudal nobles, perhaps Shivaji, the low-caste Hindu Maratha leader, sent him a truly remarkable letter requesting that he adopt Akbar's policy of cherishing and protecting "all the people" and not just Muslims.

If your Majesty places any faith in those books by distinction called divine, you will be instructed God is the God of all mankind, not the God of Mussalmans alone. Pagan and Mussalman are alike in His Presence. Distinctions of color are His ordination. In your mosques, to His name the voice is raised in prayer; in a house of images, when the bell is shaken, still He is the object of adoration. To vilify the religion or customs of other men is to set at naught the pleasure of the Almighty. When we deface a picture we naturally incur the resentment of the painter and justly the poet has said, "Presume not to arraign or scrutinize the works of Power Divine." [42]

But what was the word of a Hindu, however eloquent, when set against the word of God? And who would deny that the Hindus were polytheists and consequently infidels? Did not God send his Prophet, in the words of the Qur'an, "with the guidance and the true religion that He may make it prevail over all the religions"? Could Islam be made to prevail among the Hindus by admitting that the Hindu religion was also true? This argument must have been received by Aurangzeb as a case of special pleading. As the Qur'an says, "Say to those who disbelieve, you shall soon be vanquished." [43]

Aurangzeb followed the teachings of Shaykh Ahmad, the great restorer of traditionalist Islam, and Shaykh Ahmad read his Quar'an with a definite and literal eye. "As for the infidels, neither their wealth nor their children shall profit

[42] Rawlinson, p. 345.
[43] Qur'an 3:11.

them anything against God: they shall be the fuel of hell-fire." [44] If the consignment has been made, what should God's representative do but hurry it along? Aurangzeb was a traditionalist Muslim who sincerely cared; he was also a Mughul emperor, faced with the practical problems of politics. All his life he remained caught between the urge for tolerance and the urge for successful Muslim action, between assuring all of the requirements of a Muslim state based on his understanding of the shari'a and assuring that he did not overreach his resources. The difference between the expulsion of Roger Williams from the Massachusetts Bay Colony and Aurangzeb's treatment of the Hindus is, in a sense, only one of degree. The pious fathers of Massachusetts could not enforce their particular concepts of God and His word against a small minority; Aurangzeb could not enforce his concepts of God and His word against a vast majority, but he could indicate that he would like to—and he did.

Aurangzeb's reign represents the culmination of Shaykh Ahmad's teachings. He was motivated throughout his reign to bring the state, and the life of every Muslim, into strict agreement with the shari'a as interpreted by Shaykh Ahmad. This could not be done without affecting non-Muslims, and although Aurangzeb does not seem to have treated the Hindus with cruelty because they were Hindus, he did not do that which they most desired: he neither treated them as equals nor did he let them alone. He could not, for the Muslims and the Hindus lived side by side in the same society; the laissez-faire policy of his Mughul predecessors had developed some kind of roots. Aurangzeb, in the belief that it was required by his faith, devoted himself to establishing the absolute dominance of Muslims in India. During his reign Hindu officials no longer appeared in the upper policy-making positions;

[44] Qur'an 3:9.

taxes were weighted in favor of Muslims; and the whole society was pointed toward the shari'a, for only by following
that could Muslims become strong. This insistence upon the
dominance of Muslims has been, in Muslim eyes, his greatest
triumph. Years after the Mughul power had been wasted
away the Muslims of India looked to Delhi as their great hope.
While the Hindus accepted, assimilated, adapted themselves
to new conditions and new rulers the Muslims of India, on
the whole, remained mesmerized, their eyes on Delhi, as
though they in the present could expect great sustenance to
come to them from the past. And while they waited, their
power steadily diminished.

The poll tax, too, was re-established, despite frantic opposition from many Hindus. To be sure, the tax was light—it
apparently ranged from about 5 to less than 1 per cent of the
annual income, and was not levied on any non-Muslims who
received an income of less than fifty-two rupees a year, thus
excluding all of the peasantry. Nor was any man who paid
the poll tax liable for military service.[45] Nevertheless, the tax
was collected in the Deccan only by force, and in three
strongly Hindu areas—Rajputana, Udaipur, and Jodhpur—
the attempt to enforce the tax was abandoned.[46] The tax was
reimposed from the best of motives. Aurangzeb believed that
Akbar, in abolishing it and simultaneously making all of his
subjects liable for military service, was legislating in opposition to Islam, for military service cannot be required of non-
Muslims. On the other hand, the tax in practice was not so
much a revenue tax as a mark of discrimination. The Hindu
sensed this, and it was the source of his objections. Indeed,
in Aurangzeb's empire the Hindu felt he could be only a
second-class citizen. Almost three centuries later the tables

[45] Pakistan Historical Society, *Short History,* pp. 239–240.
[46] Dunbar, p. 41.

had turned and the State of Pakistan was created because many Muslims felt they could be only second-class citizens in a Hindu-dominated independent India.

To the emperor, however, the tax was part of the shari'a and was, therefore, essential to a Muslim state. Similarly, because no good Muslim could accept tainted money, he abolished long-standing taxes on non-Muslim religious festivals, as well as on gambling houses, houses of prostitution, and alcoholic spirits.[47] At Agra he ended the pilgrim tax his predecessors had imposed on Hindus visiting the temple there, applied the poll tax—and destroyed the temple. Here he was motivated by a desire to suppress idolatry, but his treatment of Hindus seems often to have been determined by his fears for Muslims.[48] Muhammad Saki, a contemporary chronicler, reports:

It reached the ear of His Majesty, the protector of the faith, that in the provinces of Thatta, Multan, and Benares, but especially in the latter, foolish Brahmans were in the habit of expounding frivolous books in their schools [by which he meant Hindu texts], and that students and learners, Musulmans as well as Hindus, went there, even from long distances, led by a desire to become acquainted with the wicked sciences they taught. The "Director of the Faith" consequently issued orders to all the governors of provinces to destroy with a willing hand the schools and temples of the infidels; and they were strictly enjoined to put an entire stop to the teaching and practicing of idolatrous forms of worship.[49]

It is likely that these orders were meant as warnings; they were certainly not enforced. Yet Aurangzeb, as Defender of

[47] Stanley Lane-Poole, *Aurangzeb* (London, 1896), pp. 65, 81.

[48] *Kanzu-l Mahfaz*, in Elliot and Dowson, VIII (London, 1877), 38.

[49] Muhammad Saki Musta'idd Khan, *Ma-asir-i 'Alamgiri*, in Elliot and Dowson, VII (London, 1877), 183–184.

the Faith, did go to extremes. He destroyed the temple of
Madura—which had been built with the approval of Jahangir
—erected a mosque on the spot, and the "richly-jewelled idols
. . . were transferred to Agra, and there placed beneath the
steps leading to the Nawab Begum Sahib's mosque, in order
that they might ever be pressed under foot by true believers." [50] It may well be, as some have claimed, that this
temple had become a center of intrigue against the emperor
and of support for the ideas of Dara Shikoh; nevertheless, the
humiliation of the punishment went far beyond statesman-
ship, although the ghost of Shaykh Ahmad must have ap-
plauded long.

The intensity with which Aurangzeb adhered to his traditionalist faith may have served to weaken his empire, but it
is doubtful if problems of religion were primarily responsible
for the collapse of the Mughuls. Aurangzeb was not the only
Muslim ruler in India who tried to live according to traditionalist Muslim ideas, but because he was the last great
Mughul ruler he has been assailed as one whose religious
bigotry led to the fall of an empire. This does not seem to
be true. Even though he lived into the eighteenth century,
Aurangzeb was a medieval monarch, very much of a parcel
with the medieval monarchs of Europe. He cannot be fairly
blamed for not thinking of nationalism in modern terms, nor
for thinking of religion in medieval terms. Prince Henry the
Navigator, a very Christian medieval prince, sent his Portuguese sailors south along the coast of Africa, hoping to out-
flank the Muslims so he could annihilate them and thus achieve
a great victory for Christendom. Aurangzeb had no need to
go so far to find infidels, yet no critic has accused him of trying to annihilate them. He only wanted, if they would not

[50] *Ibid.*, p. 185.

accept Islam, to follow a common medieval concept, and keep them in their place, somewhere well below the Muslims.

Aurangzeb suffered because the Turks and the Mughuls never solved the problem of succession, thus ensuring intrigue and conspiracy as a natural concomitant of the reign. At one time or another he imprisoned all but one of his five sons.[51] He inherited an empire already too large for his armies to protect. This did not matter so long as opponents raised themselves, and could be put down, one by one. But when revolts broke out simultaneously in far-flung stretches of the empire, the problems of policing became almost insurmountable. We can accuse Aurangzeb of failing to realize that his strength lay in shortening his lines, rather than in trying to keep them extended, but he was operating in the Mughul tradition, so well expressed by Akbar when he said that a monarch should "ever be intent on conquest, otherwise his enemies rise in arms against him." [52] The Mughuls had to maintain an administrative system that would assure the supremacy of an armed minority, and they paid dearly to support it. The wonder of Aurangzeb is that he was able, by playing one man against another, to maintain his power to his death. For this, however, he paid a high price—to look upon every man with deep suspicion. His has been described as a "lonely unloved life" [53]; his suspicious temperament created suspicion in others, and served to ensure that his could not, politically speaking, be a constructive reign. His religious faith, while it was unquestionably a tremendous personal solace, neither promoted unity nor invited loyalty from the non-Muslim citizens of his empire. His own strict views of Islam were not shared by

[51] J. Sarkar, *Studies in Aurangzib's Reign* (Calcutta, 1933), p. 23.
[52] Rawlinson, p. 304.
[53] Lane-Poole, p. 202.

all the Muslims, but his authority was so great that all tendencies toward innovations were ended. Islam in India was straitjacketed, and it became the function of the next great figure in Indian Islam, Shah Waliullah, while maintaining traditionalist concepts, to find some way to reintroduce elasticity into the faith. Shah Waliullah's success in these efforts was such that traditionalists and modernists alike in Pakistan can claim to be his spiritual inheritors.

For all Aurangzeb's great pursuit of the faith, his success was strangely limited. His son and successor, Bahadur Shah, had definite leanings toward Shi'ism. Aurangzeb ruled over an empire still reflecting its past glories; his successors ruled over a mere shadow. Bahadur Shah, finally succeeding to the throne at the age of sixty-five, faced an unending chain of insurrection from Rajputs, Marathas, and Sikhs. He soon gave up, devoting the last six months of his reign to gardening, and when he died in 1712 the empire fell apart. "The story of the next fifty years," it has been said, "is one of the most piteous in all history. . . ." [54]

Bahadur Shah's successor, Jahandar Shah, invited discord and rebellion by combining brutal vengeance, prolific squandering, and absolute incompetency. He gave his concubine an allowance of twenty million rupees a year, plus clothes and jewels, and spent much of his own time in drunken orgies. Naturally enough, his throne was never secure; in less than a year he was murdered. The court split into Turanian and Iranian factions, and the government's efficiency vanished amid its feuding parts. Five emperors followed in seven years. The chief noble of the court left for the south, where he set up a state of his own in Hyderabad in the Deccan—an area as large as Italy; another set up a state for himself in Oudh; the governor of Bengal acted as though he were independent.

[54] Rawlinson, p. 352.

The Marathas whom Aurangzeb had been unable to subdue appeared in 1737 before the gates of Delhi, but as suddenly withdrew. Two years later Nadir Shah of Persia, aware of the unsettled conditions to the south, marched to Delhi, and the emperor, Muhammad Shah, "the asylum of negligence," [55] saw his capital sacked. "For a long time," ran the metaphor of a contemporary historian, "the streets remained strewn with corpses, as the walks of a garden with dead flowers and leaves. The town was reduced to ashes, and had the appearance of a plain consumed with fire." [56] Then Nadir Shah left, carrying all the imperial gold plate, the Koh-i-noor diamond and other jewels, the gem-studded Peacock Throne, and anything else he could carry on the innumerable horses, elephants, and camels he also took back to Persia. So far had the mighty Mughul Empire fallen! Muhammad Shah, with a tired eye toward the future as the riches of his empire traveled slowly northward and westward, issued a royal order to the effect that "all public officers should occupy themselves in the discharge of their ordinary duties, except the historians. These should refrain from recording the events of my reign, for at present the record cannot be a pleasant one." [57] From this blow (delivered, interestingly enough, by other Muslims) the empire never recovered.

After the departure of Nadir Shah the condition of the government was worse than before. "The *amirs* took what they liked. The Emperor spent what remained to him in sports and pastime." [58] In 1757, within twenty years of this defeat, Delhi was captured by the Marathas, but the triumph was ephemeral. Four years later the third Muslim victory at

[55] *Tarikh-i-Hindi of Rustam Ali,* in Elliot and Dowson, VIII, 60.

[56] *Tazkira of Anand Ram Mukhlis,* in Elliot and Dowson, VIII, 89.

[57] *Tarikh-i-Chaghatai of Muhammad Shafi' Teherani,* in Elliot and Dowson, VIII, 21–22.

[58] *Tarikh-i-Ahmad Shah,* in Elliot and Dowson, VIII, 105.

Panipat—this one led by Ahmad Shah Abdali, the founder of Afghanistan—crushed for all time the power of the Marathas in northern India. Nothing else came of the victory, however, for the sick and unpaid Afghan soldiers insisted on returning home.

Babar in 1526 and Akbar in 1556, at the first and second battles of Panipat, had each won an empire, but even though the third battle in 1761 was also a victory for Muslim arms, it is as good a date as any by which to mark the end of the Mughul Empire as a live force. It lingered on—that is, the court lingered on—but both Muslim and Hindu were exhausted, and in the last half of the eighteenth century the British began to establish their supremacy over each.

Chapter Three

The Initial Reaction to Decline and Foreign Domination

The painful collapse of the Mughul empire forced into extended reflection those orthodox Muslims who were not content merely to hide themselves in the swamps of *kismet*. All Muslims were bewildered, even though they continued to look to Delhi as the final arbiter, but the matter must have been doubly perplexing, because the collapse followed so suddenly, indeed, in some ways preceded, the death of Aurangzeb—to the traditionalist the most truly Islamic of all the Mughul rulers. The waning of the empire revived again the questions that had plagued Indian Muslims from at least the fourteenth century. It also produced a second great Muslim theologian on the subcontinent, whose traditionalism was beyond reproach but whose emphases, as a result of his study of the circumstances in which he lived, differed slightly from theologians before him.

Ahmad ibn 'Abdur Rahim, more commonly known as Shah Waliullah, "the deputy of God," was born four years before the death of Aurangzeb and died in 1762, the year after the third battle of Panipat. His life spans the period when the deterioration of the empire and, consequently, of Muslim society was most rapid. He searched for some way by which his society could be strengthened, could, as a theologian saw it, once again be reconciled with Islam.

Shah Waliullah's father was a sufi and a scholar who had at one time worked in Aurangzeb's court, helping to compile a code of Hanifi law—one of the great achievements of that monarch's reign. Court life did not appeal to Shah 'Abdur Rahim, however, and he soon left to set up a school of his own, where he tried to find some way by which the sufis and the traditionalists—the mystics and the legalists—could be brought together, a pursuit his more famous son was to carry on after him.[1]

When Waliullah was seventeen his father died; by that time the boy had memorized the entire Qur'an, had been married, had completed the highest course offered in any Muslim school in Delhi, and had begun teaching the study of hadith literature—the collection, criticism, and analysis of traditional tales of Muhammad's life—at his father's school. He continued teaching until 1730 when he went on pilgrimage to Arabia, staying there for fourteen months to further his studies of the hadith. In 1733 he returned to Delhi. For the last thirty years of his life he devoted himself to the study of Islamic subjects, to attempts to buttress the waning empire, and to writing.[2]

Shah Waliullah was a transitional figure between the medieval and the modern age, somewhat as Dante was in Europe

[1] 'Ubaidullah Sindhi, quoted in Pakistan Historical Society, *A History of the Freedom Movement*, I (Karachi, 1957), 493.

[2] Muhammad Ishaq, *India's Contribution to the Study of Hadith Literature* (Dacca, 1953), pp. 172–178.

and, like Dante, he was far more medieval than modern.[3] Waliullah was not a modernist; but his analysis of his own troubled times formulated a position modernists were later able to develop for their own ends. His religious viewpoint was genuinely traditionalist and did not differ much from that of the first great Muslim theologian of India, Shaykh Ahmad of Sirhind. Indeed, Waliullah and Sirhindi were both members of the Nakshbandi order of sufis. Shaykh Ahmad, however, lived at a time when Muslim power was approaching its zenith; Shah Waliullah lived at a time when that power was close to its nadir. Each man applied himself to the same question—how can Islam be strengthened?—from the same religious position, but Waliullah's mind seems to have been more far-reaching and approached the question of the dynamic character of Islam from a more analytical—or, perhaps, less Arabic—point of view.

Waliullah can best be described as a scholar-reformer, but the effect of his efforts proved revolutionary. His times cried for revolution, and he patiently and continually wrote letters and pamphlets noting what was wrong with his society and

[3] There is very little literature in English on Waliullah. Most accessible are the two chapters in *A History of the Freedom Movement,* I, by S. M. Ikram and by Khaliq A. Nizam; Muin-ud-Din Ahmad Khan, "Shah Wali-Allah's Conception of Ijtehad," *Journal of the Pakistan Historical Society,* VIII, 3 (July, 1959), 165–194; Fazlur Rahman, "The Thinker of Crisis—Shah Waliy-Ullah," *Pakistan Quarterly,* VI (2), 44–48; Muhammad Mazharuddin Siddiqui, "Shah Waliullah of Delhi: His Life and Work," *The Islamic Literature,* 1st year, no. 2 (Sept., 1949), 39–42; Aziz Ahmad, "Political and Religious Ideas of Shah Wali-Ullah of Delhi," *Muslim World,* LII, 1 (Jan., 1962), 22–30. Hasan al-Ma'sumil, "Shah Wali Allah . . . ," *Islamic Culture,* Oct., 1947, pp. 341–343. Passing notice may also be found in the chapter by Mazheruddin Siddiqui in *Islam—the Straight Path,* Kenneth W. Morgan, ed. (New York, 1958), pp. 310–315, and in Mohammad Yasin, *A Social History of Islamic India* (Lucknow, 1958).

suggesting means by which conditions might be improved. Some strong action was necessary if the power of the Muslims was to be regained, and all his life Waliullah worked to achieve that end. His pen may have been instrumental in bringing about the third battle of Panipat, in 1761. He wrote to Ahmad Shah Abdali, inviting him down from Afghanistan to destroy the Maratha army: "We appeal to you in the name of God to divert your attention to this affair and to earn the glory of waging a holy war and rescue the Muslims from the hands of unbelievers. The undertaking should not resemble the invasion of Nadir Shah who destroyed the Muslims and left the Marathas and the Jats intact. I fear the day when if the Muslims become still weaker no trace of Islam would remain." [4] Action such as this represented an attempt to save the Muslim community from being overrun before it could regenerate itself. Of far greater interest are Waliullah's ideas as to the nature of the regeneration.

For a sincere and pious Muslim theologian only one solution to the problem of the Muslims in India was possible: to re-create the government of the Muslims during their golden days. This did not mean returning to the balmy days of the Mughul empire, but to the days of the early Muslim caliphate in Arabia. It has often been pointed out that while Christians have generally sought their utopias in some unknown future, Muslims have generally sought theirs in a definite past. Quite likely this reflects less an essential difference between the two faiths than a stage in historical development, for neither did the medieval Christians write utopias, although they looked with longing on the Church Fathers.

Religiously speaking, the golden days of the Muslims were those twenty-eight years of the early caliphate ending with the assassination of 'Ali, the fourth caliph and Muhammad's

[4] Quoted in Yasin, p. 175; see also *Freedom Movement*, I, 512–544.

son-in-law, in the year 661. Waliullah believed that one of the great causes of the weakness of Muslims had been the substitution of kingship for the early caliphate. Homage was paid to a king whether he deserved it or not, but the early caliphs, he believed, had been chosen on the basis of ability. What he wanted was to regenerate the spirit behind the social and political organization of those times when Muslims were filled with faith and acted with unity.

He did not believe that a literal return to the conditions of the early caliphate was possible nor, in itself, particularly Islamic so far as India was concerned. He thought of Islam as a pure universal religion, but one presented to the world in an Arabic pattern. No religious tradition, he argued, can occur in a vacuum, and because a religion is presented in one cultural pattern—in this case, Arabic—does not mean that it is forever tied to Arabic customs and procedures. In different cultures the pure religion will be expressed in different ways and even at different times by the same culture. "The code of law of a prophet," he wrote, "should be such as to appeal to the commonsense of the reasonable people of all lands of temperate climate, who, in spite of many differences in their habits and social practices, would at once recognize in it a *natural religion* and willingly accept it as such. Secondly, in the formulation of the Shari'a he keeps in view the cultural background, the mental aptitude and the social usage and practice of his contemporary society in which he is born." [5]

The great problem, of course, is how to pluck that which

[5] *Hujjatullah al-Baligha* (Urdu translation; Lahore, 1953), I, 567–568, quoted in Bashir Ahmad Dar, *Religious Thought of Sayyid Ahmad Khan* (Institute of Islamic Culture; Lahore, 1957), pp. 49–50. This aspect of Waliullah's thought was seized upon by Maulana Iqbal in his efforts to develop a dynamic concept of Islam; see *The Reconstruction of Religious Thought in Islam* (Lahore, 1951), pp. 171–172.

is the pure religion from that which is merely the cultural pattern. To this Shah Waliullah apparently had no answer, but in raising the question (although it had earlier been reflected in Hanifi thought, and even earlier in the Sunni-Shi'a split) he opened the doors for almost unlimited speculation.

In an attempt to secure the diffusion of Islamic ideas outside of the Arabic cultural pattern, Shah Waliullah translated the Qur'an from its original Arabic, which few Muslims in India understood, into Persian, the language of the aristocracy. This move, while it incensed many of the traditionalist theologians (who believed God's word should not be tampered with in any way), proved to be popular. Each of two of his sons made his own translation of the Qur'an in Urdu, the new language rapidly replacing Persian in India as the Mughul power eclipsed. Perhaps these later translations in the vernacular of the people were even more revolutionary than Waliullah's pioneering effort. The medieval Muslim aristocrat, like his medieval Christian counterpart, distrusted the influence of widespread knowledge. Nothing should be done that might encourage the lowborn to move from their place. It was felt that learning would prove too equalitarian, rulers would lose prestige, and God's social order would be ruined.[6] The translations of Waliullah's sons indicate that this medieval concept, so far as it related to enough learning as to be able to read the Qur'an, had been overthrown.

One reason why his own society was weak, Waliullah believed, was the excess of high living—part of the price paid for the success of the Mughuls. If only the truly Islamic customs and practices might be re-established, then most certainly the power and authority that were fast seeping

[6] Barni, *Fatawa-i-Jahandari*, folio 130a; Muhammad Bakir Khan, *Mau'iza-yi-Jahangiri*, folios 29–31, quoted in W. T. deBary, ed., *Sources of Indian Tradition* (New York, 1958), pp. 517–518.

away from the Muslims in India would be restored to them. By strengthening Muslim society Waliullah meant to strengthen the Muslim faith—that was his ultimate purpose, for if the faith were strong, so too would be the community. The strengthening of Muslim society would mean that many Hindu customs that had been accepted by Muslims on the subcontinent—such as the ban on the remarriage of widows —would be abolished. Waliullah wrote in opposition to expensive engagements, expensive weddings, the high cost of alimony, and expensive funerals. None of these things were a part of early Islam, and their removal could only strengthen the Muslim community in India. It is indicative of the man, however, that his opposition to such practices was not because they were Hindu, but because they were un-Islamic. He was not motivated by the bigotry that was part of Shaykh Ahmad Sirhindi. In his greatest work, the encyclopedic *Hujjat-Ullah al-Baligha*, he cites reasons for the decline of the Roman and Sassanid Persian empires: the problems of succession, high living, unjust taxation, misery among peasants and artisans, the influence of social parasites. But there is no need to repeat these old stories, he wrote, "when you are seeing now all these things in the lives of the rulers of your cities." [7] Repent! cried Waliullah to the nobility—reform your ways! To the lower classes he advised prayer, work, and sound economic practices so that the religious injunction to pay alms might be met and that there would still be a little saved for emergencies.

Waliullah saw, too, that more than high living, and more than the absorption of Hindu customs, had weakened his society. There was no real unity among the Muslims; indeed, the community was divided against itself. The four principal sufi orders paid little attention to one another, yet all sufis

[7] *Hujjat-Ullah il Balighah*, I, cited in *Freedom Movement*, I, 519.

faced a running battle with the traditionalists who, in turn, warred on both the sufis and the Shi'as. Waliullah hoped to achieve unity among the divergent Muslims by emphasizing early Islam—before the sufis had become important, and before the Sunni-Shi'a split. The scholar in him constantly emphasized the spirit of balance and he took pains to point out that balance, in the sense of justice or fairness, exists in all aspects of life. He never became, like Shaykh Ahmad Sirhindi, or like his contemporary reformer in Arabia, Muhammad ibn 'Abd al-Wahab, the pure revolutionary who sees things only as black or white. Indeed, it is not an unfair comparison to say that Shaykh Ahmad is to Xavier as Waliullah is to Erasmus.

Conciliation, except in dealing with elements of political disruption that seemed to threaten Islam—such as the raging Marathas, Jats, and Sikhs—was the hallmark of Waliullah. One of the problems over which traditionalists and sufis quarreled was one that had appeared long before, and one that Shaykh Ahmad Sirhindi thought he had effectively settled. Shaykh Ahmad had maintained that the mystics were wrong when they argued in such pantheistic terms as the unity of existence; this was all illusion. There was instead, he argued, a duality of existence: creator and created were separate. Nevertheless, many sufis did not accept his argument, and this old dispute continued to simmer. Waliullah sought to resolve it by showing that both sides were right, depending on the viewpoint.

Both views were based on true revelations, he maintained, and that of Shaykh Ahmad actually confirmed that of ibn Arabi. "If real facts," he wrote, "are taken into account and studied without their garb of simile and metaphor, both doctrines will appear about the same." [8] It has been said that

8 *Visva-Bharati Annals*, IV (1951), 35–36, quoted in deBary, p. 462.

Waliullah did give a philosophical and sufistic base to Islamic orthodoxy.[9]

He tried to resolve the disputes not only between sufis and traditionalists, but among sufis themselves. He was too much the Indian himself to reject mysticism, but he did hope to promote cooperation among members of the mystic orders. Having been initiated himself into each of the four primary sufi orders on the subcontinent, he started the practice of initiating novices into all the orders simultaneously—a practice that has been continued by the Muslim theological school established at Deoband in the wake of his influence.

A further example of the conciliatory technique of Waliullah is that contrary to the customary practice of the traditionalists of his day, he never maintained that the Shi'as were not Muslims. He steadfastly refused not to classify them as Muslims, and as a consequence was awarded one of the lowest epithets in the traditionalist vocabulary—that of being a Shi'a! [10] The profound respect and esteem in which Waliullah was held in all Muslim religious circles, however, greatly weakened the effect of any opposition taken against him.

Besides high living and internal dissension, Muslim society, in Waliullah's opinion, suffered from a rigid conformity to interpretations made in other ages and other areas. Waliullah recognized that growth and change were essential for a healthy society; he did not believe that Muslim society was strengthened by a blind acceptance of one or the other of the four schools of Muslim jurisprudence. In this respect he did not differ from Shaykh Ahmad Sirhindi, nor from Muhammad ibn 'Abd al-Wahab in Arabia, who also considered the blind following of the medieval authorities to be an ele-

---

[9] S. M. Ikram, in *Freedom Movement*, I, 498.

[10] *Freedom Movement*, I, 499–500. The source of this story is 'Abd-ul-'Aziz, one of Waliullah's sons.

ment of weakness in Islam. Perhaps the greatest impact Waliullah's thought had on the Muslims of India stemmed from his views concerning the right of an individual to form an independent judgment on a legal question—to exercise the right of *ijtihad*. To most of the traditionalist theologians the individual scholar had no such right: the last word on the subject had been said by the end of the tenth century, and since then the "gates of ijtihad"—the gates on the path leading to independent judgment—had been closed. So long as the rigid conformity existed, however, the social elasticity recognized by his sense of balance as essential for good health could not exist. This elasticity he tried to introduce through his interpretation of the principle of independent judgment.

All in all, perhaps the most striking thing about Waliullah was that, although completely the theologian, he thought of society in sociological terms. Religious injunctions, he maintained, were to be observed not necessarily because they were divine in origin, but because of the benefits they were calculated to confer both on the individual and on society. Islamic commandments, he wrote, are not tests merely to reward if passed and to punish if failed. The purpose of the commandments is social. This view was not un-Islamic; indeed, the celebrated historian ibn Khaldun had held much the same one four centuries earlier. For if religion encompasses all things, as Islam teaches, then it must certainly encompass this interpretation. By his revival of this emphasis, and because of his own tremendous reputation as a scholar and a pious Muslim, Waliullah provided a nontheological foundation upon which later thinkers, more removed from strictly theological premises, could build. If Islamic commandments exist to provide social benefits, then the test of a commandment is the degree of success with which it does this.

In a world in which cultural patterns are being buffeted from all sides, the test becomes a very severe one.

Waliullah believed that slavish adherence by the learned theologians to the opinion of the medieval jurists endangered his society. It was their job to search in the hadith literature and the Qur'an for the pure religion itself, and to apply it to their own time and place. This, of course, might involve bypassing the medieval jurists, a really radical suggestion, although hardly unique in his time. As for the individual who has not properly studied his faith—that is, one who has not devoted his entire life to Muslim theology—the assistance of a learned man is essential, but only because of his knowledge of the Book of God and the sunna. Waliullah, although he believed in the absolute clarity of the Qur'an, never went so far as to say that no more was needed. Characteristically, however, he did offer a conciliatory alternative to the theologians, hoping to achieve at least a little gain. The four primary schools of Muslim jurisprudence, he said, should be treated equally by the theologians, and exclusive attention should not be given to any one of them.

Waliullah hoped by breaking the rigorous hold of the medieval jurists on Islamic thought to introduce sufficient elasticity into Islam in India to permit it to adapt itself to new times and new conditions. He wanted a reform, but he does not seem to have wanted any major change. He pointed out the ways by which individuals, more involved in the ripening social changes than the Muslim theologians, could logically advocate reforms far in excess of anything of which he dreamed. What Waliullah considered as "sufficient" elasticity later reformers considered hopelessly insufficient. Actually, two strong movements developed as a result of Waliullah's teaching. One, more directly connected with him, became increasingly conservative, increasingly literal in its approach; the other became increasingly liberal and abstract in its Islamic interpretations. His own efforts to rejuvenate the Muslims of his time—except, perhaps, in an ephemeral manner in the political field—were largely failures, yet for all this he remains one of the greatest of all influences on Indian, and Pakistani, Muslim thought.

Beyond his part in organizing the forces that won the ephemeral victory at Panipat, Waliullah's efforts had no appreciable effect in halting the Muslim decline in India. After he died, his teachings were carried on to some degree by his sons, under whom the school at Delhi was continued. Early in the nineteenth century there was incorporated within it another famous school of hadith, that originally founded by Shaykh Ahmad of Sirhind.

Muslim leaders hoped for an Islamic renaissance, but none of them was able to picture it apart from a renewal of Muslim political strength. The Muslims continued to measure their religious strength in terms of their political success, an attitude that has been at various times assailed as reflecting the materialism of Muhammad or the absolutely unitarian worldview of Islam. Both interpretations are open to question, for even medieval Christianity, despite its trinitarianism, was most distinguished for its concept of, and its emphasis upon, Christian unity—a unity that was certainly thought of in political as well as religious terms. Nevertheless, it is true that the decline of the Muslims became, to Muslim theologians, something that could be stopped by avoiding those military defeats which led to the loss of political position and of religious strength. The glory of Waliullah is that he saw much deeper than this; his failure partially lies in the fact that few of his contemporaries did. But Waliullah insisted on looking at Islam not through the eyes of a seventh-century Arab trying to unite the Arabian peninsula but through the eyes of a non-Arab living and ruling in a land in which Muslims were a minority. The breadth of Waliullah's traditionalist approach was remarkable. But Waliullah, too, believed that the decline could not be stopped until Muslims won victories on the battlefield—otherwise they would be swamped by the infidels in every way. He urged soldiers to abandon their un-Islamic habits and to develop the spirit of crusade and the character of soldiers fighting for Islam.[11]

In the south of India Tipu Sultan, the Muslim ruler of Mysore, tried to strengthen the force of his opposition to the British by stirring up the crusading spirit among his soldiers. A manual he had prepared for his forces described warfare "against the aggressive disbelievers for the triumph of the Faith" as true Islam.[12] Elsewhere in his manual he urged every Muslim to resist disbelievers so long as they had the power to resist. Whatever effect Tipu's remarks may have had on stirring up his soldiers, they do not seem to have overly inspired his Muslim contemporaries. More than once his armies fought against the Muslim troops of the Nizam of Hyderabad. So far as the practical politics of south India were concerned, the unitarian concepts of Islam did not seem to apply. Tipu's defenses finally crumbled, and in the British victory at Seringapatam in 1799 he died while, as he had urged his soldiers, resisting to the last. The wavering Nizam of Hyderabad, who had been on every side at one time or another, ended up on the side of the victors. He became known as the "Faithful Ally" of the British, and as he forfeited whatever power he had, the British asserted their role as the leading power in southern India.

In the north of India the idea of an Islamic renaissance

[11] *Freedom Movement*, I, 520.
[12] *Ibid.*, p. 486.

through jihad was taken up, not by a Muslim ruler, but by a mercenary soldier who accepted his Islam deeply, sincerely, and literally. Sayyid Ahmad Shahid was born in the village of Rae Bareli in 1786, twenty-four years after the death of Waliullah. He spent three years at the local mosque school, beginning at the traditional age of four years, four months, and four days; twelve years later he went to Delhi and studied for two years under Shah 'Abd-ul-Qadir, and proclaimed himself a disciple of Shah 'Abd-ul-'Aziz, both sons of Waliullah.[13] This constituted all of his formal education.

When he returned to his native village from Delhi he was hailed as a saint, partly, no doubt, because of his exemplary character, partly because he was an epileptic, and partly because he basked under the halo of every man who had studied under 'Abd-ul-'Aziz and who had absorbed the deep mysticism of son and father. After two years he joined the cavalry forces of Amir Khan Pindari, one of the bandit leaders of Rajasthan, and eventually was placed in charge of Amir Khan's bodyguard. After seven years of this work he returned to Delhi, once again visiting 'Abd-ul-'Aziz. The latter must have been much impressed by the now mature Sayyid Ahmad, for he advised both his nephew, Shah Isma'il Shahid, and his son-in-law, Maulvi 'Abd-ul-Hai, to adopt the Sayyid as their spiritual adviser. Nothing could have added more to the reputation of Sayyid Ahmad Shahid; invitations to visit and to preach were showered upon him, and the voice of Shaykh Ahmad of Sirhind (by way of Waliullah) was heard throughout the Muslim north. Adherents flocked to him by the thousands. So many were his disciples that a permanent organization, called "The Path of Muhammad" (*Tariqah-i-Muhammadi*), complete with taxes, was established in 1818. In Calcutta so many people wanted to

[13] *Ibid.*, p. 567

touch his hand, thus signifying themselves to have become his disciples, that he abandoned tradition to the extent of stipulating that one might be initiated into discipleship, and into membership in "The Path of Muhammad," by touching not just his hand, but any part of his yards of turban which he unrolled for the purpose.[14]

"The Path of Muhammad" was identified by some Muslims as an Indian version of the puritanical Wahabi movement in Arabia; the British in India seized on this idea and expanded it to represent a great Muslim renaissance almost without bounds; others have identified the group as just a new sufi order among the Muslims of India. Actually, it was no more than a mystically ordered Islamic revival movement, stressing the importance of the principle of independent judgment (ijtihad) and rejecting the principle of blindly following the decisions of the medieval jurists (*taqlid*). The reform movement in Arabia known as Wahabism agreed in all these points, but was not mystical. This preference for following the Prophetic tradition rather than accepting the prescriptions of the Muslim schools of jurisprudence was accepted by both Shaykh Ahmad of Sirhind and Waliullah. Indeed, Sayyid Ahmad Shahid said, "My way is the way of my grandfather" —referring to Waliullah, and using the term *way (tariqah)* in a general sense, not to exclude other ways.[15] The Sayyid was in reality carrying on the implied protest of Waliullah against the traditionalism of his time, particularly as it had been tightened through the code of Hanifi law compiled under Aurangzeb.

To this point Sayyid Ahmad Shahid seems to portray the typical itinerant preacher, possessing tremendous magnetism. Do not compare anything to God, he urged, for that is the

[14] W. W. Hunter, *The Indian Musalmans* (Calcutta, 1945), p. 5.
[15] Muinuddin Ahmad Khan, thesis in preparation, Dacca University.

greatest sin, and observe only the practices that were observed by Muhammad, for in accretions to the Faith lies its weakness.[16]

He denounced all innovation in Islam. Such changes, he said, sprang from corrupt sufis or were heretical in themselves or were acquired by the imitation of other cultures. Had not Muhammad said, "This day have I completed your religion"? What can be added to that which is already complete and perfect, except that which will weaken it? He spoke vigorously against excessive dependence upon one's spiritual mentor, essential as a guide but limited in usefulness. His limits are found in the injunctions laid down in the Qur'an and the traditions. "Follow no one," he said, "be he *mujtahid, imam, ghaus, qutb, maulvi, mashaikh,* king, minister, *padri,* or pundit against the authority of the *Qur'an* and the *Hadis.*"[17] Sayyid Ahmad Shahid was a sincere evangelist among Muslims. Just as Waliullah was a sufi tinged with social feeling, Sayyid Ahmad was a puritan tinged with mysticism. Shah 'Abd-ul-'Aziz had once declared that there was nothing unlawful about learning English, or in attending schools in which English was taught, but even his great authority had no influence on the tremendous surge of defensive reaction personified by Sayyid Ahmad Shahid of Rae Bareli.[18] The danger of English, as seen by most Muslims of the time, lay not in its being a pathway to modern science or even materialism, but in being the first step toward conversion to Christianity. Shah Waliullah had maintained that the true religion cannot be tied to regional customs and procedures; it must be universal. The comment of his son, 'Abd-

[16] Hunter, p. 46. See also Murray T. Titus, *Islam in India and Pakistan* (Madras, 1959), pp. 191–193.

[17] *Freedom Movement,* I, 569; the quotation is from *Taqwiyat-ul-Iman.*

[18] Dar, *Religious Thought,* p. 56.

ul-'Aziz, was certainly in the spirit of his father, but it apparently elicited favorable response from few Muslims. From this point on, however, the Muslims of India were increasingly forced to come to grips with the issues involved in cultural change. It was as though the mountain were coming to Mahomet, because Mahomet was unwilling to go to the mountain. The initial reaction in India was the use of force. When that failed, a policy of isolation and aloofness was tried, and, when that proved too expensive, the Muslims indulged in politics. But not until the creation of Pakistan, when the responsibilities of independence were felt, were the Muslims really forced to argue the question as to how much of the old tradition and how much of the new world were essential.

Sayyid Ahmad Shahid was one of the first to call the Muslims to arms. It was obvious to him, as it had been to Waliullah, that all his preaching to the Muslims was not going to influence the Sikhs—or the Christians, either. He became convinced that more than mere preaching, more than merely amassing disciples, was needed to resuscitate the Faith and to improve the status of Muslims. Before any Islamic revival could be successful a sound political and social environment had to be created. This could only be done, he believed, by warfare; it could only be done by calling for a crusade, a jihad for Islam. It is this emphasis on jihad that really distinguished the Sayyid from other sufis of his time.

In 1826, two years after returning from a pilgrimage to Mecca, on the authority of Shah 'Abd-ul-'Aziz, he declared the existence of a holy war against the Sikhs in a manifesto.

The Sikh nation have long held sway in Lahore and other places. Their oppressions have exceeded all bounds. Thousands of Muhammadans have they unjustly killed, and on thousands have they heaped disgrace. No longer do they allow the Call to Prayer from the mosques, and the killing of cows they have entirely pro-hibited. When at last their insulting tyranny could no more be endured, Hazrat Sayyid Ahmad (may his fortunes and blessings ever abide!), having for his single object the protection of the Faith, took with him a few Musalmans, and, going in the direc-tion of Cabul and Peshawar, succeeded in rousing Muhammadans from their slumber of indifference, and nerving their courage for action. Praise be to God, some thousands of believers became ready at his call to tread the path of God's service; and on the 21st December 1826, the Jihad against the Infidel Sikhs begins.[19]

The jihad, as one might suppose, was far more spectacular than it was successful. That a holy war was considered so enthusiastically by so many traditionalists at this time may indicate the poverty of rational thinking among them. Tipu in the south, with highly trained armies and good leadership, had not been able to persuade his fellow Muslims to carry out a crusade against the British. Even there, the odds seemed too great. The odds were even greater in the north; Sayyid Ahmad Shahid was dependent upon the influence of his own personality, the organizational ability of his disciples, espe-cially Shah Isma'il Shahid and Maulvi 'Abd-ul-Hai, and the penchant for fighting that marked the tribesmen of the northwest.

Nevertheless, the position of the Sayyid was little different from that of Pope Pius V, who decided in 1569 that he had to resort to active measures if Catholicism were to be saved in England. He accordingly encouraged rebellion. What else could the Pope have done, other than meekly to admit the triumph of Protestantism in England? What could Sayyid Ahmad Shahid have done, other than meekly to have ad-mitted the decline of Islam and the rise of the Sikhs and the

[19] Hunter, pp. 6-7.

British? The Pope was fighting for Catholicism rather than for any particular prince. Sayyid Ahmad was fighting for Islam, not for the Mughuls or any other princely house. Perhaps each faith offered alternative forms of action that might have proven successful under the particular conditions; neither Pope nor Sayyid conceived of them: each advanced an essentially negative argument when the times cried for something positive. Like Pius V, the Sayyid was wrong, for the conditions which had made excommunication and deposition effective in medieval Europe no longer prevailed, and the conditions which had made medieval jihads successful no longer prevailed, either.

Viewed as a military operation, there is very little that can be said for this jihad, although its aftereffects thoroughly frightened the British. Sayyid Ahmad Shahid began it with five or six hundred companions. He sought support from the Muslim Mirs of Sind, but they were suspicious; the ruler of Bahawalpur refused to commit himself, even though his subjects were exceptionally enthusiastic toward the Sayyid; and while the chieftain of Baluchistan was interested, no active support was forthcoming.[20] This refusal on the part of the leading Muslim nobles to engage in the Sayyid's crusade must have been based on the absolutely inadequate preparations he had taken. His training had been as a freebooter, but he was too emotionally involved to realize that this was not a freebooting operation. From Baluchistan he wandered into Afghanistan, looking for military assistance. Although he did gather a few hundred soldiers, he found there more division among the Muslims, but he trusted that once a jihad was proclaimed, Muslims would flock to his support as they had flocked to touch his turban.

[20] This brief discussion of Sayyid Ahmad's jihad is largely based on the discussion in *Freedom Movement*, I, 556–600.

His crusade, from beginning to end, was an *ad hoc* matter; the character of his forces prevented it from being anything else. At the peak of his success he formed an *imamat*, a central organization to help prosecute the war. But although Sayyid Ahmad was acknowledged the leader, no chieftain surrendered any of his powers, and the jihad was a hodge-podge. He was able, at one time, to assemble 80,000 fighters, but he was never able to secure the loyalty of the tribesmen upon whom he most depended. They poisoned his food; they deserted on the battlefield; and they leagued with the Sikhs. The Sayyid's forces were marked neither by discipline nor by unity, and at last, in May 1831, caught by surprise in the mountainous village of Balakot, he and his disciple Shah Isma'il Shahid, with six hundred of his men, were killed during a Sikh attack.[21]

Thus ended the first phase of the jihad. Although it was a failure, it represented the first attempt to appeal to Muslims over the heads of their rulers. The doctrines the Sayyid had preached had all been translated into simple language to appeal to the masses, and his appeal was doubtless greatly increased because the period of his activity coincided with the crest of a wave of Urdu vernacular development in India.

Part of his appeal, too, lay in the fact that he was in tune with his times. This was a period of religious reform in India, as it was in most other parts of the world. Among the Hindus the men who organized the Brahma Samaj played a somewhat similar role as reformers. This awakening interest in religious reform on the subcontinent has often been explained by the influence of Christian teaching, especially by the early missionaries. The Brahma Samaj (Society of God) seems to have been a response to the activity of the Christian missionaries.

[21] *Freedom Movement,* I, 597–598.

As such, it had to be more than defensive. Thus Rammohan Roy emphasized an ethical monotheism he found in the Hindu scriptures, a positive theology to meet that of the Christian missionaries. The roots of the Muslim reform movement go much deeper. Waliullah was not apparently influenced by Christian thinking, nor were his sons 'Abd-ul-'Aziz and 'Abd-ul-Qadir. The Muslim revival, meeting a different challenge from that which Rammohan Roy recognized, sought only to return to the original faith. It was assumed that everyone knew the nature of that original faith, and not until Sir Syed Ahmad Khan in the late nineteenth century did a Muslim offer a new emphasis, a new reading, of his faith. Sayyid Ahmad Shahid merely echoed what he had been taught; he carried on what was really a thoroughly Muslim tradition, developing it only in terms of organization and mass appeal. Nevertheless, it may still be true that the tremendous response he received from some groups of Muslims represented a reaction on their part to the stimulus provided by the activity of Christian missionaries. It is also true that the Sayyid's supporters were well distributed throughout northern India, whether Christian missionaries had been in the area or not.

Those Muslim rulers who had refused to join an ill-prepared jihad proved to have been right; the Sayyid's forces were no match for the disciplined, well-equipped, and ably led troops of the Sikhs.[22] But despite his mistakes and his shortcomings, the Sayyid was a tremendously popular figure among many Muslims. His popularity even increased after his death, for his body was not found at Balakot, and the rumor spread that he had escaped, that he was alive and pre-

[22] Some of the Sikhs were officered by Europeans cast adrift after the ending of the Napoleonic wars.

paring yet another jihad. But his body had not been found because the Sikhs, recognizing it on the battlefield, had burned it.

Sayyid Ahmad Shahid of Rae Bareli represented one aspect of the effort of the Indian Muslims to reassert themselves. He did serve as a rallying point for many of the dissatisfied in the Muslim community. When the dissatisfaction some-times expressed itself in violence, it generally took the form of peasant revolts, especially in Bengal—revolts essentially agrarian and economic in nature, but almost invariably pro-fessing certain revivalist religious attitudes as well. Frequently these revolts, in one way or another, were connected with the activities of Sayyid Ahmad Shahid. He had founded The Path of Muhammad in 1818 to promote his revivalism; later it was utilized to advance the religious war he had proclaimed on the authority of Shah 'Abd-ul-'Aziz against the Sikhs. After his death at Balakot the organization split into two, and eventually into three, amorphous groups of scholars divided from one another by differences in theological opin-ion. Each was essentially traditionalist, although it could be argued that one group, the least strong, described a new mental approach for its day and place, although its tenets were almost as old as Muhammad.

The main body of The Path of Muhammad centered at Patna. It was led by Maulana Wilayat 'Ali, the chief successor to the Sayyid. This group showed quite clearly the effects of Waliullah's teaching, for it held that the blind acceptance of the teaching of any of the medieval schoolmen was not permissible for any person in a position to decide for himself. Truth, Wilayat 'Ali maintained, is to be found in the Qur'an and the hadith, and is best derived directly from its source rather than in a second-hand fashion through the opinions of tenth-century jurists. The person who was capable of forming independent judgments, rather than being in a position in which he had to trust the judgment of a spiritual guide, was called a *mujtahid*.[23] To reach this level of interpretation the mujtahid had to have spent most of his life in a study of the Qur'an and the hadith, and to be familiar, as well, with many other theological tools and subtleties—the Arabic language, the use of analogy, the problem of abrogating and abrogated ordinances, and so on. It was the belief of the Patna school, however, in common with almost all of India, that if one had to depend upon a spiritual guide, preference should be given to one trained in the Hanifi law; Wilayat 'Ali's contention was not that the studies of the medieval jurists should be ignored, but (like Waliullah before him) that each school should be considered equal.

This emphasis on independent judgment, guarded as it was, and admired as Waliullah may have been, was much too radical for most Muslims, including many who had listed themselves among the followers of Sayyid Ahmad Shahid. It was not a problem that particularly bothered the Sayyid, partly because he was not of a temperament to be interested in such distinctions, partly because he was always accompanied by learned mujtahids; his followers, called "fanatic Hindustanis" by the British, were often called "the mujahids" by Muslims. At any rate, dissidents from the position of Wilayat 'Ali, led by Maulana Karamat 'Ali, broke off from The Path of Muhammad to form their own group, known as the *Ta'aiyuni*.[24] Rejecting Waliullah in part, this group

---

[23] The word "mujtahid" refers to a teacher and scholar. There were many mujtahids in Sayyid Ahmad Shahid's army in the hills, but the army as a group was referred to as "the *mujahids*," a word which means "warriors of the faith," perhaps "crusaders."

[24] Muinuddin Ahmad Khan, thesis in preparation, Dacca University. See also H. A. R. Gibb and J. H. Kramers, *Shorter Encyclopaedia of Islam* (Ithaca, 1961), p. 217; Titus, p. 194.

insisted that one of the medieval schools of jurisprudence
had to be followed by every scholar, no matter how finely
trained he might be, or how diligently he had studied the
Qur'an. The Ta'aiyuni considered the position of the Patna
group on this question as somewhat in the way of a drastic
reform—if "reform" is the proper word—and nicknamed his
followers "Wahabis" after the puritanical and sometimes excessive reform movement founded by Muhammad ibn 'Abd
al-Wahab in eighteenth-century Arabia.[25] After the death of
Wilayat 'Ali in 1852 the sobriquet became popular in government circles as well.

Karamat 'Ali believed that Sayyid Ahmad Shahid was the
teacher born in his century to renew the faith; his teachings,
therefore, were to be followed until a new renewer appeared
in the next century. He believed that India under the British
was not a "country of the enemy," and that, consequently,
holy war against the British was unjustified. As a reformer
Maulana Karamat 'Ali was vigorous in combating supersti-
tions and Hindu customs that had been adopted by the
Muslims of Bengal, but otherwise he was thoroughly traditionalist. He differed from 'Abd-ul-'Aziz and Sayyid Ahmad
Shahid largely in wanting to keep the Muslim reform movement away from political controversy. It was a case, perhaps,
in which two parties disagreed as to whether or not reform
could be effected in the existing atmosphere. Karamat 'Ali
believed that it could. He was, incidentally, a teacher of
Sayyid Ameer Ali, author of *The Spirit of Islam*, and a leading
reformer of a later generation.

It is true that the Wahabis of Arabia were also opposed
to learned theologians being blind imitators of their tenth-
century predecessors, just as were members of the Patna

25 L. Bevan Jones, *The People of the Mosque* (London, 1932), p.
206.

school; the latter, if they had a preference, usually sided with the decisions of the Hanifi school (upon which Aurangzeb's codification was based), while the Wahabis similarly tended to support the Hanbali school. The essential difference between the two is that between India and Arabia, between Waliullah and his contemporary 'Abd al-Wahab. The Patna school, like Waliullah, did not discount mysticism, but thought of it as a phenomenon that could be utilized to enhance one's spiritual development. The Wahabis of Arabia had no use for mysticism whatever. Mysticism was never appealing in Arabia, but it was the life-blood of religion in India—whether Muslim or Hindu. Karamat 'Ali, in opposition to the views of the Patna group, thought that the term "The Path of Muhammad" (Tariqah-i-Muhammadi) was a collective name for the four leading sufi orders in India, rather than a fifth mystic sect itself; it was, he maintained, only a higher level of mystic realization within these orders.[26]

The Arabian Wahabis and the Indian revivalists were alike in that each wanted to divest Islamic practice of the accretions and customs that had been acquired since Muhammad, but this was little more than what Shaykh Ahmad of Sirhind had been preaching: "Away from Plotinus and his host, and back to Muhammad!"[27] It was, however, a narrower concept than Waliullah apparently maintained. Both were revival movements, and both thought of jihad in terms of physical force. It was this similarity that led the British to accept the identification of the Patna school as a wing of the Wahabi movement itself. In time, the term *Wahabi* was used to describe any Muslim reformer in India. Sir Syed Ahmad Khan,

[26] See Muinuddin Ahmad Khan. The main sufi orders in India were the Kadiriya, Chishtiya, Nakshbandiya, and Mujaddidiya.
[27] Burhan Ahmad Faruqi, *The Mujaddid's Conception of Tawhid* (Lahore, 1943), p. 127.

the most independent Muslim thinker in nineteenth-century India, and the founder of most modernist groups today, referred to himself as a "Wahabi." "My motto," he said, referring to that of the Wahabis, "is to speak the truth boldly without fear of consequences." [28]

The identification of the Patna group with the Wahabis was furthered by the belief that Sayyid Ahmad Shahid had contacts with the Wahabis during his pilgrimage to Mecca. The Wahabis had but recently been expelled from Mecca by the forces of Muhammad Ali of Egypt when the Sayyid arrived on his pilgrimage. His own reform teaching seemed to the Meccan authorities to smack so much of Wahabism that he, too, was expelled from the holy city.[29] It is not likely that he was thus, as Hunter maintains, converted to Wahabism overnight; he had been the student of 'Abd-ul-'Aziz too long for that. But 'Abd-ul-'Aziz had also preached the need for reform, and it is likely that the Sayyid was attracted to reformers.

Maulana Wilayat 'Ali carried on the belief of Sayyid Ahmad Shahid that the condition of the Muslims in India had deteriorated so far it could be improved only by force, only through a religious war. India, once the land of Islam, now under British control was the land of the enemies of Islam and had to be rewon for the faith. For some years the Patna group served as a center through which the remnants of the jihad were maintained in the northwestern hills. Again the "Hindustani fanatics" excited more fear in the British than their numbers seem to justify.

The first real action between the mujahids in the hills

[28] Dar, p. 127. "Syed" is the form of *Sayyid* preferred by S. A. Khan.
[29] Hunter, p. 52.

and the British took place in 1853. Not until 1857, following the Mutiny, did any large military action take place. From 1857 on the mujahids were forced to seek refuge in first one and then another tribal area. The British collected guarantees from the various tribes in the area not to lend assistance to the band, and when some of the tribes seemed to have relapsed in observing their guarantees, the Ambela campaign of 1863 was undertaken to end the disturbances.

Once again, as they had under Sayyid Ahmad Shahid, the tribesmen deserted the religious fighters after having given the British forces a severe drubbing in the process. But the strength of the mujahids was broken. The jihad was not truly ended by the Ambela campaign, which directly led to a series of trials of "Wahabi" leaders that extended over a decade, but it ceased to be a matter of any importance. Most Muslims of the subcontinent realized that if they were to redeem themselves they could not hope to do so by a blood-and-thunder jihad. It was a truism to all that the flintlocks of the Muslims were no match for the British Enfields.

Sometime in the 1860's The Path of Muhammad split again. Its members could admit the need of no particular spiritual guide for one sufficiently learned and religious, but it couldn't agree as to what the existing schools were equal in. One section of the scholars maintained they were equal in the validity of their decisions; one section thought they were equal in error. Most of the scholars were strongly Hanifi, but the tendency within the group was for one part to move toward establishing the Hanifi law as supreme—moving, in other words, closer to the position of the Ta'aiyuni—and for another part to move toward the denial of the practice of accepting only one, or at least toward repudiating the propriety of following any single school. This latter group argued that the medieval jurists had evolved their decisions from a study of the Qur'an and hadith; why should a nineteenth-century scholar not be free to evolve his own decisions from a similar study? This group was known as Ahl-i-Hadith—"the people of the hadith," or the people who belonged to no recognized Sunni school of law. They were directly in line with the teaching of Waliullah, emphasizing an extremely strict unitarianism (this was not only Islamic, it was a reaction to the worship of saints—a practice which continually creeps into Islam in India), urging the abolition of un-Islamic customs and practices, and relieving this generally harsh picture by asserting the freedom of every learned Muslim to follow his own interpretations of the Qur'an.[30] To the Ahl-i-Hadith no Islamic legal opinion is fixed for all time—every generation must search out its own interpretation. The Ahl-i-Hadith, at least as a group, never attained much strength in India and Pakistan; their ideas, however, gained increasing acceptance.

On the surface nothing really new appeared in any of the three groups: The Path of Muhammad, the Ta'aiyuni, or the Ahl-i-Hadith. Each maintained what might be called an essentially traditionalist attitude toward Islam, for medieval Islam cannot be limited to a single classification. In a sense, before the medieval schools were established, everyone was Ahl-i-Hadith because there was nothing else. In the nineteenth century, however, the Ahl-i-Hadith was the least influential; at the same time it demanded the most in the way of individual self-confidence, whether rightly or wrongly placed, and even if only for a very few scholars.

The Path of Muhammad and the groups that split from it

[30] A short summary of the tenets of the Ahl-i-Hadith can be found in Titus, pp. 195–197.

represent most of the movements of traditionalist Islamic revivalism in nineteenth-century India. Another such movement occurred in Bengal, however, and was known as the Fara'idiya. Started by Hajji Shari'at Allah early in the nineteenth century, the Fara'idiya aimed at enforcing the obligatory religious duties (*fara'id*) and at eliminating un-Islamic practices among the Muslims of Bengal. The Fara'idiya program under its founder was almost exclusively one of religious reformation, but during the middle of the century when the program was under the direction of his tall, handsome son, Dudu Miyan, social and economic elements were added. This was a natural outgrowth, for the membership of the Fara'idiya was largely of Muslim peasants, weavers, and oil-grinders. The group, provided by Dudu Miyan with a tighter, more hierarchical organization, tried to develop safeguards for its members from the demands of landowners, most of whom were Hindu, and to promote social justice among its own membership. Landowner opposition to the sect not unnaturally began to appear, and Dudu Miyan began to exert an increasingly strong hand. Consequently the sect channeled itself in waters familiar to every religion: agree with my position or stand persecution. Not only Hindu landlords, but Muslim farmers who did not join his movement were subject to its wrath. As a matter of fact, the Fara'idiya began, religiously speaking, emphasizing the oneness of God, absolute adherence to the Hanifi school, and acceptance of mysticism as beneficial to Islam. With the death of Dudu Miyan in 1862, however, the movement lost its strong leader and became ineffective.

Nine years after The Path of Muhammad was founded, the movement appeared in rural Bengal under the leadership of Mir Mithar 'Ali, who was also called Titu Mir, and who had become a disciple of Sayyid Ahmad Shahid in 1822. Titu Mir began preaching the pure doctrines of Islam—that the attributes of God must not be applied to human beings, and that only the rites or ceremonies approved by the Qur'an and prophetic tradition should be observed. His high point was reached when he led a Muslim revolt against landowners who, in retaliation for his activity, had imposed a tax on beards—a distinguishing mark among Muslims. Bengal was the scene of peasant disturbances through most of the middle years of the nineteenth century; nevertheless, the fact that these outbreaks were strengthened by religious and doctrinal ties seems incidental to their basic nature of social protest. The movements in Bengal seem to have been much more deeply grounded in social and economic unrest than the movements to the west. Someone has said that the Punjab breeds prophets and Bengal breeds social reformers; the truth of that remark seems to be supported by an analysis of both the Fara'idiya movement of Dudu Miyan and the Hajjis, as they were called, of Titu Mir. So far as religious change was concerned little can be said for either movement. Each was thoroughly traditionalist; each represented views Islam had known for more than a thousand years.[31]

It was obvious to many Muslims that the military aspects of these revival movements in nineteenth-century India had no chance of success. Yet while India was no longer considered the land of the faithful, was it not obligatory upon Muslims to take up jihad against the English? No uniform

[31] A summary of these movements in Bengal is to be found in the thesis by Muinuddin Ahmad Khan. See also his *Muslim Struggle for Freedom in Bengal* (Bureau of National Reconstruction; East Pakistan, 1960); and his article, "The Struggle of Titu Mir, A Re-examination," *Journal of Asiatic Society of Pakistan*, IV (1959), 113–133.

agreement was reached among Muslims on this question; the difficulty that Sayyid Ahmad Shahid had struck in forming his jihad is merely one of many indications of this. It is sometimes argued that the part played by the Muslims in the rebellion of 1857 rested in this belief. It may very well be that some Muslims looked upon the 1857 revolt as a splendid opportunity to be developed into a religious war to overthrow the British. But little evidence is provided to indicate that the 1857 rebellion was the result of any organized effort; it blazed brightly after lighting accidentally. But not for long, and not everywhere, in fact, was there any fire. It has become the practice in both India and Pakistan to refer to this struggle as "Our War for Independence," but the phrase, considering the event, seems ill-chosen. It is a mistaken assumption to assume that the active disciples of Sayyid Ahmad Shahid, Shah Isma'il Shahid, and Wilayat 'Ali were either blind followers or represented a majority of the Muslims in India. The Shi'as, for example—perhaps 10 per cent of the Indian Muslims—cannot be included. Many Muslims found it easier to contribute funds for the jihad, and so avoid any social obliquy and even earn a reputation for piety, than not—so long as they were not required to do more. The fact still remained, however, and it was increasingly clear to most thinking Muslims, that the British were in a paramount position, that the Muslims could not hope to match their military might, and that the British were not trying to interfere with the religious sensitivities of the people of India. Under such circumstances, these Muslims asked, could there be any religious justification for jihad?

The Hanifi views were quite clear on the matter. A country turns from a land of Islam, a land of safety (*Daru'l-Islam*), to a land of the enemy, a land of war (*Daru'l-Harb*), not because it is taken over by non-Muslims, but because three conditions are fulfilled: the laws and regulations of non-Muslims are enforced; the country is completely surrounded by others which are lands of war; and Muslims cannot live under the new regime in the same security as they lived under the previous Muslim government.[32] The Muslim theologians of Lucknow discussed the propriety of religious war in 1870, and decreed that "the Musalmans here are protected by Christians, and there is no jihad in a country where protection is afforded. . . . Besides, it is necessary that there should be a probability of victory. . . . If there is no such probability, the Jihad is unlawful."[33]

The Muslim Society of Calcutta, led by Karamat 'Ali, perhaps in reply to the Patna school's advocacy of jihad, decided that religious warfare by the Muslims was illegal because India was still the land of safety; they proceeded further to stipulate that "if any misguided wretch, owing to perverse fortune, were to wage war against the Ruling Powers of this country, British India, such war would be rightly pronounced rebellion; and rebellion is strictly forbidden by Muhammadan law."[34] Sayyid Ahmad Shahid, of course, raised his jihad against the Sikhs rather than against the British, but he looked upon the matter only as one of putting first things first, and first he thought he could defeat the Sikhs. The remnants of his followers still maintained arms in the hill regions in 1868 and were able to form temporary alliances with various tribesmen. Their numbers were swelled by individuals who, fearing reprisals for their part in the events of 1857, had fled from northern India. Sir Syed Ahmad Khan maintained that Hindus

[32] A. Rahim, *Muhammadan Jurisprudence* (Lahore, 1958), p. 395.
[33] Hunter, Appendix II, p. 209.
[34] Hunter, Appendix III, p. 210.

were among them.[35] It seems a mistake to assume that they represented any idea of resistance shared by the majority of Indian Muslims—or that, by this time, they were still an essentially religious movement in themselves.

Another refugee from the struggle of 1857, in which he had played some part, was Muhammad Qasim Nanautvi, a scholar of the hadith belonging to Waliullah's school. After the British had successfully overcome the rebellion, Nanautvi migrated to Mecca. In 1867 he returned and led the establishment of a theological school at Deoband, near Delhi, to keep alive the true Islamic teaching. In truth, the founding of the school was an attempt to save the Muslims of India from the secular influences of the British. Although conceived to carry on the teaching of Waliullah, it seized upon the more conservative aspects of his thought. For many years Deoband was one of the great centers of conservative Muslim teaching; its graduates spread out over India, and served as a major influence in persuading the mass of Muslims to remain traditionalist and to reject the modern world. In a sense, Deoband represents the coming together again of the schools that separated out of The Path of Muhammad. They converged again, as they had diverged in the first place, strictly traditionalist, and uneasy in the changed conditions that marked British India in the twentieth century. This uneasiness was a natural concomitant of the insistence of the traditionalist leaders that a man could understand Islam, and so be in a condition to be a guide to someone else, only if he had spent long years of studying the hadith, the juridical opinions of the medieval scholars, and the meaning of the Qur'an as explained by its many commentators. Unfortu-

[35] Mahmud Husain, "The Ambela Campaign, 1863," *Journal of the Pakistan Historical Society*, I, part II (April, 1953), 105-117.

nately, the individual who could satisfy these requirements could not be in a position to assess adequately the new world and its changed conditions. When new approaches to Islam were taken, they were led by men who were not theologians —men who had some firsthand experience in the world the masters of Deoband chose to renounce.

Chapter Four

The Beginning of a
Positive Response

After the death of Sayyid Ahmad Shahid, traditionalist
Muslim thought in India was divided theologically and politically. Maulana Karamat 'Ali, who led the largest of the
divisions, admitted the paramountcy of the British but maintained that India was not, as a result, the land of the enemy;
his religious position, strongly Hanifi, was certainly as traditionalist as that of Maulana Wilayat 'Ali, the leader of the
second division. The latter's activist group was finally defeated by the British through a combination of military and
economic pressure and was forced to content itself with carrying on, at the theological school at Deoband, the anti-
British tradition as well as Waliullah's combination of mysticism and the acceptance—for the learned few—of independent judgment. Only a few traces remained in the northwest
of the jihad organization developed by Sayyid Ahmad Shahid
and continued so long after his death by Maulana Wilayat
'Ali. The third group, the people of the hadith, was equally
zealous in urging first principles and puritanical reform, but

its extremist position placed it somewhat outside the recognized limits of authority. With the passing of time, however, the Ahl-i-Hadith became accepted—perhaps "tolerated" is a better word—as only another wing of traditionalist thought, advanced beyond that of the Deoband wing because it rejected the legal opinions, decisions, and judgment of any of the four recognized medieval schools of canon law. They contended, as did Waliullah, that every age must seek its own interpretation of the Qur'an and the traditions.

These traditionalist positions were alike in that each was determined to preserve Islam from non-Islamic encroachments, and each reacted defensively against the increasing efforts of Christian missionaries to win converts for their faith at the expense of Islam. Fear of Christian conversion may very well have played as large a role in the decline of the Muslims under the early British administration as any other single factor. Certainly for large elements the tendency was to keep away from the Christians—a tendency that inevitably fostered distrust and promoted wishful thinking as the Muslims romanticized the days of the Mughuls, drew into themselves, and refused to cooperate with the new rulers of India.

The picture is not as simple as this, however, and many other elements entered into the fact that the Muslims were largely ignored, and the Hindus favored, by the British. The British did feel that in asserting their dominance in India they had replaced that of the Mughuls, and naturally enough looked for support among other peoples. It is also true that the Hindus were more accessible to Christian missionaries. The original entry points of the Europeans into India were largely Hindu areas; the predominantly Muslim areas were farther inland. Calcutta, for example, was largely Hindu; so were Bombay and Madras. Missionaries, who had much to do

Star Mosque, Dacca. Built in Mughul times, it is sometimes called Mirza Ghulam Pir's mosque, after its architect. (Photograph by Freeland Abbott.)

The Pearl Mosque, built by Aurangzeb in the Red Fort, Delhi, 1659. The building in the foreground is the emperor's private audience chamber (the Diwan-i-Khas) in which was placed the gem-studded peacock throne; over the entry is the inscription, "If there be Paradise on earth, this is it, this is it, this is it." (Photograph by Freeland Abbott.)

A village mosque near Bahawalpur in West Pakistan. The niche in the center pillar indicates the direction of Mecca. (Photograph by Freeland Abbott.)

Eid prayers at the Badshahi Mosque, Lahore. The principal Muslim religious oc-
casions are the two Eids, which occur just before and just after Ramadan, the month
of fasting. The Badshahi Mosque was built in 1674 by Aurangzeb. (Courtesy of the
Pakistan Press Information Department.)

Emperor Akbar (1542–1605). The greatest Mughul ruler, Akbar built a sound framework of political and military institutions for the empire; he reacted against the political demands of a militant, traditionalist Islam and searched instead for ways to achieve religious tolerance. (From a Mughul painting; courtesy of the Pakistan Press Information Department.)

Emperor Aurangzeb (1618–1707)—the last great Mughul ruler. During his lifetime the empire fell into decline, as the unsolved problems of his predecessors proved insurmountable. (From a Mughul painting; courtesy of the Pakistan Press Information Department.)

A view of Balakot today. Here in 1828 Sayyid Ahmad Shahid met h
death. The village marks the entrance to the Kaghan valley, one of th
loveliest in the Himalayas. (Courtesy of the *Pakistan Quarterly*.)

Left: Khalifa 'Abdul Hakim (1894–1959), philosopher, educator, and publicist of a modern approach to Islam. (Courtesy of the *Pakistan Quarterly.*)

Above: Maulana Abu'l A'la Maudoodi (1903–), founder of the Jama'at-i-Islami (the Community of Islam), an opposition group in Pakistan dedicated to establishing an Islamic state of a more traditional form. (Courtesy of the Pakistan Press Information Department.)

Left: Sir Syed Ahmad Khan (1817–1898), the greatest Indian Muslim of his century. He strove to bring Muslims out of their backwardness by introducing them to modern sciences, and in 1875 founded a college at Aligarh that later became Aligarh University. (Courtesy of the Pakistan Press Information Department.)

Left: Mirza Ghulam Ahmad (c. 1835–1908), founder of the Ahmadiya, the Muslim sect most active in missionary activity. (Courtesy of the Ahmadiya Movement in Islam.)

Above: Muhammad Iqbal (1873–1938) poet and philosopher whose ideas animated the movement to found an independent Muslim state in northwestern India. (Courtesy of the Pakistan Press Information Department.)

Left: Mohamed Ali Jinnah (1876–1948) who is sometimes called Quaid-i-Azam ("the Great Leader"). He was the founder of Pakistan and its first governor-general. (Courtesy of the *Pakistan Quarterly*.)

with the spread of western education, and who found Hindus easier to locate, existing in greater numbers, and easier to convert, concentrated their efforts on them. Funds were limited, too, barely sufficient for Calcutta alone, and Calcutta was all for English education. The Committee of Public Instruction in Calcutta seldom saw beyond the city's horizons.[1] To the Christian missionary the Hindus were exotic and therefore appealing; the Muslims, on the other hand, based their beliefs on arguments, and scriptures, too, with which the missionaries were all too familiar. The first schools teaching western ideas were run by the missionaries, and the first students in those schools were, naturally enough, Hindus or converts from Hinduism. As late as 1893, when over 45 per cent of the population of Bengal was Muslim, less than 4 per cent of the graduates of western-type schools were Muslim.[2]

British officials did not generally promote western education in India until after 1813, when the British Parliament, probably responding to missionary influence, insisted that the East India Company set aside 10,000 rupees every year for "the revival and improvement of literature and the encouragement of the learned natives of India, and for the introduction and promotion of a knowledge of the sciences among the inhabitants of British territories in India."[3] That these educational funds were to be spent in support of western learning rather than in that of the traditional schools—whether Muslim or Hindu—was not finally decided until 1835, when Thomas Babington Macaulay, the newly arrived Law Mem-

[1] Yusuf Ali, *Cultural History of India* (Bombay, 1940), p. 118.

[2] J. M. S. Baljon, Jr., *The Reforms and Religious Ideas of Sir Sayyid Ahmad Khan* (Leiden, 1949), p. 42.

[3] The quotation is from the 43d section of the renewed Charter of 1813; H. G. Rawlinson, *India, A Short Cultural History* (London, 1952), p. 408.

ber of the Governor-General's Council, threw his decisive
vote as President of a newly reconstituted Committee of Public Instruction in support of western education over oriental
learning. This decision was inevitable, sooner or later, for the
traditional institutions of learning, whether Muslim *madrassah*
or Hindu *pathshala*, were little more than narrow theological
schools; they were archaic for their times, offering very little
in the way of practical studies so far as statecraft in the nineteenth century was concerned. The British had actually debated the problem for many years, but in an age of utilitarian-
ism, and in an age when the horizons of science and technological development seemed limitless, there was no question
as to how the decision would finally fall.

The question was originally brought to the fore in 1816
when Rammohan Roy, a cultivated and progressive Hindu,
along with two prominent Englishmen, established the Hindu
College in Calcutta, the first regular English school in India.[4]
The general attitude of those Englishmen who supported
westernized education is reflected well in an 1823 dispatch
objecting to the subsidization of oriental studies at the recently established Poona Hindu College, a school whose en-
rollment was originally limited to Brahmans between the ages
of ten and eighteen.[5]

With respect to the sciences, it is worse than a waste of time
to employ persons either to teach or learn them, in the state in
which they are found in the Oriental books. As far as any historical documents may be found in the Oriental languages, what

[4] V. V. Oak, *England's Educational Policy in India* (Madras, 1925),
pp. 5–6; Edward Thompson and G. T. Garratt, *Rise and Fulfillment
of British Rule in India* (Allahabad, 1962), p. 266; C. F. Andrews,
Zaka Ullah of Delhi (Cambridge, 1929), pp. 34–35.

[5] Kenneth Ballhatchet, *Social Policy and Social Change in Western
India, 1817–1830* (London, 1957), pp. 255–256.

is desirable is that they should be translated, and this, it is evident, will be best accomplished by Europeans who have acquired the requisite knowledge. Beyond these branches, what remains in Oriental literature is poetry, but it has never been thought necessary to establish Colleges for the cultivation of poetry.

The typical argument of the Orientalists, that the eastern languages were "rich, melodious, and elegant," filled with "admirable works," and that they had been spoken in "the politest courts" was overruled by the utilitarian arguments of the westerners.[6] Macaulay's vote, supported by an engaging and satiric minute in which he argued that western learning was the seat of all civilized knowledge, "I have never found one among them [the Orientalists] who could deny that a single shelf of a good European library was worth the whole native literature of India and Arabia," and that no one could conscientiously be urged to waste his time learning how to purify himself "after touching an ass," or how "to expiate the crime of killing a goat," merely assured the immediate success of the westerners. It did not, unfortunately, assure that increasing funds would be provided by the government; as late as 1854 the government still hoped to withdraw entirely from educational work and let private individuals and institutions carry on.[7] One must remember that in England, and in much of the continent at this time, the government played no hand in the support of education. It was assumed that a child's education lay wholly within the province of his parents and church—an attitude not at all unlike that prevailing among the Muslims and Hindus of India, or the supporters

[6] See the Orientalist argument of Sir William Jones in W. T. deBary, ed., *Sources of Indian Tradition* (New York, 1958), pp. 590–592, from which these quotations are taken.

[7] Oak, pp. 28–29.

of parochial schools in the United States. The remarkable thing about many of the British civil servants in India was that they *were* able to recognize the necessity of state support for education, despite the fact that many of them recognized that such education might very well lead to independence.[8]

The British decided to support western education in the schools receiving government money in India, but they also decided that they could not afford to support mass education, and, indeed, were not really sure they wanted to. This was, after all, almost half a century before anything approaching mass education was effected within England itself. Mountstuart Elphinstone, Governor of the Bombay Presidency, observed in 1823 that "the missionaries find the lowest castes the best pupils"; he felt, however, that these classes were so despised in their society that "if our system of education first took root among them, it would never spread further."[9] The government hoped that through education of the upper classes, those "whose influence on the rest of the countrymen is the most extensive," the new learning would filter down to those below—a hope that eventually proved unrealizable, at least in the amount of time available, because of the structural characteristics of Indian society.[10] The decision was easier made, no doubt, because only the upper classes were clamoring for an English education.

Such emphasis upon secular education had the effect of weakening still more the mosque-schools of the Muslims (as well as the pathshalas of the Hindus), particularly as the early English educational efforts, with the partial exception of the

[8] Ballhatchet, pp. 249–250.

[9] Ballhatchet, p. 258. Yusuf Ali observed that mass education in the vernacular had been considered, p. 122.

[10] Pakistan Historical Society, *A History of the Freedom Movement,* I (Karachi, 1957), 203.

founding of the Calcutta Madrassah in 1781 by Warren Hastings, were primarily directed toward Hindu institutions. Yet the original plea by Calcutta Muslims for a school was to ensure that their children could be educated to hold jobs in the British administration; the Calcutta Madrassah, however, began as a traditional school. After 1835, as a result of the victory of the westerners, government funds were appropriated only to nonreligious schools, that is, those teaching English and other western subjects. There can be no doubt that the British administrators were thoroughly sincere in this, but it is also true that under the circumstances every subject had its effect upon the religious premises of the Muslims and Hindus of the time. The ideal of noninterference in matters of religion was impossible of realization in practice. In trying to be purely secular, and so avoid religious conflict, the government was prejudicing the Muslim and Hindu faiths, for the secular education reflected a different society, a different time, and different values from those current in these religions in India.

Traditionally the mosque-schools, called madrassahs, were the basis of Muslim education. Their curriculum included Arabic and usually Persian, logic, philosophy, Muslim law, hadith, and commentaries on the Qur'an. Most of the teachers tended to gravitate to the cities, and the larger madrassahs appeared in great numbers in a very few centers. It is reported, not without hyperbole, that during the reign of Muhammad ibn Tughluq there were a thousand madrassahs in Delhi alone— 999 of which were of the Hanifi school of jurisprudence; the other belonged to the Shafi school.[11] There were at least thirty in the city of Jaunpur, in what is now the United Provinces of the Republic of India, and a sixteenth-

[11] *Freedom Movement*, II, Part I (Karachi, 1960), 171.

century English traveler, visiting Thatta—now a picturesque ruin near Karachi—reported four hundred large and small madrassahs there.[12]

The quality of these schools must have varied tremendously; the nature of their instruction did not. The Emperor Akbar once ordered that the madrassahs emphasize secular subjects, but the order was a dead letter, and they remained essentially schools of Arabic and theology. Aurangzeb is said to have reprimanded his former teacher for having taught him Arabic, grammar, and philosophy rather than subjects practical for a future ruler of a vast empire.[13] His tirade, however, does not seem to have affected the nature of the courses taught at the madrassahs, even those maintained by grants of money from the emperor's purse. Early in the eighteenth century the mullah Nizam-ud-din Sihalawi drew up a curriculum for the madrassahs which became standard, and which is still the basis for instruction in many such schools.

The syllabus of mullah Sihalawi, and indeed, of the entire madrassah system, may be compared with education in Europe before the rise of the universities—before any great demand for education in the new, secular professions such as law or medicine, or the new philosophy itself, had become manifest. The demand in Europe for formal education other than of a religious nature arose as a result of royal attempts to buttress thrones by recourse to that which was known of the old Roman law, propitiously borrowed at this time from the Byzantines. The demand in Europe was pressed, too, by the needs of the rising merchants, and of the money economy

[12] *Ibid.*, p. 189; Abdul Qayun Malik, "Popular Education in Pre-British India," *Proceedings of the Pakistan History Conference*, 1952, p. 203.

[13] François Bernier, *Travels in the Mogul Empire* (2nd ed.; London, 1914), pp. 154–161.

they were introducing. So medical schools, at first based on knowledge borrowed from the Arabs, began; and so arose the serious study of other secular subjects in medieval Europe.

Such demands did not receive any great support in Muslim India, although the Muslims had themselves introduced a money economy. It was throttled by the extremely efficient control the traditionalists exerted over the majority of the Muslim population (and the same is true of their counterparts in Hindu society), and by the absolutely monopolistic position maintained by the government—the "oriental satrapy" of western imagination. The personal whim of the ruler, whether Muslim or Hindu, remained an uncertain but nearly absolute law.

Many of the mosque-schools were financed by the emperor. Muhammad Shah granted "a few villages" to pay the expenses of the madrassah founded by the mullah Hamdallah at Sandila; he also helped support the madrassah founded by Shah Waliullah's father, and promoted its expansion under Shah Waliullah.[14] Others, of course, were privately financed by wealthy patrons. As the Mughul Empire declined so did the funds that provided for the upkeep of the schools; as the Muslim nobles lost their own sources of income, their support for madrassahs fell off. The educational system that had been outstanding during the high periods of Muslim rule in India, certainly in comparison with that of medieval Europe before the rise of universities, had progressively fallen off through the nineteenth century, both in numbers and quality. Warren Hastings, in justifying the establishment of the Calcutta Madrassah, told the Directors of the East India Company that this madrassah was "almost the only complete establishment of the kind now existing in India, although they were once

[14] *Freedom Movement,* II, Part I, 178–180.

in universal use, and the decayed remains of these schools are yet to be seen in every capital, town, and city of Hindustan and Deccan." [15]

Almost every village mosque had its own school, known as a *maktab*. Less pretentious than the madrassah, these served as the primary fount of what was required for a Muslim's elementary education: to learn to recognize Arabic letters, to pronounce prayers in Arabic, and to be familiar with some qur'anic stories and some of the hadith. As in the madrassahs, students were not divided into classes, but each progressed at his own rate—or, as did the youthful Sayyid Ahmad Shahid, stopped attending after a short time. Even so, for one who applied himself, the actual amount of learning a boy would acquire at a typical maktab was more than likely to be small. Maulana Mohamed Ali of Rampur, who was born in 1878, reports in his autobiography that "had the curriculum of our maktabs provided *all* the knowledge of his religon that such a Muslim youth could acquire, his religious equipment would have indeed been scandalously small. . . ." He goes on to say that most religious education was acquired by living in an atmosphere in which people talked continually and sincerely of religion. For most of the Muslims of India, even in the great periods of Muslim rule, this must also have been the case.[16]

While Sayyid Ahmad Shahid was trying to save Islam in India by waging a holy war against its enemies and by stimulating a religious revival among the masses, and while the mosque-school system that had once spread a network across India was trying to preserve itself against the new demands

---

[15] G. R. Gleig, *Memoirs of the Life of Warren Hastings* (London, 1841), III, 159.

[16] Maulana Mohamed Ali, *My Life: A Fragment* (Lahore, 1944), p. 10.

of a changing society, the often vituperative efforts of the Christian missionaries to convince the Muslims that their faith was blind, irrational, and wrong proved the strongest influence in focusing the best Muslim minds upon the problems facing their religion. The defense of Islam in a society that was changing, as Waliullah seems to have perceived, required as well some new thinking about Islam in terms of the new society. This was not likely to come from the mullahs, steeped as they were in the medieval teachings of an age beginning to disappear. It came, in fact, from individuals who were well acquainted with Islam and yet aware of the nature of western thought and who tried to reconcile the two. In the European Reformation two opposing religious views concerning Christianity, their differences sharpened by the social changes also taking place, were split upon the rock of nationalism. Heresies had appeared in Christendom before the sixteenth century, but they had always been successfully suppressed, or they had succumbed to the lethargic nature of the society in which they appeared. In early nineteenth-century India nationalism in the sense in which it had existed in sixteenth-century Europe did not exist. Religious change here, so far as the Muslims were concerned, while it also concerned two varying views of Islamic jurisprudence (the block to new interpretations), split on the rock of western science and learning. Heresies had been suppressed or ignored in Islam, too; one of the greatest of them was that so crudely promoted by Akbar, now reappearing in changed form.

The beginnings of a movement toward reconciliation of traditional Islamic teaching and modern knowledge appeared in the "Delhi renaissance" in the years just before 1857. This movement was increasingly stimulated by the revolution in language going on in northern India as the use of the vernacular Urdu became more and more widespread.

At the suggestion of the British Resident, English classes were added in 1827 to the course of instruction offered at the Delhi madrassah.[17] The College was thus divided into an English section and an Oriental section, all under one principal; in the Oriental section western science and knowledge were also taught, but in Urdu. One of its students described this new experience by saying, "The doctrines of ancient philosophy taught through the medium of Arabic were thus cast in the shade before the more reasonable and experimental theory of modern science. The old dogma, for instance, that the earth is the fixed center of the universe, was gradually laughed at by the higher students of the Oriental as well as by those of the English Department of the Delhi College." [18] The teaching in English at Delhi College did have an unsettling effect upon the traditionalist beliefs of many students; certainly the Muslims of Delhi believed so, for during the riots of 1857 it was attacked and closed. Nevertheless, the graduates of the College seem to have been genuinely religious men.[19]

Many of them achieved renown for their services to Islam, but often the services promoted a viewpoint somewhat at odds with that maintained by the fundamentalists. Altaf Husain Hali, one of the greatest Urdu poets, spread through his verse the rationalist ideas of Sir Syed Ahmad Khan; Maulana Nazir Ahmad, a pioneer Urdu novelist, emphasized the evils of illiteracy, ignorance, and frustration—he preached, in effect, against the social status quo; Maulana Zakaullah was a freethinking Muslim who emphasized that the spirit of the law should triumph over the letter of the law. Religious tolera-

[17] *Freedom Movement*, II, Part I, 178.

[18] Andrews, pp. 39–40, quoting Professor Ramchandra's *Memoirs.* Zaka Ullah used to say much the same thing.

[19] Cf. Andrews, pp. 40–41.

tion, he believed, was the most important thing for India. This small group was eclipsed by the Mutiny of 1857.

For lack of anyone better, and in obedience to long-established habits, the revolutionists of 1857, both Muslim and Hindu, had tried to center their activities around Bahadur Shah, the last of the Mughul emperors. Bahadur (ironically enough the name means "warrior") was never equal to the task; indeed, it can hardly be said that he ever took it on, but the British chose to look upon the Mughul ruler and the Muslims as persistent threats to their own position of power. The distrust and punishment bestowed upon the Muslim community served to sink them still farther into the mudflats of self-pity. The position of the Muslims in India descended far below its previous nadir, when, in the days of Waliullah, Nadir Shah had come marching down from Persia to ransack Delhi. In these days, too, a man appeared to urge the Muslims to new heights and new ways. Although Sir Syed Ahmad Khan dominated the Islamic society of his day as Shah Waliullah had dominated that of his, there was a tremendous difference between the two men. Shah Waliullah was the last of the great medieval theologians; Sir Syed may be considered the first of those thinkers tinged with an awareness and understanding of the modern world who devoted themselves to rejuvenating Islam. He was a government servant, not a professional theologian, and he was a practical man of affairs, not a mystic. Shah Waliullah, while he did meet with some opposition from other theologians, in general had their support. Sir Syed, so far as his religious views were concerned, was almost always being attacked. But no man has had so great an influence in determining the nature of modern movements in Islam.

Three great problems faced the Muslims of India in Sir Syed's day. Each reflected the lack of self-confidence overcoming the Muslims, and each was marked by the tendency of Muslims to withdraw into isolation behind what were really ghetto walls largely of their own making. Their government had succumbed to non-Muslims (although the blow of Nadir Shah had certainly been telling), their traditional education was being ridiculed or ignored, and their religious precepts were being attacked. These problems were not new in the late nineteenth century; but all the methods of meeting them had failed. Even though Tipu Sultan was largely interested in his own aggrandizement, both he and Sayyid Ahmad Shahid had tried to protect the Muslims by means of crusades, and each had himself died in battle. Sayyid Ahmad Shahid had tried to revitalize the masses by a huge evangelical campaign, and while his success might arouse the envy of Billy Graham, it was not enough. Waliullah alone had seemed to realize that more than patchwork repairs were needed.

The problems could be met in one of two ways: either by retreat or by attack. Retreat, so far as it was deliberate, was negative; by denying or ignoring the significance of western learning, its effects were to worsen, rather than to improve, the lot of the Muslims in India. For all the physical force involved in Sayyid Ahmad Shahid's crusade, his method was essentially negative; it was essentially a holding operation against insuperable odds. Attack was an attempt to show that Islam had been misinterpreted, that Islam was a great and useful religion and not at variance with that which was best in the culture and learning of the West—that, indeed, the foreigners might in some ways be even more truly Islamic than the Muslims themselves. Syed Ahmad Khan was the leading proponent of this positive method of attack.

Born at Delhi in 1817, Sir Syed received a traditional Muslim education, although he also indifferently studied astronomy, mathematics, and medicine. Upon the death of his father in 1838 he accepted a position as a minor judge in the organization of the East India Company. From this time to 1857 he devoted himself to traditional studies. He was obviously influenced by Shah Isma'il, one of the disciples of Sayyid Ahmad Shahid, and wrote favorably of the jihad in the northwest.[20] He published several tracts, most of them religious, and not remarkable for any great degree of originality (one attempted to prove Ptolemy's theory that the earth does not move). At the same time, however, he did demonstrate the quality of his mind in critically editing an account of Akbar's reign. Ghalib, perhaps the greatest master of nineteenth-century Urdu, remarked of this book that it was a waste of Syed Ahmad's time, for it was much more important to popularize English institutions than the Institutes of Akbar.[21] But Sir Syed was not untouched by that hypnosis which caused the Muslims of India still to look to Delhi, and to feel a compensating pride in recollecting the glorious past of the Mughuls, an attitude exhaustively portrayed in a study of the historical monuments of Delhi. The Mutiny of 1857 finally woke him out of these dreamy visions of the past, made him aware of the harsh reality of Muslim decline, and converted him into a tireless, dedicated defender—and interpreter—of Islam.

For each of the three problems facing Islam in India Sir Syed Ahmad Khan found a definite answer; he spent his life promoting those answers. First of all, he insisted that the British rule had to be acknowledged; the Muslims were in no position to regain the political control that had once been theirs—nor would they ever be in such a position unless they gained some understanding of, and insight into, western learning and science. So insistent was he upon this point that he refused to support any activity on the part of Muslims toward

[20] S. M. Ikram, *Mawj-i-Kawthar* (Lahore, 1952), p. 263.
[21] Baljon, p. 5 n. 14.

constructing any kind of political organization. Secondly, he urged with outstanding success the adoption of western education side-by-side with Muslim religious education in order that this insight might be provided. Finally, he preached an interpretation of Islam showing that these western ideas were not at all un-Islamic, but on the contrary were genuinely Islamic. In addition, he met the attacks of the Christian missionaries with trenchant criticisms of Christianity as it was preached by the missionaries—criticisms that in themselves lent confidence to those Muslims whose faith was being weakened.

His most outstanding success was in the realm of education. No Muslim today, whether modernist or traditionalist, denies him credit for his herculean efforts in this field. The college which he established in 1875 at Aligarh, in north central India, became the training ground of Muslims all over India and the East. After the partition of India in 1947, the great majority of college-trained officials in Pakistan were graduates of Aligarh. The drive and impetus that led to the successful foundation of Aligarh College (which became Aligarh University in 1922) spilled over into other educational areas. Even before the college was founded Sir Syed had established a Literary and Scientific Society to translate English books into Urdu, and to support a periodical which printed material in both English and Urdu, a device designed to educate not only the Muslims in English, but the English in the ways of the Muslims.

Of greater significance than the Literary and Scientific Society was the Muhammadan Educational Conference established in 1886 to spread his educational ideas among all of the Muslims of India, and to lend support to needy madrassahs and maktabs. This last function may have been included to pacify the theologians, for the emphasis of the Conference was on western education. It must be realized, however, that Sir Syed was himself a sincere Muslim and had no intention of abandoning the great tradition of Islam. He saw that tradition in a manner somewhat different from that of the theologians of his day, but he was not in the least abandoning Islam for the West. After a schoolboy had eulogized him one day, Sir Syed replied, "Remember that Islam, for which you live and for which you would die, must be maintained for national survival. My dear boy, should you progress sky-high, yet not remain a Muslim in the process—then of what use would all this prosperity be to you, for you would no longer be a fellow national." [22]

Although Sir Syed Ahmad Khan is most revered in India and Pakistan today as an educator, it would be rash to say that, in the long run, his influence has been any less great in the field of religious interpretation. He offered little new in specific interpretation; his contribution lay in his new approach to the matter. True, his ideas of Islam never appealed to more than a very few contemporary upper- and middle-class Muslims, but he did stir up a swell of criticism and questioning that served to create more questioning minds. He stimulated the effective reaction in India against the medieval-minded Muslim theologians. Sir Syed's was the initial assault on the scholasticism of the theologians, an assault that reached its first intellectual peak in the writings of Muhammad Iqbal.

Sir Syed's position resulted from pressures of practicality. He was just as deeply Muslim, and just as positive of the truth of his faith, as the most pious mullah, but he recognized the validity of much of the western experience—even as the Muslim theologians at this time generally disparaged it. The result was that Sir Syed was forced to rethink his faith and to reconcile it with this new learning. "A new science of logic is

[22] S. M. Ikram, p. 164.

needed in these times," he said, "by which we may either refute the doctrines of modern science, or prove them to be of doubtful validity, or show that they are in conformity with the tenets of Islam." [23] Sir Syed, believing that Islam came from God, and believing that all nature, as well as all of nature's laws, was the handiwork of God, was sure that the science and learning of the West, so far as it was true, was in conformity with Islam. If this were not so, then Islam had no future, which was impossible to conceive. First and last, Sir Syed was the defender of Islam; his defense was made through reform. His reform was to shift the traditionalist emphasis from an approach determined by the customs and attitudes of Arabia before the eleventh century to an emphasis more in keeping with the thought of nineteenth-century Europe, as he understood it.

The position of Sir Syed in this respect is not dissimilar from that of the medieval dialecticians of Europe who set up reason against authority, but who believed no genuine conflict existed between revealed truth and rational truth. Revealed truth, they believed, could be made intelligible, but in the last analysis, if reason failed, then revealed truth had to be taken on faith. Sir Syed, however, was operating from the rational truth of the nineteenth century rather than from that of the eleventh century; his Muslim opponents were often not far removed from the habits of eleventh-century European thought. It was Sir Syed, however, who provided the first strong arguments against those of the Christian missionaries in India.

The dispute between Muslims and Christians in India had begun as early as Akbar's reign, but the nature of the argument was such that victory for either side was impossible. The Christian missionaries argued against Islam and the Mus-

[23] *Ibid.*, pp. 165–166.

lims argued against Christianity on very much the same terms; each assaulted the other on rational grounds and defended its own beliefs in terms of the supernatural.[24] Dr. Pfander, an energetic worker for the Church Missionary Society, unwittingly summed up the final argument of both Christians and Muslims when he declared: "The Word of God is not under the dominion of reason, but, on the contrary, reason must submit to the Word of God." [25] These words might also have been spoken with equal zest by the dialecticians, whether Christian or Muslim, of a much earlier period.

By the middle of the nineteenth century this dispute had passed into new realms, propelled by the force of nineteenth-century rationalism. Christians in England found themselves forced to find some sort of reconciliation between the bounds they had known and the new horizons opened up by such scientific discoveries as Darwin's theory; Christians in India discovered that some Muslims were trying to use the new European thought for the benefit of Islam. Syed Ahmad, himself trained in his youth by mystics, ignored all mysticism in his interpretation of Islam. He tended to slight the hadith literature, too, neither accepting it nor rejecting it entirely, but treating it as a mass of stories not above suspicion, and hence better left alone. He maintained that he was as capable as the medieval jurists at interpreting the legal side of Islam. In short, Sir Syed insisted on going back to the Qur'an—the fundamental authority—as the basis for his own interpretation of Islam, and he insisted on the right of the Muslim to read and interpret the Qur'an in the light of the time and place in which he lived.

[24] See L. Levonian, *Muslim Mentality* (London, 1928), pp. 182–204, for an outline of the missionaries' arguments.

[25] Quoted in Bashir Ahmad Dar, *Religious Thought of Sayyid Ahmad Khan* (Institute of Islamic Culture; Lahore, 1957), pp. 88–89.

The Qur'an, however, had to be interpreted from a new point of view. The interpretation of the medieval scholars, continued by the traditionalists, was neither unthinking nor illogical. They customarily used the stories of the hadith literature to support a particular interpretation derived from the Qur'an, if only because it seemed to be more clear. Because of this, students at the best madrassahs often spent their time studying methods of interpreting the Qur'an, rather than in actually reading it. But the learned theologians and Sir Syed were looking for something quite different. The theologians assumed that all religion was to be found in, or deduced from, the Qur'an—and the hadith; they tried to begin their study with no previous assumptions, for they believed that all that was necessary about religion was to be found in the revelation, and in the explanation of the revelation, the role in which the hadith literature was cast. God does not do things, they maintained, in a halfway manner. Sir Syed Ahmad Khan, however, had his own idea of what true religion was before he read the Qur'an.

If religion is true, he asserted, it must be in conformity with God's handiwork—with nature. If a religion is against man's nature and his constitution, "against his powers and the rights which follow from these powers, and stands in the way of putting them to useful purposes, then undoubtedly that religion cannot be claimed to issue forth from the hands of the Author of Nature, for religion, after all, is made for men. . . ." [26] Sir Syed believed that once the accretions of the ages were removed, Islam was above all other religions in its simple, rational, and natural qualities. He believed, in short, that nineteenth-century rational thought was the epitome of the original Islam, and he set out to show that this was so.

[26] Quoted in Dar, p. 150, from Majmu'a Lectures (Urdu), pp. 284–286.

In sociological terms Sir Syed was unconsciously trying to reshape the symbolism of Islam to fit a new age, which is what Luther and Calvin were doing to sixteenth-century Christianity, or what the Roman Church was accomplishing in a much more quiet and cautious way from 1543 on. He did not question the revelation; the unchanged character of the Qur'an since its revelation to Muhammad is a matter of tremendous pride to Muslims. He merely tried to read out what he considered the mythology and the irrationality that had been erroneously read into it over the centuries.

Nor did he create a new interpretation out of hand. The greatest single work in which his ideas of Islam are developed is his unfinished commentary on the Qur'an; in six or seven volumes it covers about two-thirds of the Qur'an. It contains fifty-two individual interpretations with which the majority of theologians disagreed, but for only eleven of these does there appear to have been no support whatever from other commentators.[27] For these eleven cases Sir Syed quoted other verses of the Qur'an in his support, and some hadith. His friend and biographer, the poet Hali, believed that Sir Syed did little more than reveal ideas and opinions known to the more learned theologians, but either ignored or suppressed by them.[28]

Because he did try to present Islam as a rational religion, he relied heavily on those commentators who had tried to interpret Islam in rational terms. He denied, for example, the traditional story, based on many hadith, and on several qur'anic verses, that Muhammad had one night been physically carried from Mecca to Jerusalem; he interpreted this story as a dream. In this opinion he had all kinds of support,

[27] Baljon believes that in only three cases did he actually add new theories to Muslim dogma: for the qur'anic teaching regarding slavery, the crucifixion of Christ, and personal prayer. Baljon, p. 92 and n. 28.

[28] S. M. Ikram, p. 167.

including not only eminent theologians, but the statement of Muhammad's wife, Aisha, although the incident reportedly took place before Aisha was born.[29] Similarly, he argued that Satan and the angels were not physical beings, but forces controlling nature, motivating elements of God's laws; nor were the jinns of the Qur'an ghosts or demons, but references to the wild barbarians who lived in the mountains of Arabia —this particular interpretation was one of those eleven that seem to have been unique with him. He maintained that the qur'anic picture of paradise as a land flowing with milk and honey and filled with voluptuously beautiful women was no more than a metaphor, an attempt to suggest what could not possibly be described: the pleasures of the next world, and no more real than the Christian heaven of pearly gates, melodious harps, and golden streets.

Muslim critics accused Sir Syed of ignoring sound and reliable hadiths for questionable ones which supported his views. In a sense the criticism was just, but Sir Syed had no faith in the mass of hadith literature, no matter how carefully its origins and antecedents had been checked. The Qur'an, he insisted, could be explained only by reference to the Qur'an itself. The validity of any story of the hadith, he maintained, could be measured only by whether or not it agreed with the Qur'an. But his Qur'an was one that was to be interpreted as an exposition of a natural and rational religion. As far as the traditionalists were concerned, this was little short of revolutionary.[30] Sir Syed was claiming that the Qur'an explained the

[29] Sayyid Ahmad Khan, *Essay on Shaqq-i-Sadar and Miraj* (Lahore, 1959). This is one of the twelve essays from Sir Syed's *Essays on the Life of Muhammad*.

[30] Ibn Taimiya, a controversial theologian of the thirteenth century, was quoted by Sir Syed in his commentary on the Qur'an as having said that "the truly traditional is always consistent with the truly rational." See Dar, pp. 246, 140.

hadith, rather than that the function of the hadith was to explain the Qur'an. And the Qur'an was itself to be explained in the light of man's God-given reason.

This, of course, was a tremendous responsibility, and Sir Syed treated it as such. He believed the Qur'an was God's verbal inspiration to Muhammad, unique not so much because of the music of its language as because of the guidance it contains for all mankind, whether learned or illiterate. In the Qur'an were two kinds of injunctions: those fundamental to Islam, none of which is contrary to Natural Law, and those of secondary importance, the function of which is to enable man to realize the true spirit behind the fundamental injunctions. To pray, for example, is fundamental, but to pray in a certain direction is not, for "whithersoever you turn, there is the Presence of God." [31] The direction serves only to unite the community, not to validate the prayer, and need not be strictly enforced—except in ordinary circumstances. It was not to be completely ignored, for it was from God.

Holy war, he insisted, had to be based on purely religious considerations. He admitted that the Qur'an urges Muslims to resort to violence, but he felt that this was a better balance than the idealism of the Christians which had not ended bloody warfare, even between Christians, but if anything had encouraged hypocrisy. To turn the other cheek is an unnatural principle, he averred, for it denies any remedy for one's grievances. He believed that jihad was a purely defensive device, the purpose of which is to establish peace and order. Those passages in the Qur'an which had been interpreted to imply the use of jihad to secure conversions to Islam had been, according to him, improperly interpreted, for the Qur'an did not call for conversion to Islam but for freedom of conscience.

[31] Qur'an 2:115; see also 2:142.

Sir Syed deduced from his reading of the Qur'an that only in exceptional circumstances was polygamy permitted in Islam; that Muhammad had, in effect, abolished slavery; that cutting off the hands as a punishment for theft was to be used only by a nation that could not afford a prison system; and that the Qur'an does not forbid all interest, but only forbids charging exorbitant interest to those "who are poor and miserable and need help and sympathy." [32]

The heart of his revolution lies in reading the Qur'an and the hadiths in this manner. Having implicitly accepted the Qur'an on faith, he believed God would show faith in him by expecting the Qur'an to be read in the only manner he could read it—in the light of his reason. So far as the hadith were concerned, he was insisting upon a new criticism, based not upon the personal reliability of those who had relayed the tradition, but upon the relationship of the tradition, the modern mind, and the Qur'an as interpreted in what he considered a rational manner. Sir Syed maintained that he was doing nothing really new, and he cited al-Ghazali, the great eleventh-century theologian, who had said that every school of thought among Muslims interpreted the Qur'an rationally in the light of its time. [33]

His Muslim opponents were incensed, for they had been brought up to believe that the opinions of the medieval jurists were not to be questioned. Even Waliullah had not shaken the majority of theologians from this belief. Some now questioned whether or not Sir Syed was still a Muslim. For a time the success of Aligarh was threatened, and Sir Syed very wisely excluded his own interpretations from the re-

[32] Dar, p. 265. These three paragraphs are largely derived from the discussion in Dar, pp. 249–266.

[33] Dar, p. 160.

quired courses in Muslim theology at his school. All Muslim students had to pray five times daily and, except with a reasonable excuse, to fast during the month of Ramadan.[34] He also adamantly refused to consider women's education or to make any pronouncements in favor of the subject, knowing that it would only cause an uproar that would take attention away from what he felt must come first. Sir Syed was a gradualist in a hurry. To him education came first, and he was not willing to jeopardize it in any way; on the other hand, he recognized that "with the spread of this new learning for which I am striving my utmost . . . there will appear a sort of indifference, rather positive reversion, towards what are usually called the doctrines of Islam, though I am equally sure that it will not in the least affect the true religion of Islam." [35]

Without the new education the Muslim community was doomed; with the new education the traditionalist view of Islam was doomed. This was the situation Sir Syed Ahmad Khan so clearly saw, and he reasoned that a true religion does not stand in the way of true progress. It was his role to show the Muslims of India that Islam need not be a barrier to progress as it was developing in the West, that the Muslim could be modern and still be proud of his faith.

The Reformation in Europe in the sixteenth century developed into a great armed feud between Protestants and Catholics, and into several smaller feuds between various Protestant groups. Only over a period of years, after the religious wars of the sixteenth and seventeenth centuries had shown that national or dynastic states were not necessarily

[34] Baljon, p. 41.
[35] Quoted in Dar, p. 148, from Majmu'a Lectures (Urdu), pp. 21–22.

based on an absolute unity of religious belief, did the armed
feud between Catholics and Protestants subside; not until the
effects of eighteenth-century rationalism had had time to be
absorbed were the dissident sects somewhat reluctantly accepted as full-fledged members of the body politic. No great
armed feud between Muslims on the Indian subcontinent
broke out over religious questions, however; perhaps because
another religion could be used to absorb such passions—in
a mutual way—for Hinduism, too, was going through the
same pangs of development as was Islam in India.

The Reformation in Europe was a matter of fighting within
one religion itself. Sir Syed Ahmad Khan believed that Martin
Luther was influenced by reading the Qur'an, but even if one
accepts the extremely doubtful argument he advances, one
must admit that Islam, outside of the military threat posed
by the Ottoman Turks, played no direct role in the religious
machinations of sixteenth-century Europe.[36] Christian missionaries, however, did play a direct role in stimulating Muslim thinking in India; the arguments of the Christian missionaries served to put the advocates of Islam on the defensive,
and their defense served in turn not only to strengthen their
own faith, but to lead to a re-examination of it. Out of this
concatenation of historical, social, economic and religious
forces arose several specific responses.

Most prominent was the hardening of traditionalism. Religion is essentially conservative; inasmuch as it reflects social
values, its organization is a device to secure those values for
its own society. An attack on social values becomes an attack
on religion. This is the same response that the Catholic
Church initially demonstrated at the Council of Trent; in
India it is best demonstrated by the educational institution

[36] Sir Syed Ahmad Khan, *Whether Islam Has Been Beneficial or
Injurious to Human Society in General* (Lahore, 1954), p. 41.

that in its own way set out to rival Aligarh—the theological school developed out of the Deoband madrassah by Maulana Muhammad Qasim.

Eventually compromises were developed between the Aligarh position and that of Deoband. Sir Syed, as we have noted, began with nineteenth-century rationalism; the Deoband school began with a thoroughly scholastic approach that tried to interpret Islam from the Qur'an and the hadith; it did not insist on the absolute supremacy of any single school of jurisprudence. Deoband refused to look at the West, except to regret it; Sir Syed looked at the West and was so impressed he was sure Islam could not be inconsistent with it, and tried to prove it. Others, less sure, preferred to analyze the West in the terms in which they understood Islam. Foremost among such men was Muhammad Shibli Nu'mani, a traditionalist who had taught Persian and Arabic at Aligarh for sixteen years. Shibli hoped to revive the great traditions of the golden days of Islamic civilization, and so encourage a new vigor in the Islam of the present. Because he believed that Aligarh was too secular, he founded a theological school at Lucknow, the Nadwat-ul-Ulama, hoping to retain some elements of the Aligarh spirit, but to incorporate a much greater religious emphasis. It was still too early for a program meant to be both rational and religious; before long the Lucknow school had little to distinguish it from Deoband except the English subjects taught there.

Another institution that reflected a compromise attempt on the part of those who wanted to appreciate the advantages of western ideas and concepts, but did not want to lose the old-time religion, either, was the nationalist-inspired Jamia Millia Islamia. This autonomous university was established at Aligarh in 1920 and five years later moved to the outskirts of Delhi. It hoped to create both a good Muslim in the tradi-

tional sense and a good citizen of a united and independent
India.

Despite such compromise attempts, the conservative influence of Deoband remained dominant in the cities, and
the even more conservative influence of the Bareilly theological school dominated most of the rural areas. The adherents
of Sir Syed Ahmad Khan comprised only a very small percentage of the literate Muslim population in India, mostly in
the middle- and upper-class urban groups.

Although Deoband is described as a theological school, it
should not be thought of in terms of the typical American
graduate school of theology. Deoband students were—and
are—admitted at the age of seven and usually graduate between the ages of seventeen and twenty-one. During those
years they study a great deal of Arabic and theological subjects; as a last, and optional course, the reading of the Qur'an
is assigned. The Jamia Millia Islamia offers sixteen years of
instruction, beginning with kindergarten; the last four years
approximate the level of an American college or university.

The supporters of Deoband were firm in their conviction
that even if society was changing, *they* would not change.
It was a religious principle with them that Islam, the true
religion, did not and could not change; it was a religious
principle that true religion cannot be divorced from its society—there is no separation of church and state. From these
two premises of the syllogism, the master of Deoband deduced that social change, unless it were a return to the conditions of seventh-century Arabia, could not be countenanced
because it would affect the faith. And social change most
clearly meant the acceptance of western learning. The Deoband school was really caught up short in its own unitarianism: it insisted upon retaining a theological outlook in times
that cried for a social outlook; its masters remained scholastics

when scholasticism no longer appealed to men's minds. This was a problem Waliullah saw, and only in this sense can he be considered a modernist. But Waliullah did no more than indicate the problem; he did not himself take any decisive steps to meet it, other than the translation of the Qur'an, or the equal acceptance of all four medieval schools of jurisprudence. Very likely he could not have taken any decisive action and remained strictly traditionalist. Sayyid Ahmad Shahid did take action, to be sure, but he saw a different problem. He was fighting to preserve what existed from further depredations by external forces, not to effect an adjustment to a new social and intellectual milieu. It was Sir Syed Ahmad Khan who saw the problem in its social and intellectual terms, and who did take decisive action to meet it, but to do so he had to abandon the traditionalist position.

The shift in emphasis from a theological to a social point of view has been *the* great change in the interpretation of Islam. The great change of Protestantism in respect to Catholicism in the sixteenth century was essentially social, too. The role of the individual, the self-confident man of the Renaissance, and the diversity he encompassed, were given precedence over the medieval conception of the unity of society at the cost of the submersion of the individual. Protestantism demanded more freedom for the individual in reading and interpreting the Bible, and more responsibility for the individual in his relations with God: that is, the need for an intercessor between man and God was not acknowledged.

A second response, exemplified by Sir Syed among others, was a demand that Islam be returned to its original purity, to "the true religion"—the cry of Luther and Zwingli and Calvin for Christianity, and the cry of every reformer of every religion everywhere. It is not surprising that this soon developed into a "Back to Muhammad!" movement, but its approach was through the thorny problem of the reliability of the hadith literature.

Shaykh Ahmad of Sirhind had attacked Akbar and his innovations under this "back to the true religion" banner. Shah Waliullah had supported the ideal of independent judgment in legal matters—ijtihad—because he believed its application would restore the purity of Islam; he had recognized that society was changing and could not successfully remain bound to old rules. Sir Syed went further, for he applied his independent judgment not only to legal matters but to the Qur'an itself. Waliullah, who had been raised on the hadith, and was perhaps the greatest scholar of hadith of his day, had searched for a compromise between the teaching of al-Shafi'i and Abu Hanifa, believing that the jurisprudence of the former was more in keeping with the hadith, but admiring the Hanifi school as being more rational.[37] Sir Syed was not so attached to the hadith; he recognized that many of them—and those most respected—were strong arguments in favor of the traditionalist viewpoint. He respected hadith which seemed to him to agree with the Qur'an as he interpreted it but was extremely suspicious of all others. The hadith were soon to be thrown out entirely by one group, who considered them to be a barrier in the way of achieving the original Islam.

The People of the Qur'an (Ahl-i-Qur'an) movement was founded in 1902; it was far too radical for its day and never gathered much support outside the Punjab where it started. The People of the Qur'an discarded both the jurisprudence of the four schools and the literature of the hadith—the sunna—itself. Only the Qur'an is God's revelation, its founder asserted, and only God's revelation need be heeded. The

[37] He was also strongly attracted to the Maliki school. Maudoodi to author, October 19, 1959.

movement was further weakened by the religious peculiarities by which its founder, Maulvi Abdullah Chakralvi, tried to give it distinction—as though being so far leftwing was not distinctive enough!

Nevertheless, the position of the People of the Qur'an was thoroughly logical, for there was no doubt, even among traditionalists, that many of the hadith were questionable—and who could tell which were or which were not? Knowing the Qur'an to be true, and unwilling to accept the rule-of-thumb test of Sir Syed, the People of the Qur'an insisted that the pure faith could be found only in a pure source—the Qur'an itself and by itself. One follower of the People of the Qur'an was Hafiz Aslam Jaraighpuri, a professor at the Jamia Millia Islamia in Delhi who, in turn, exerted a warm influence on Ghulam Ahmad Parwez, the most active Islamic reformer in Pakistan today.

The demand for the return to the original religion, of course, raised the fundamental question: what *was* the original religion? To the traditionalists this was crystal clear, made even more so because the best minds of Islam, in days much nearer to those of the Prophet, had studied the Qur'an and the hadith and had decided just exactly what interpretations were called for.

On the other hand, some Muslim mystics—among them the thirteenth-century Persian, Rumi—had long maintained that Islam had been presented as a series of steps, that the Qur'an was read at different levels by everyone depending upon the step he had achieved, and that each level revealed more of God's truth than that which preceded it. To insist that there could be only one interpretation was to deny one of the most remarkable things about the book: that it was indeed written for everyone. But the mystic was harmless so long as he alone held his view and did not spread it very far. This was usually the case in a society without printing and when books were customarily transcribed into a language most people were not able to read.

In the nineteenth century, as the Urdu vernacular came into its own, the printing press made it possible to spread divergent opinions easily. One of the main reasons for Sir Syed Ahmad Khan's influence was the quantity of his writings—about 6,000 pages—in Urdu, much of which received a wide circulation for the time. Little objection was raised to the presentation of modernist views in English—almost none of the traditionalist theologians could read it, and fewer still of the masses. S. Khuda Bakhsh, in Calcutta, translated several studies by German Orientalists into English and wrote several provocative English essays of his own on Islam, but his over-all influence was minor, for he was writing in a language that did not, in the early twentieth century, claim any large following. The development of Urdu, replacing the Persian that had been the language of the aristocracy alone, played a role in the recent development of Islam on the subcontinent similar to the development of modern German in the time of Martin Luther. The use of English, meanwhile, provided a medium by which modernist ideas could be advanced within modernist circles without eliciting too much controversy from traditionalists.

The great exception to the ineffectiveness of writing in English was Sayyid Ameer Ali's book, *The Spirit of Islam*. Something of the reason for this exception lies in the contrast between his presentation and that of Sir Syed Ahmad Khan and his supporters. The latter were such thorough-going rationalists that their arguments often lacked emotional appeal, while *The Spirit of Islam*, written to show the superiority of Islam over all other religions, possesses an enthusiasm and a depth of emotional feeling that moves everyone who reads it. Something of the reason for this exception, too, lies in the fact that the book—which appeared only seven years before Sir Syed's death—represents the second phase of the reform movement. Sir Syed was essentially defensive; he was arguing that Islam is not inimical to progress, that the Muslim and his faith are the equal of any.[38] Ameer Ali, however, carried the argument of Sir Syed onto positive ground: he did not argue that Islam was not inferior; he argued that it was superior. He supported his arguments with a critical examination of Christian belief in particular in which the angry polemics of an earlier day are pleasantly missing, although the gist of the argument is much the same. Ameer Ali avoids dogmatism; his is really a rational appeal to intuition. In this he had little choice, for the dogma of Islam had been developed by the advocates of an interpretation he could not himself accept. Like all reformers, he maintained that the spirit loses—rather than gains, as the traditionalist would say—by a blind observance of ritual. He believed that whenever Islam ruled in the true spirit of Muhammad, a civilization of unequal richness appeared.[39] Back to Muhammad, that humble, kind, understanding servant of men and beloved of God! cried Ameer Ali. Thus he shifted the emphasis of the reformers from qur'anic quibbling to appreciations of the Prophet.

It was a strong position, for it was attractive to both traditionalists and modernists. It appealed to a quickening historical sense which in itself marked the bare beginnings of a sense of criticism—a historical sense marked in English writing by the translations of Khuda Bakhsh, and in Urdu by the ex-

[38] See Wilfred Cantwell Smith, *Modern Islam in India, A Social Analysis* (London, 1946), p. 49, for further development of this point.

[39] G. E. von Grunebaum, "Islam, Essays in the Nature and Growth of a Cultural Tradition," *The American Anthropologist*, Vol. 57, No. 2, Part 2, memoir no. 81 (April, 1955), pp. 189–193.

tensive, if not very searching, religious biographies of Muhammad Shibli Nu'mani. It satisfied the feelings of Muslims who worried about the attacks of the Christian missionaries because it portrayed Muhammad in very much the same terms as the missionaries were portraying Christ, except, of course, that Ameer Ali clung to the stern unitarianism of Islam, and would not concede that the term "Son of God" was to be applied literally to anyone. To the Muslim, God is One, and Father and Son, in his experience, have always been two; on this point every Muslim, whether traditionalist or modernist, prefers to be thoroughly rational and to indulge in absolutely no metaphysics.

Even so, the emotional appeal of *The Spirit of Islam* had its greatest effect in India not because many Indian Muslims read it, but because it became the accepted reply to Christian arguments. It is as an apologetic work that the book is most frequently cited by non-Muslims, and it is certainly this. Indeed, it was written for an English audience. But it is also something more, for it released the reformists from the entanglements into which they were falling through Sir Syed Ahmad Khan's commentary on the Qur'an.

Ameer Ali's book was thoroughly grounded in the thought of Sir Syed, but he presented the new thought generated by Sir Syed in a new format, one with a vast appeal for the self-conscious Muslims. Sir Syed, for example, had said that Islam forbids slavery; Ameer Ali said that Islam was the *only* religion that did so. "Christianity, as a system and a creed," he wrote, "raised no protest against slavery, enforced no rule, inculcated no principle for the mitigation of the evil." [40] But Muhammad had utilized every opportunity to improve the conditions of slaves—they were in most respects to be treated as equals of their masters—and to secure their liberation.

[40] Syed Ameer Ali, *The Spirit of Islam* (London, 1922), p. 259.

Sir Syed had said that Islam is not opposed to science; Ameer Ali pointed out that the theory of evolution had been proposed by the eleventh-century mathematician Hasan ibn Haitham,[41] and detailed at length the rationalistic and scientific spirit that had marked the golden days of Islamic civilization.

Sir Syed had maintained that polygamy was permitted in Islam only under exceptional circumstances; Ameer Ali emphasized that no religion has abolished polygamy, and that St. Augustine did not disapprove of the practice if it was a legal institution of a country. But, Ameer Ali argued, "to suppose that Muhammad either adopted or legalized polygamy" is a great mistake.[42] Muhammad found it in existence and curbed it, raising the status of women to new heights. There is undoubted truth in this, but Ameer Ali was unfair when he wrote, "Of Christianity, in its relation to womankind, the less said the better." [43] He was willing to attribute the backward position of Muslim women to a want of culture in the community generally, rather than to any religious laws, but he was not willing to make the same concession to Christian communities.[44]

As the dispute between traditionalists and modernists intensified, another response began to emerge. It was the argument of the agnostics, or secularists. They were neither numerous nor organized. Mostly, they were submerged in the upper, and often English-educated, levels of the large urban Muslim community and remained quiet, desirous of little more than not being labeled dissenters.

The agnostic was a secularist because he recognized that

[41] *Ibid.,* p. 424.
[42] *Ibid.,* pp. 225–227.
[43] *Ibid.,* p. 251.
[44] *Ibid.,* p. 257.

the most pressing task facing the Muslims of India lay not in the mosque itself, but in social and economic fields. Intellectually moved by the appeal of western science and learning, and emotionally drawn by the spirit of Islam, the agnostic could not see where the line should be drawn between the two, or was not willing to enter the fray concerned with drawing the line. He was an individual who could not reconcile the sometimes strained interpretations of Sir Syed with his own actual reading of the Qur'an, or he was an individual who constitutionally reacted against prolonged theological discussion—because he saw either no answer to it or no sense in it. What good was religion, the agnostic asked, if it contributed to hell on earth at the price of a later heaven? He was an individual who was no longer satisfied with the ends portrayed in medieval philosophy, but was not sure, either, of the goals of modern philosophy.

A parallel might be drawn between the Politiques of the European Reformation and the agnostics within the Muslim community in India. The Politiques of Europe appeared as the result of a stalemated war between the French Catholics and the Huguenots; they were Catholic realists who placed the welfare of the state above all questions of dogmatic religion. The "politiques" of the Muslim community appeared in reaction to a stalemate in their minds between a medieval approach to religion and an approach to life that was no longer medieval. They remained deeply religious, but rationally they could not countenance the strife and quarreling produced by questions of religious dogma.

Outside the exclusive circle of Islam and its traditionalists and modernists, one would have to identify another group as being similar to the Politiques: those Muslims who believed they could live in peace and prosperity with the Hindus. In this sense every Mughul emperor was a politique; so, too,

were the founders of the Jamia Millia Islamia, who believed
that peace, understanding, and prosperity were the fruit of
true education, and who sought by their course of study to
end religious discord between all faiths, while teaching students to be good Muslims.

While the response of most literate Muslims lay in between
the position of Sir Syed Ahmad Khan and that of the Deoband
school, there was very little response at all from the mass
of Muslims, 90 per cent of whom were illiterate. Mostly
rural folk, these Muslims implicitly followed the local Imam,
or some local saint, in matters of religion and observed an
Islam that was based on little formal instruction, but—as
Maulana Mohamed Ali has indicated—on living in an atmosphere that was "religious." The rural Muslim believed
what he was told, but his instruction, for the most part, came
from individuals who had been trained in schools to the right
of Deoband.

The ideas of Sir Syed Ahmad Khan, buttressed by the
warmth and historical approach of Ameer Ali, represented
the heart of the reformist position. Other reformers would
come, but each would jump off from the thought of these
two men. Interestingly enough, they seemed to jump in almost
every imaginable direction.

Chapter Five

A Variety of
Twentieth-Century Responses

There can be no doubt that Sir Syed Ahmad Khan stands as a dividing line between Muslim thinkers on the subcontinent. An occasional and isolated freethinker is to be found before his time, mostly among the sufis; afterwards, freethinkers, no longer primarily confined to the sufis, are more often to be found. Yet Sir Syed himself did not so much inject novelty as encourage processes already at work. Waliullah, for instance, had emphasized the significance of hadith over the actual decisions of the jurists—a position echoed by the school at Deoband. Sir Syed took the next step and emphasized the significance of the Qur'an over that of the hadith.[1] Nevertheless, very few of the differences in qur'anic interpretation utilized by Sir Syed originated with him. In Sir Syed's view the security of Islam was dependent upon breaking down the habits of isolation and aloofness into which

---

[1] Mazheruddin Siddiqui, "Muslim Culture in Pakistan and India" in Kenneth W. Morgan, ed., *Islam—The Straight Path* (New York, 1958), p. 319.

Muslims had fallen. Islam, he believed, had lost the resiliency it needed always to be in accord with the times: that resiliency could once again be found by returning to the Qur'an, to the pure revelation. Nor was there anything truly new in this. What Sir Syed provided more than anything else was an attitude. For he, responding to the rationalism of Europe, believed that man's knowledge was expanding and that it could not be confined within previously established limits. He read the Qur'an in a manner supporting his belief in expanding knowledge.

His own program did not differ in its essentials from that of the great Egyptian reformer, and contemporary of Sir Syed, Muhammad 'Abduh. The latter's program has been summarized by Professor Gibb as including the purification of Islam from corrupting influences and practices; the reformation of Muslim higher education; the reformation of Islamic doctrine in the light of modern thought; and the defense of Islam against European influences and Christian attacks.[2] Sir Syed's emphasis lay primarily in the second and third of these points, but was not, of course, limited to them alone. In fact, however, the placing of the emphasis lent color to the nature of the reform. Other reformers had emphasized the first and fourth points—the Wahabis, for example—but they did not stimulate the new thinking that appeared after the time of Sir Syed. Mirza Ghulam Ahmad, founder of the most controversial sect in Islam, who was usually considered a modernist, placed his emphasis almost entirely on the first and fourth of these points. Ghulam Ahmad accepted many of the ideas of Sir Syed, but specifically objected to the intellectual attitude—the truly distinguishing characteristic—from which Sir Syed evolved his views. Both men accepted the assumption that Islam is the perfect religion; Ghulam

[2] H. A. R. Gibb, *Modern Trends in Islam* (Chicago, 1947), p. 33.

Ahmad based his analysis primarily on theological arguments, while Sir Syed insisted that the proof was not to be found in theologically based arguments alone, nor could it be based primarily on scholastic reasoning. In this sense, because he justified the thinking and knowledge of his age in terms of Islam, Sir Syed may be described as a secular thinker. Mirza Ghulam Ahmad did not think such an effort meaningful; operating from theological premises, he argued very much like a medieval logician in love with his syllogisms. The two men represent extreme opposites, and the Ahmadiyas have a point when they maintain that "in the history of Indian Islam we find two separate movements among Muslims. The movement of Sir Sayyid Ahmad of Aligarh and of Mirza Ghulam Ahmad of Qadian." [3]

There are, in fact, more than two movements in the recent history of Indian Islam, and it is difficult to make meaningful comparisons among them, especially as the movement generated by Sir Syed has had its effects upon all subsequent movements, including that of Mirza Ghulam Ahmad. The latter began his career by trying to prove dialectically that no other religion could compare with Islam. In the process of making his argument he found himself forced onto paths somewhat removed from those of traditionalism and which led to the creation of a new Muslim sect.

Mirza Ghulam Ahmad was born about 1835 in the Punjab village of Qadian.[4] His family had originally owned extensive

[3] Maulana Muhammad Ali, *True Conception of Ahmadiyyat* (Lahore, n.d.), p. 66.

[4] This short sketch of Mirza Ghulam Ahmad is largely based on the following works: Maulana Muhammad Ali, *The Founder of the Ahmadiyya Movement* (Lahore, n.d.); Maulana Muhammad Ali, *Mirza Ghulam Ahmad of Qadian*, trans. by S. Muhammad Tufail (Lahore, 1959); H. A. Walter, *The Ahmadiya Movement* (Calcutta, 1918); Phoenix, *His Holiness* (Lahore, 1958).

estates in the area and had been favored by the Mughul emperors, but most of the holdings had been lost to the Sikhs before Ghulam Ahmad was born. The boy received no formal religious instruction. He learned Arabic and Persian and studied the Qur'an under private tutors; from his father he learned some elements of native (Unani) medicine. The first forty years of his life were undistinguished, marked by four years (1864–1868) during which he worked as a clerk in the office of the Deputy Commissioner at Sialkot. He seems never to have taken any interest in his clerical work, much preferring to spend his time reading religious literature or debating with Christian missionaries. In 1868 he returned to Qadian to help on his family's estates. After his father died in 1876 Ghulam Ahmad was finally able to follow his own inclinations. Three years earlier the idea had come to him of writing a book in which he would prove the superiority of Islam by sheer logic. The publication, in 1880, of the first two parts of *Barahin-i-Ahmadiya* (The Proofs of Muhammad) was met with general favor by the Muslim community, although it caused no particular excitement. The two parts consisted of little more than a restating of the rational arguments by which Muslim traditionalists had supported Islam in the past. By the application of reason and logic to the investigation of Islam, Ghulam Ahmad tried to establish the superiority of the Qur'an over all other revelations. Once this was accepted, he was confident that the triumph of Islam would be assured.

And should a seeker-after-truth bring forward and adduce some religious verities from any scripture in Latin, Hebrew, English, Sanskrit, etc., or produce from his own brain any fine and subtle truth on theology, we take it upon ourselves to show the same from the Holy Qur'an, provided he gives us a written undertaking beforehand of accepting Islam if he is convinced, and the intimation of this declaration is communicated to us in time to be inserted and published in this book.[5]

The challenge was not as limited in time as one may suppose. Additional parts of the study appeared at intervals over a period of four years. In the third part, published in 1882, Ghulam Ahmad claimed to have received a revelation from God that he was the great reformer of Islam's fourteenth century—the *mujaddid* of his time, as Shaykh Ahmad Sirhindi and Shah Waliullah had been the great Islamic reformers of their times. Even this does not seem to have disturbed the traditionalist theologians—an indication, perhaps, of the respect with which they accepted his book. The direction Ghulam Ahmad's thought was taking was indicated by the manifesto he published asserting his claim to be the mujaddid of the century, and in which he added that spiritually his "excellence resembles the excellence of Messiah, the son of Mary, and that the one of them bears a very strong resemblance and a close relation to the other." [6]

In 1889, about four years after the publication of the last part of *The Proofs of Muhammad*, Ghulam Ahmad announced that he would accept as personal followers all who would accept his leadership. This was the beginning of the organized Ahmadiya movement, named not after Ghulam Ahmad, but after the prophet Muhammad, who was also known as Ahmad.[7] There is nothing particularly striking

[5] Mirza Ghulam Ahmad, *Barahin-i-Ahmadiyya*, trans. by Mirza Masum Beg (Lahore, 1955), p. 53.

[6] Mirza Ghulam Ahmad, quoted in Maulana Muhammad Ali, *The Founder of the Ahmadiyya Movement*, p. 21.

[7] Ghulam Ahmad said that the Meccan period of Muhammad's life, marked by patience, persecution, and forbearance, was a manifestation of the name Ahmad; the Medina period, during which retributive justice was dealt out to the opponents of Islam, exemplified the name Muhammad. See "True Significance of the Name Ahmadiyyah," trans. from Mirza Ghulam Ahmad, *The Light*, June 1, 1958, pp. 7–8.

about the conditions demanded by Ghulam Ahmad of his followers—except for a requirement not to injure any person, no matter what his religion (a denial of jihad by physical force), even Sayyid Ahmad Shahid would have been in complete agreement with them.

The two men do, in fact, make interesting subjects for comparison. Sayyid Ahmad Shahid, sure that his faith was in jeopardy, leaped to its defense with the only means he knew: recourse to arms. Ghulam Ahmad, equally sure that his faith was in jeopardy, also leaped to its defense with the only means of which he was capable: recourse to rational argument. Each was inspired to a large degree by the Sikhs, and each formed a central organization to promote his efforts in the defense of the faith. Each was essentially traditionalist in his approach and opposed to western concepts. Sayyid Ahmad Shahid was a sufi who believed, unlike almost every other sufi, in jihad; Ghulam Ahmad, who was not a sufi, believed that jihad in the traditional sense (which was the sense in which it was accepted by Sayyid Ahmad Shahid) was not applicable to the Islam of his time. Each in his own way was revolutionary. And if Ghulam Ahmad felt he had been divinely commissioned, so, too, did Sayyid Ahmad Shahid.[8] It is at this point that the similarities cease. Sayyid Ahmad made nothing that could be considered an innovation in the faith; a wild cacophony has surrounded Ghulam Ahmad and his claims. Sayyid Ahmad's organization was in effect another mystic order; its members made no attempt to exclude themselves from the rest of Muslim society. Ghulam Ahmad's organization, like his teaching, was not at all mystical, and at least one wing of

[8] Cf. W. W. Hunter, *The Indian Mussalmans* (Calcutta, 1945), p. 6, who remarks that Sayyid Ahmad Shahid's recruiting for the jihad was furthered "by the assurance that he was divinely commissioned to extirpate the whole Infidel world, from the Sikhs even unto *the Chinese*."

it did develop into an exclusive sect. The efforts of Sayyid Ahmad were in effect almost entirely defensive—his jihad was little more than a last-ditch stand. Ghulam Ahmad's efforts were not only defensive; he took the offensive as well, and established an extensive, highly organized missionary enterprise to carry the truths of Islam as he understood them to all parts of the world.

Ghulam Ahmad recognized that the customary means of defending Islam were fruitless. Like Karamat 'Ali, he recognized that a jihad with no chance of success was purposeless —a position aptly expressed by Sir Syed Ahmad Khan when he said, "If you have power, *jihad* is incumbent upon you; if you have no power, it is unlawful." [9] To Ghulam Ahmad this attitude was not enough. It implied giving up the struggle, and did not the Qur'an urge Muslims to "strive hard against the unbelievers"? [10] The abandonment of jihad because there seemed to be no hope of success meant also the setting aside of a qur'anic injunction. He met the dilemma by emphasizing that the true meaning of jihad was *moral struggle;* it was false doctrine and a "wrong conception," he said, to think of it as meaning the spread of Islam by arms. [11] "The Jihad of this age," he wrote, "is to strive hard for the cause of Islam and reply to the objections of the opponents and spread the beauties of Islam and the truth of the Holy Prophet in the world." [12]

This definition of jihad was not particularly new. Mu-

---

[9] Bashir Ahmad Dar, *Religious Thought of Sayyid Ahmad Khan* (Institute of Islamic Culture; Lahore, 1957), p. 82.

[10] Qur'an 66:9; 9:73.

[11] Analyst, *Facts About the Ahmadiyya Movement* (Lahore, 1951), p. 2.

[12] Letter from Ghulam Ahmad to Mir Nasir Nawab, quoted in *ibid.,* p. 5.

hammad is reported to have said that the best jihad is to speak a just word before a tyrannical authority.[13] No theologian disagreed as to this meaning of the term, but none of them maintained, as did Ghulam Ahmad, that it was the primary meaning. This dispute, engendered by traditionalists in each instance, reached into the fundamentals of qur'anic interpretation.

The traditional scholars accepted the premise that later revelations of Muhammad sometimes abrogated earlier ones— a line of reasoning based upon certain verses of the Qur'an. Waliullah had considered the matter and had reduced the number of supposedly abrogated verses by explaining away the seeming contradictions. Ghulam Ahmad maintained that because the Qur'an was God's word, and as such eternal and everlasting, and of necessity true, no part of it could possibly be abrogated by any other part. The theologians believed that the verses advocating the primary meaning of jihad urged by Ghulam Ahmad had been abrogated by later verses which specifically urged the use of jihad in the sense of physical force. On these grounds, of course, the quarrel became intense, for each side could with equal justice insist that the other was repealing an existing law of the Qur'an. Although the problem of the abrogation of verses was largely academic, and sometimes pertained only to the chronological order of the verses, it became something more than a theologians' quarrel when individuals were accused of ignoring a portion of revelation under the pretext of abrogation just to suit their modernist inclinations.

The repudiation of the doctrine of jihad by the sword, not only for the present but "at any future time," was a

---

[13] *Sayings of the Prophet Muhammad*, introduction by Mirza Abu'l-Fazl (Allahabad, 1924), p. 76. This hadith is related in four of the six collections most favored by Muslims.

distinctive mark of Ghulam Ahmad's organization.[14] Sir Syed had held that armed conflict was included within the wider definition of jihad, but that it was to be used only when a chance of success was indicated. He did not renounce physical force forever.

Over the course of time Mirza Ghulam Ahmad's interpretation of jihad did win some support, especially with the continued supremacy of non-Muslim arms. Two distinct opinions can be found today among Muslims—apart from that of the Ahmadiyas themselves. One group believes that given proper conditions physical force is part of jihad; the other believes that jihad does not ever properly include the idea of physical coercion, except in self-defense.

Few conservative theologians would consider the qur'anic verse "There is no compulsion in religion" to have any application to the problem of jihad. The Ahmadiyas maintain that it applies to conversion *from* a faith—even Islam—as well as to conversion *to* a faith. The traditionalist believes it refers only to conversion *to* Islam; once a man becomes a Muslim he must remain a Muslim. The penalty for apostasy is death, because the traditionalist acknowledges no distinction between the state and the faith and looks upon apostasy as a form of treason. In general, the attitude toward apostasy is one of the clearest points dividing the traditionalist from the modernist today.

An even greater controversy centered around Ghulam Ahmad's assertion that Jesus had not died on the cross, but had been removed while still alive, nursed back to health, and then had emigrated to Kashmir, where he died at the age of 120. Muslims had long believed that Jesus was alive in heaven and would reappear to save them in days of distress. To

[14] Mirza Ghulam Ahmad, "True Significance of the Name Ahmadiyyah," p. 7.

Ghulam Ahmad such an idea was little short of anathema, for it seemed to him to mean that in the last resort Jesus and not Muhammad would be the real savior of Islam. Obviously, this could not be true, and the belief of the Muslims had to be in error. It was necessary to show that Jesus had died like any man, and so could not be physically waiting somewhere in the heavens to make a second appearance on earth. The second coming of Jesus, said Ghulam Ahmad, refers not to the reappearance of his body but to that of his spirit, and he insisted that he personified Jesus' spiritual nature.

This was just another doctrinal matter within Islam about which there was opportunity for rival arguments; and alone it was nothing with which the traditionalists could take serious issue. In 1942 the religious leaders of Al-Azhar, the highest authority among Muslim theological schools, issued a declaration stating that it was impossible to establish, on the basis of the Qur'an and the hadith, which of these two interpretations was true. Either view, said the scholars of Al-Azhar, should be considered thoroughly Islamic.[15]

What the Muslim community as a whole could not tolerate was Ghulam Ahmad's claim to be something more than a reformer; nor could the community reconcile itself to the exclusivist characteristics his organization soon developed. Just what Ghulam Ahmad claimed is not clear. One group of his followers insists he never considered himself as other than a mujaddid, although as mujaddids go he was the greatest; the larger group insists that he was a prophet. Islamic theology, of course, rests upon the principle that Muhammad was the last of the prophets. Sir Muhammad Iqbal believed that the Ahmadiyas should have been recognized as a distinct religion. The three main elements of Islam, he said, were "belief

[15] *The Ulama of Egypt on the Death of Jesus Christ, A Fatwa* (Lahore, 1959).

in the Unity of God, belief in all the Prophets, and belief in the Finality of Muhammad's Prophethood"; he thought the Ahmadiyas denied the last, and really decisive, demarcating element.[16]

There can be no doubt that Ghulam Ahmad used the term "prophet" when speaking of himself, but his meaning of it is unclear. It would seem that he believed Muhammad was the last prophet in the sense of one who would bring a complete code of law for mankind; he thought of himself as a prophet whose function was to sharpen and emphasize that code to secure the safety and success of Islam. His words appeared to equivocate, however, and the tremendous claims he made as to his revelations and prophecies created still more uncertainty; even his own disciples do not agree as to what he meant.[17] In 1914 his organization split into two groups,

[16] Letter to *Statesman*, June 10, 1935, in "Shamoo," *Speeches and Statements of Iqbal* (Lahore, 1948), p. 108.

[17] See *Report of the Court of Inquiry . . . to Enquire into the Punjab Disturbances of 1953* (Lahore, Government Printing, 1954), p. 189. This is commonly referred to as the Munir Report. Both groups of Ahmadiyas continue to publish pamphlets extensively quoting Mirza Ghulam Ahmad in support of their respective views. See Hazrat Mirza Ghulam Ahmad, *A Misunderstanding Removed* (Rabwah, n.d.); and Maulana Muhammad Ali, *Prophet of Mujaddid?* (Lahore, n.d.). See also Stanley E. Brush, "Ahmadiyyat in Pakistan," *The Muslim World*, XLV, 2 (April, 1955), 145–171.

A typical statement by Mirza Ghulam Ahmad is here translated from *Haqiqatul Vahi*, pp. 149–150, by A. G. Soofi, former head of the American Fazl Mosque, Washington, D.C.: "Similarly in the beginning I held the belief that since the Messiah, son of Mary, was a prophet (nabi) and of the close elect of God, I held no comparison to him, and whenever something appeared that related to my superiority, I would treat it as a minor qualification. But when later the revelation of food descended on me like rain, it did not let me persist in that belief, and I was granted clearly the title of prophet (nabi) with the qualification that in one sense I was a prophet (nabi), and in another sense a follower (ummati)."

one of which maintained that his use of the term "prophet" was literal, and the other, known as the Lahoris, maintained that it was metaphorical. While the split involved questions of internal politics as well as internal dogma, it also seems to have reflected a greater tendency on the part of the Lahore group toward acceptance of Sir Syed's new attitude. Nevertheless, in both factions the basic interest remained the defense and propagation of Islam through the avoidance of armed conflict and through extensive dialectics and missionary zeal.

But Ghulam Ahmad's claim involved more than prophethood, and he thought of himself as incorporating not only the spiritual essence of Jesus and of Muhammad, but that also of Krishna and Zoroaster. On the face of it, he would appear to represent a continuation of the syncretist movement in India marked by Kabir, Nanak, and Akbar. Actually, this is not so. Ghulam Ahmad was thoroughly Muslim and made no real efforts other than this that might lead toward a union of the faiths. His son wrote of him that "he was the Promised Prophet of every nation and was appointed to collect all mankind under the banner of our faith." [18] He was all for union, provided everyone else became Muslim.

[18] Mirza Bashiruddin Mahmud Ahmad, *Ahmadiyyat or The True Islam* (Rabwah, 1959), p. 10. Ghulam Ahmad's last lecture—written a day or two before his death—urges Hindus and Muslims to learn to live together, for *"the teaching of Islam is not necessarily opposed to the Vedic teaching. Nearly everything that Islam teaches is to be met with in one or another of the Vedic schools"* Hazrat Mirza Ghulam Ahmad, *A Message of Peace* (Lahore, 1947), p. 10 (the italics are in the original). In this interesting and sincere lecture, Ghulam Ahmad rather typically proposed that Hindus and Muslims should sign agreements always to speak respectfully of the others' faith. "And if we fail to fulfill this agreement," the proposed Hindu agreement reads, "we shall pay to the Head of the Ahmadiyiyya [sic] Movement Rs. 3,00,000, as a penalty for breach of agreement" (pp. 27–28). Of course, Ghulam Ahmad could not, and did not pretend to, speak for Muslims outside the Ahmadiya Movement.

Mirza Ghulam Ahmad did claim that God had singled him out over all men to promote unity among them. He could not have come to any other conclusion, once having decided from the basis of his studies that 6,000 years had passed since Adam, that 1,000 years of Satan's supremacy had ended (that is, the period of decline of Islam from its halcyon days during the early 'Abbasid caliphate), and that God's prophecies stipulated that at the end of these times the Messiah would appear. "I am," he said, "that Messiah: let him who will accept me." [19] He then tried to convince the Muslim body of the validity of his claim, basing his arguments for the most part on his exemplary character, his accomplishments, and the accuracy of his prophetic revelations.

These revelations are an interesting study in themselves. Many of them are reminiscent of the kind of story that was the stock-in-trade of every Christian evangelist—no food for the family, despair in the heart, then prayer to God and a check in the next mail. Many of Ghulam Ahmad's prophecies have an unsavory aspect, as when he prophesied the death by murder of Lekh Ram, a particularly vitriolic Hindu opponent. Lekh Ram was murdered some years later by an unknown assailant. There is a strong Old Testament flavor to be found in the teaching of Ghulam Ahmad.

As Ghulam Ahmad battled against the indifference and hostility of the Muslim community, his organization became more and more separated from it, although Ghulam Ahmad decreed that no one becomes a Kafir by rejecting his claims. His followers, the Ahmadiyas, then became a tightly closed corporation, marrying among themselves, attending their own mosques, and increasing the hostility of Muslims against them by their very exclusiveness. Indeed, this seems to be the pri-

[19] *Review of Religions,* III, 131, quoted in H. A. Walter, p. 26.

mary reason why the Ahmadiyas have elicited so much ill-feeling among Muslims.[20]

The claims of Ghulam Ahmad were not accepted by the mass of the community. Yet his was an attempt, too, to find the position of Islam in the modern world. He could not accept the approach of Sir Syed Ahmad Khan simply because Sir Syed did not start with the Qur'an and the traditions, but used them to buttress his own intellectual position, which Ghulam Ahmad did not share. Ghulam Ahmad did accept some of the particular interpretations of Sir Syed—enough so that a critic could write of him that he "played the plagiarist to Sir Syed Ahmad."[21] One could argue as well, and the Ahmadiyas do, that Mirza Ghulam Ahmad drew all of his ideas from the Qur'an, the hadith, and the writing of past imams; any similarity between the ideas of the two reflects their use of the same sources. Sir Syed, for instance, had maintained that Jesus had died (a view reflected in one of the early hadith); he had maintained that apostasy should not be punishable by death. Even more significantly, Ghulam Ahmad agreed with Sir Syed in avoiding political entanglements with the British and boasted of his loyalty and service to the British government in India. Cynics point out that any Hindu or Muslim government would have curtailed his activities, and that this loyalty (like his interpreta-

---

[20] See *Report . . . into the Punjab Disturbances*, p. 198. The feeling against the Ahmadiyas is expressed in Abu'l A'la Maudoodi, *The Qadiani Problem* (Lahore, 1953). The Ahmadiyas point out that these prophecies are no more "unsavory" than the warning to Moses to lead the children of Israel by the sea in order that many of Pharaoh's men would drown, and the children of Israel could gloat. The Lahoris, it should be noted, do not prohibit marriage with non-Ahmadiyas. See "Ahmadiyya Movement's Role as seen by a Western Scholar," *The Light Weekly*, XLIV, 12 (April, 1965), 4.

[21] Phoenix, p. 56.

tion of jihad) was a measure of self-preservation. Nevertheless, one has to admit that Ghulam Ahmad's position was
eminently sensible and not at all unique among Muslims in
India. It did, however, possess certain revolutionary elements,
for it amounted to separating Islam from politics. It was a
tacit admission to a kind of separation between church and
state. Even this was nothing new, however; Muhammad ibn
Tughluq in the fourteenth century had insisted upon the same
thing.

But not all Muslims agreed with this nonpolitical approach.
In 1906—a year and a half before Mirza Ghulam Ahmad's
death—the Muslim League was founded at Dacca to safe-
guard the rights of Muslims through political intervention.
Strangely enough, this was established by a group of Muslims
who were themselves mostly attracted to the teachings of Sir
Syed Ahmad Khan.

The primary significance of the Ahmadiya movement lay
in its missionary emphasis. Every Muslim believed that Islam
was the only religion free from error. The Ahmadiyas made
it part of their principles to show the errors of other religions
to their adherents and to proselytize energetically for Islam.
In a sense, the Ahmadiyas represent the Muslims emerging,
religiously speaking, from the withdrawal that had begun
with the arrival of the British, just as the Muslim League
represents the political emergence from that same withdrawal.

In the course of time the Ahmadiya arguments against
other religions were wholeheartedly accepted by even their
most vociferous critics. In this sense, Ghulam Ahmad was
pursuing the same course as Ameer Ali, although with less
charm and subtlety; at the same time he repudiated the
"higher criticism," the ability to look at the Qur'an in a de-
tached manner, that Ameer Ali had absorbed from Sir Syed

Ahmad Khan. Through the vigor of their proselytizing and their incessant and highly publicized attacks on Christianity, they instilled a stronger faith in many Muslims. They developed a confident belief that Christianity does not explain the strength of Europe, and that the true religion remained Islam, even though the personal claims of Ghulam Ahmad were not accepted, and his organization was in general scorned. This is the essential significance of the Ahmadiya movement. It is somewhat ironic that the sect most attacked by Muslims in India and Pakistan has also been that which has worked hardest, in both its branches, to defend and extend Islam against the competition offered by other faiths.

On the whole, whatever may have developed within the Ahmadiya community after him, it seems a presumption to consider Ghulam Ahmad as a modernist; despite this, or because of this, the Ahmadiyas seem to have picked up much of their support from among the more educated Muslims. They wanted reform, but they did not appreciate the dynamic concept of knowledge assumed by Sir Syed Ahmad Khan, and many of the interpretations advanced by Sir Syed seemed to them strained. Even so, the Ahmadiya movement could not develop into a strong force for modern reform because it elicited nothing but hostility from the Muslim community at large. The Lahore group, although it insisted that Ghulam Ahmad was not a prophet, and although it showed many elements of modernism, was in the eyes of most Muslims tarred with the same brush.[22]

The force of the movement was weakened as its adherents exerted their efforts to defend the person of Ghulam Ahmad or to attack one another over the question of prophethood. While missionary enterprise went on and techniques of organ-

[22] Both groups discourage intermarriage outside the movement. See Mazheruddin Siddiqui, in *Islam—The Straight Path*, pp. 324–325.

ization became highly developed, the movement as a whole remained too isolated from the Muslim community to exert any direct effect, at least in the first seventy-five years of its existence.

Mirza Ghulam Ahmad seems to have been initially motivated to defend Islam by attacks being made by outsiders—particularly Christian missionaries and Hindu, especially Arya Samaj, preachers. Following the success of Aligarh and the entry of Muslims into political areas, an attack developed which was essentially internal. This was the cynical, agnostic, more rarely atheistic reaction of some educated Muslims who could accept neither the views of the traditionalists nor the rationalizations of Sir Syed. They were intellectual exiles—displaced persons who, seeing weaknesses in two different lines of approach, were unable to discover a third.

The pressures affecting them came from all sides. They had been stirred by the poetry of Altaf Husain Hali, an admirer of Sir Syed Ahmad Khan. Hali's most famous poem, *The Flow and Ebb of Islam*, more commonly called *Musaddas*, became an Urdu classic, "the Bible of the new movement, and in creating a widespread awakening amongst the Muslims, its contribution is considered next only to that of the Aligarh College and the Muslim Educational Conference." [23] The later, and greater, Muslim poet Muhammad Iqbal continued the theme developed by Hali, adding themes of his own as well. Iqbal attacked passivity—he was all for action.

> The life of this world consists in movement;
> This is the established law of the world.
> On this road halt is out of place;

[23] A. H. Albiruni, *Makers of Pakistan and Modern Muslim India* (Lahore, 1950), p. 70; see also Abdul Qayyum in Percival Spear and S. M. Ikram, *The Cultural Heritage of Pakistan* (Oxford and Karachi, 1955), p. 87.

A static condition means death.
Those on the move have gone ahead,
Those who tarried only a little while got crushed.[24]

Sir Muhammad Iqbal (knighted for his poetry in 1922) is perhaps best known in the West through his series of seven lectures, *The Reconstruction of Religious Thought in Islam*. There can be little doubt that these lectures, at least initially, made a far greater impression in the West than among the Muslims of India, who generally didn't bother to read them. Among the orthodox it was frequently believed either that in the nine years between the delivery of these lectures and his death in 1938 Iqbal changed his views, growing more in keeping with the traditionalist interpretation, or that Iqbal was merely trying to explain Islam to the modern world in terms that the world could understand.

After the partition of India, Iqbal, who as president of the Muslim League in 1930 had expressed a demand for "the formation of a consolidated Muslim state in the best interests of India and Islam," [25] was elevated to something like the patron saint of Pakistan. His ideas were highly publicized and his writings were extensively quoted—by almost everyone. That Iqbal in his long life expressed a wide variety of views may have had a subsequent effect of helping to intensify a questioning, uncertain attitude among some Muslims.

Syed Abdul Vahid, the leading student of Iqbal, has estimated that 75 per cent of the people of Pakistan have some idea of Iqbal's poetry, but very few understand his philosophy

[24] *Bang-i-Dara* (The Call of the Road), quoted by Abdul Qayyum in *The Cultural Heritage*, pp. 196–197.

[25] The quotation is from an extract of the speech reproduced in Mohammed Noman, ed., *Our Struggle* (Karachi, n.d.), p. 14. See also W. T. deBary, ed., *Sources of Indian Tradition* (New York, 1958), pp. 763–768, for other extracts of this speech.

or know that he did not believe in heaven and hell.[26] His most important message was not philosophical; it was simple and direct, addressed to the Muslims of India: "Wake up!" This is a dynamic universe, he cried, and it calls for positive action! Believe in yourself, for only in the development of the self can success be found. Some of his ideas are very close to those of Emerson.[27] The self could best develop to its fullest capacity only within the circle of a righteous community, such as the community of Islam. Yet Islam—properly the best of all righteous communities—was deep in a dogmatic slumber that denied intellectual freedom.

The problem Iqbal raised he never answered. How does one break the bonds of tradition? How does one reactivate a society that has become static?

> Being afraid of the new order
> And sticking rigidly to the old order—
> This is a very difficult stage
> In the life of nations.[28]

It was a difficult stage for Iqbal, too, who was too much the poet to be able to recommend any specific line of action. He welcomed the liberal movement in modern Islam, but warned that it could easily lead to excesses. He emphasized the elements of change in life, but warned that there are elements of conservation as well.[29] There should certainly be evolution, he thought, but he hesitated to say where it should

[26] Syed Abdul Vahid to the author, September 28, 1959. Iqbal's concept of heaven and hell appears at the end of his fourth lecture.

[27] Freeland Abbott, "A Pakistani Looks at Democracy," *Modern Age*, II, 3 (Summer, 1958), 315–319.

[28] *Bang-i-Dara*, quoted to the author by Allama Alaudin Siddiqui, head of the Department of Islamic Studies, Punjab University.

[29] Sir Muhammad Iqbal, *The Reconstruction of Religious Thought in Islam* (Lahore, 1951), pp. 162–163, 166.

begin. In a sense, Iqbal represents the modern aspect of the problem of dualism that so disturbed Shaykh Ahmad of Sirhind; he was trying to frame a philosophy of religion that incorporated mysticism but excluded pantheism.

Iqbal was also framing a political philosophy to meet a problem that had faced Waliullah, and that earlier had disturbed the followers of Timur the Lame: how to assure a healthy religious climate in India for Muslims. Waliullah had helped persuade the Afghan, Ahmad Shah Abdali, to invade India in 1761 and defeat the Maratha army at Panipat, a victory Waliullah hoped would restore Muslim solidarity. Sir Muhammad Iqbal, searching to ensure Muslim solidarity in his time, urged the creation of a separate Muslim state in northwest India. Such a step, he argued in his presidential address before the annual meeting of the Muslim League in 1930, will give Islam "an opportunity to rid itself of the stamp the Arabian imperialism was forced to give it, to mobilize its law, its education, its culture, and to bring them into closer contact with its original spirit and with the spirit of modern times." [30] It would also remove the Muslims from the Hindu political sphere in which, as he carefully pointed out, if India should become a democratic state, they would always be a minority. The modernization of Islam, however, was not a matter that could wait for politics.

Liberating Islam from its medieval shackles, Iqbal believed, required first of all liberating the concept of individual interpretation in legal matters—ijtihad—from the restrictions that had grown around it. During the early days of Islam, ijtihad was practically synonymous with "opinion"; later, it developed a particular meaning: the opinion of those with a peculiar right to form such judgments. This increasingly

[30] "Shamoo," *Speeches and Statements of Iqbal* (Lahore, 1948), p. 15.

narrow definition of the term, Iqbal believed, was the result of three things: the activity of conservative thinkers, the appeal of aesthetic sufism, and the destruction wrought by the Mongols.

In the first place, conservative thinkers, afraid of the early rationalist (Mu'tazila) movement in Islam, had utilized Islamic law to hamstring the rationalist movement. The sufis, in turn, reacted against "the dry-as-dust subtleties" of the legalists and attracted to themselves, and absorbed, the best minds in Islam. As a result, the Muslim state was left in the hands of mediocrities who "found their security only in blindly following the schools" of Muslim law. The coup de grâce, according to Iqbal, was inflicted by the Mongols whose sack of Baghdad in 1258 destroyed the center of Muslim intellectual life and threatened Islamic society as a whole. To meet this threat, and to preserve what remained, conservative thinkers tended to resist all innovation in Islamic law, no matter what the practice of the early Muslims may have been.[31] In the modern era, Iqbal insisted, there was no need for restrictions so hidebound as to be almost impossible of realization by any individual.

In this respect Iqbal was merely continuing an already old intellectual attack on the monopolistic view of the Sunni traditionalists. Waliullah had held that every qualified man had a right to follow his own judgment in legal matters, provided his decision was made according to the principles of Islamic law—*fiqh*. Sir Muhammad Iqbal echoed this, perhaps broadening the concept of a "qualified man," and urged that

[31] Iqbal, pp. 149–152. This emphasis on the effects of the Mongol invasion on the deterioration of Islamic society is commonly made by Muslims, but frequently exaggerated; the 'Abbasid caliphate had lost its vitality four hundred years before the sack of Baghdad.

a critical study be made of Muslim law, that its origins be examined, that the more than nineteen schools of jurisprudence founded in the early centuries of Islam be carefully studied, and that the four accepted sources of Muslim law—the Qur'an, the hadith, the consensus of opinion (*ijma*), and analogical reasoning (*qiyas*)—be analyzed once again. He believed that the fundamental problems facing Islam could not be solved until the law was modernized; just what he meant by modernization we do not know. He is reported to have been working on such a study when he died.

The problem of ijtihad disturbed Iqbal because he was trying to effect a change within the established order; in a sense, he was a kind of Erasmian figure. Many reformers, perhaps most, did not worry about whether or not they possessed the right of independent judgment—they just practiced it. Maulana Muhammad Ali, a leader of the Lahori wing of the Ahmadiya movement, argued in his book *The Religion of Islam*, first published in 1935, that ijtihad had always been a vital part of Islam; "it was the only way," he wrote, "through which the needs of succeeding generations and the requirements of the different races merging into Islam could be met." [32]

Maulana Abul Kalam Azad was another reformer who did not question his own right of independent judgment. Qur'anic interpretation, he asserted, is not the monopoly of imams and mujtahids.[33] Abul Kalam, a publicist and political figure, Mahatma Gandhi's adviser on Muslim affairs, became the first education minister of the Republic of India. He believed

[32] Maulana Muhammad Ali, *The Religion of Islam* (Lahore, 1950), p. 113. His translation and commentary on the Qur'an first appeared in 1920.

[33] J. M. S. Baljon, Jr., *Modern Muslim Koran Interpretation* (*1880–1960*) (Leiden, 1961), p. 16.

that Hindus and Muslims had to live together—an ideal to which he remained faithful all his life. "If you wish to stay in India and remain alive," he wrote to his fellow Muslims through the columns of his newspaper in 1911, "you should embrace your neighbors." [34] In fact, Abul Kalam's conviction in this matter undoubtedly had some effect in reducing the impact his commentary on the Qur'an may have had on much of the Muslim population of India.

Abul Kalam first thought of writing a translation and commentary in 1915 and, after starting it, began to publish parts in his journal. He was soon imprisoned for political activities, and in prison, without benefit of his previous work, had completed a translation of the Qur'an by the time of his release in 1918. Three years later, he was arrested again and the carelessness of an arresting officer led to the loss of this translation. In 1927 he began again, finally finishing his commentary in 1930.[35]

Abul Kalam Azad pressed the same rational, naturalistic approach found in Sir Syed Ahmad Khan's commentary, although not in the same nineteenth-century terms. He was interested in establishing that there was not real conflict but rather a harmony between science and religion. The primary characteristic of Abul Kalam Azad's commentary is his emphasis on the universal nature of religion.

This, of course, is the teaching of every monotheistic religion, and in this sense Abul Kalam was saying nothing new. But the background of Hindu-Muslim rivalry lent a stronger emphasis to his words. The law of man's spiritual fulfillment, he said, was the same for all; the greatest error of religious

[34] Quoted in Albiruni, p. 140.

[35] J. M. S. Baljon, Jr., "A Modern Urdu Tafsir," *The World of Islam*, N.S., II, 2 (1952), 95–107; see also Baljon, *Modern Muslim Koran Interpretation*.

men was to divide themselves into mutually hostile groups.[36]
While rituals and customs vary, religion is the same for all—
for it consists in being submissive to God and in leading a
life of right action. Men are divided into innumerable artificial
groups and factions, but one relationship still holds them together: the common worship of one God. Abul Kalam Azad
pointed out that the reform and welfare of mankind are the
object of religion, and that this object can be fulfilled only
if the code of conduct suits "the circumstances of the time
and place and the social fabric and intellectual capacity of
the people for whom the code is evolved." [37] When people
begin to attach primary importance to differences, they are
beginning to stray from true religion. The Qur'an, Azad
maintained, really set out to distinguish between the principles
and the forms of religion; its purpose was to direct attention
to the essence of religion. Does not the Qur'an say:

We have set for each (group) of you a particular code and path.
Had God so willed, He could have made you one people, but He
tests you by the separate regulations which He has made for you
(according to your different circumstances and capacities). So
(do not lose yourself in these differences but) endeavor to sur-
pass each other through your good deeds.[38]

The Qur'an, Azad maintained, teaches a broad-minded and
understanding tolerance toward all other religions, for they
do not differ in that which is fundamental.[39]

Muslim reformers were grappling with much the same

[36] Ashfaque Husain, *The Spirit of Islam* (Bombay, 1958), p. 73. This
is a summary of Maulana Abul Kalam Azad's commentary on the first
surah of the Qur'an. See Maulana Abul Kalam Azad, *The Tarjumān
al-Qur'an*, trans. Syed Abdul Latif, I (New York, 1962).

[37] Ashfaque Husain, p. 67.

[38] Qur'an 5:48, quoted by Ashfaque Husain, p. 68.

[39] See Baljon, *Modern Muslim Koran Interpretation*, p. 74.

problem as that which confronted the Puritan reformers of
Stuart days in England. In each case the problem was to
transfer to their society the liberal elements in their faith and
to reject the reactionary elements. In each case a certain
latitude appeared—call it a note of freedom. Both groups
fought to remove the fetters of an external religious law, to
replace them with an internal law of the spirit. In each case,
dogma tended to break down. The Puritans maintained that
the Bible had not been properly understood until the Reformation; the Muslim modernists maintained that the Qur'an
was not being properly interpreted by the traditionalist religious leaders. Among the Muslim modernists this anti-
ritualistic tendency frequently led to a new characterization
of the "five pillars" of Islam (the creed, prayer, alms-giving,
fasting, and pilgrimage). This new characterization is particularly evident in the works of Muhammad 'Inayat Allah
Khan (al-Mashriqi) and of Ghulam Ahmad Parwez.[40]

With the increase in education among Muslims, and the
spread of the Urdu press, variant interpretations by Muslims
became more common knowledge, and the popular custodians of the faith began to lose their appeal. This development owed much to the bifurcation in education that began
about the time of Sir Syed, which ensured that all Muslims
would not receive the same education, and which thus led to
different paths.[41] 'Ubaidullah Sindhi, a teacher of hadith at
Deoband, and somewhat of a revolutionary, remarked in his
later years that the traditionalist scholars at Deoband were

[40] A. S. P. Woodhouse, "Puritanism and Democracy," *The Cana-
dian Journal of Economics and Political Science*, IV (1938), 1–21;
reprinted in Robert L. Schuyler and Herman Ausubel, *The Making of
English History* (New York, 1952), pp. 288–302. See also Woodhouse,
Puritanism and Liberty (Chicago, 1950).

[41] I am indebted to Chaudry Muhammad 'Ali, a former prime
minister of Pakistan, for this point.

like the bullocks who walked round and round in a tight circle, turning the wheel that fetched water up from the well: they thought they were always moving forward, although they were always going round and round in the same old rut.[42]

Increasingly, the word "mullah" was used in a satirical manner. Many reasons undoubtedly contributed to this shift in attitude, such as the failure of the Khilafat Movement in the early 1920's. This was a Pan-Islamic attempt, begun by Maulana Mohamed Ali, to secure the revival of the Ottoman Caliphate. The movement (important politically because it marked a brief period when Muslim and Hindu agitators worked closely together) collapsed after the Turkish president, Mustafa Kemal Ataturk, himself abolished the caliphate. Even more discouraging was the suffering endured by thousands of pious Muslims who had been persuaded to sell all their belongings and migrate to Afghanistan. Afghanistan could not accept them, and many disillusioned Muslims, now penniless and homeless, were forced to return to India.[43] Whatever the various factors involved, questioning on the part of many educated Muslims increased, to the extent that some scholars felt the faith itself was in danger. Traditional Islam had to be clothed in more modern dress if it were to hold its attraction for these questioners.

The role of Maulana Abu'l A'la Maudoodi was to show that a conservative interpretation of Islam need not be out of place in the modern world; perhaps his most important function was to weaken the extreme traditionalists, but he lent at

[42] This anecdote was told me by Allama Alaudin Siddiqui, who was at one time a student of 'Ubaidullah Sindhi, and who heard this story from him personally.

[43] Estimates on the number of Muslims involved in this unhappy migration vary from 18,000 to 2,000,000. The lower figure seems more likely to be right.

least temporary relief to many Muslims who wanted to remain traditionalists and also accept—or reject in a rational manner —the teachings of modern science.

Maulana Maudoodi was born in Aurangabad in south central India in 1903.[44] He never attended school, but was taught Arabic and Persian by his father. When he was fifteen his father died and young Maudoodi drifted into journalism. In 1932 he founded an Urdu monthly, *The Interpreter of the Qur'an* (*Tarjumun-ul-Qur'an*), and his writings attracted much attention. Among those impressed by the young Maudoodi was the poet Sir Muhammad Iqbal. The latter apparently encouraged him to move to the town of Pathankot in the Punjab, where Maudoodi found an endowed estate, complete with a printing press, at his service.

Maudoodi's position was little different from that held by the school at Deoband, although he was far more strongly set against mysticism; nor was it very much different from that of Abul Kalam Azad before World War I. Maudoodi's influence was enhanced simply because in the decades before World War II no one else was comparable—whatever the character of his persuasion—in intellectual ability, command of Urdu, and interest in religion. His appeal was to the more educated Muslim: to that Muslim, in general, who had felt the effects of the divergent educational tendencies existing among Muslims. His initial attraction was increased because he insisted that Islam could not be divorced from politics— a point of view particularly attractive to certain Muslims

[44] Freeland Abbott, "The Jama'at-i-Islami of Pakistan," *The Middle East Journal*, XI, 1 (Winter, 1957), 37–51; F. Abbott, "Maulana Maududi and Quranic Interpretation," *The Muslim World*, XLVIII, 1 (January, 1958), 6–19; Wilfred Cantwell Smith, *Modern Islam in India* (London, 1946), *passim*, esp. pp. 149 ff.; Mazheruddin Siddiqui, in *Islam—The Straight Path*, pp. 325–327, 330–331; Leonard Binder, *Religion and Politics in Pakistan* (Berkeley, 1961).

during the years between the wars. Maudoodi was a purist, however, and he lost some of his popularity when he refused to support the Muslim League, maintaining that it was only a nationalist organization, and that if one were to uphold Islamic ideology he must fight against selfish nationalism.[45] It was God's law to bring mankind together, not separate man from man, and Maulana Maudoodi looked upon nationalism as a European import that should be rejected. Oddly enough, the nationalist reaction involving the rejection of things western, and the appeal of a purely Muslim ideology in the face of western demands, in itself played a role in promoting Maudoodi's early popularity.

Maulana Maudoodi won a reputation as a modernist because he paid specific attention to some of the political and social questions of his day. Mirza Ghulam Ahmad recognized the necessity of rebutting non-Muslim critics, and, as he saw it, of correcting errors that had crept into the traditional interpretation of Islam—corrections that would also enhance its logical position so far as such rebuttal was concerned. Essentially, Mirza Ghulam Ahmad was an apologist with an offensive. Maulana Maudoodi is not an apologist; he is not interested in showing, as were Sir Syed Ahmad Khan, Ameer Ali, or Mirza Ghulam Ahmad, that Islam is better than any other religion; he just assumes it. The day of Muslim apologia in India had passed by the early 1930's—a passing that was probably as much the work of the poets Hali and Iqbal, and perhaps of the scholar Shibli Nu'mani, as of anyone.

Maulana Maudoodi's philosophy is adequately reflected in a listing of some of the words that continually appear in his

---

[45] Sayyid Abulala Maudoodi, *Nationalism and India* (Pathankot, 1947), pp. 50–51, n. Variant spellings of the Maulana's names used in different publications have been retained in the footnotes for bibliographical purposes.

writings: code, obedience, moral, whole, heaven. Because he does represent the most recent expression of traditionalist Islam, his views are worth outlining. They provide a standard against which other views may be measured.

Maulana Maudoodi believes that this universe is the kingdom of God, and that the earth is only a province of that kingdom.[46] Man is an autonomous being on earth, but his autonomy entails a responsible understanding—to him is given the power to distinguish between good and evil and to adopt whatever manner of life he will.

In fact, there are two spheres to human life: the physical and the moral. In the physical sphere man has practically no option at all; he has to adjust himself to the laws of nature. All that man can do is to discover them. In the physical sphere everything is created as it is. Personally, Maudoodi would prefer not to believe in evolution, and while he might admit that the horse evolved, he believes that man exists very much as he was created. In any case, the problem of evolution is a problem of the physical sphere; it is not the function of religion to give guidance in this—religion is confined to the moral sphere, and deals with the proper conduct of man. Progress in our knowledge of the physical sphere may be effected by scientific investigation, but progress in the moral sphere—including political, social, and economic realms—requires guidance through the prophets.

Adam, the first man, was also the first prophet, because he had all the information that was necessary at the time: the reality of the universe had been explained to him, and he had been told the code and manner of life he should adopt. Islam

[46] This discussion is based upon personal conversations with Maulana Maudoodi, and with the former secretary of Maudoodi's organization, Mian Tufail Muhammad, as well as upon translations of many of Maudoodi's writings.

does not teach that man—Adam and Eve—started in complete ignorance. This picture of the universe, and man's place in it, as well as the role of Adam, is much the same as that presented by the Ahmadiyas.

The source of human progress, Maulana Maudoodi maintains, is the adjustment of the individual to the reality of the universe. This lesson, derived from the teaching of the prophets, is the central theme of the Qur'an. Man's success in this world and in the hereafter depends on the degree to which he submits to the will of God. Superficial knowledge leads to wrong conclusions and eventually to large-scale errors—all of which must be accounted for after death. In keeping with traditional belief, Maudoodi believes that two angels are attached to every person, recording every action, word, and look. The problems involved in human progress and the way to human progress—the nature of God and of God's kingdom, the position of man within that kingdom (autonomous but with no real independence), and the coming judgment—these are what the Qur'an tries to impress on the individual; in short, everything that is summed up in the meaning of the word Islam itself: submission to God.

Because there is only one God, and because all the earth is His, submission is the only true religion. Even the universe follows Islam, for what is submission but obedience? [47] Obedience is perhaps the key word in Maudoodi's theology. In the physical realm man has little choice: he must obey. In the moral realm he does have a choice: he can follow the guidance offered by the prophets, or he can go astray.

Man goes astray only as a result of his propensity to dominate his fellow man, whether directly or indirectly. To dominate is to play God, Maudoodi insists, and to accept domina-

[47] Sayyid Abul Ala Maududi, *Towards Understanding Islam* (Lahore, 1948), p. 3.

tion is to worship a Golden Calf. Whenever man finds himself in a position from which he can dominate, "tyranny, excess, intemperance, unlawful exploitation, and inequality reign supreme." There are many ways by which man demonstrates his domineering qualities, and Maudoodi cites among others Wall Street, the Politbureau, and all clergymen who dictate to others what is lawful and what is not.[48] Indeed, the tendency toward specialization in the modern age is to be deplored because it creates experts and specialists who come to be dominated by their own limited viewpoints when a comprehensive and general outlook on life and its problems is needed.[49] This unfortunate, although natural, weakness of man (Maulana Maudoodi calls it a "dreadful disease") can be remedied only by man's repudiation of all masters and by man's explicit recognition that only Allah is the Lord. The message of all prophets since Adam has been the same—how to achieve "the demolition of man's supremacy over man." [50] The way to achieve it, of course, is to follow the guidance of the prophets.

This far in his argument Maulana Maudoodi has expressed the bases of Islamic philosophy in terms particularly appealing to a moderately educated member of a religious minority living under foreign domination in the interwar world. This far his argument has little to do with either modernism or traditionalism. The difference between the two positions emerges when the Maulana analyzes the guidance itself.

The Qur'an, in Maulana Maudoodi's terms, urges man "to seek knowledge of Reality," to master the moral order, but it also exhorts man to base his views about the world and

[48] Sayyed Abul Ala Maudoodi, *Political Theory of Islam* (Pathankot [c. 1939]), pp. 17–24.

[49] Sayyid Abulala Maudoodi, *The Economic Problem of Man and Its Islamic Solution* (Pathankot, 1947), pp. 4–5.

[50] Maudoodi, *Political Theory of Islam*, pp. 24–25.

life on the facts of the universe. The Qur'an "forbids and discourages only the fanciful and speculative" theories and philosophies.[51] It is left to the properly educated individual to determine whether a given theory does not in itself transgress revealed knowledge. It is revealed knowledge, after all, that is the basis for salvation, and that knowledge is not the product of any human experience, whether in the physical or social sciences or in philosophy. It is probably wrong, Maudoodi thinks, to quote the scriptures in support of such sciences, but it is equally wrong to maintain that Islam discourages the experimental sciences, or that Muslims ever thought they did not require anything further than divinely revealed knowledge. Yet this essentially traditionalist interpretation of revelation, and the checks imposed to protect that revelation and to ensure that "fanciful" theories are not raised, in themselves prohibit major variations on the interpretation of revealed knowledge.

There is nothing wrong with this, in Maudoodi's eyes, for the revelation is from God; God does not change, and neither does His revelation or its meaning. This can be illustrated by considering some aspects of Islam that have been cited as indication of changes being effected in Islamic concepts.

The meaning of jihad, for example, has not changed over the centuries: the term always had two parts, one connoting "striving one's utmost" and one connoting "armed conflict." Before the Muslims had achieved political power jihad could connote only nonviolent struggle, but after Muslim power had been built up, both meanings were simultaneously in use. Today Muslim power is again weak, and "Muslims have," writes Maudoodi, "become devoid of courage and capacity to wage any kind of war." Consequently, jihad has again

---

[51] These quotations, and those in the paragraphs following, are from personal correspondence of Maulana Maudoodi to the author.

been reduced to an unarmed struggle, and armed conflict has of necessity gone out of fashion. This is the same position, incidentally, as that of Sir Syed Ahmad Khan, although not that of Mirza Ghulam Ahmad.

Similarly, nothing has changed so far as polygamy is concerned. In Maudoodi's view, this is a matter not of the reinterpretation of the Qur'an, but of its distortion. He believes that only those Muslims who have been overly impressed by western civilization interpret the Qur'an as being essentially opposed to polygamy; they blindly copy the western principle of monogamy, even though it is at variance with every divine book. Monogamy, Maulana Maudoodi asserts, "is in fact the legacy of pagan Rome."

Polygamy had been the common practice in Arabia before Muhammad received any revelation, and he received no revelation that prohibited it. This, in itself, Maulana Maudoodi thinks, is evidence enough of its permissibility. The qur'anic verse relating to polygamy was revealed shortly after the defeat of the Muslims at the battle of 'Uhud in 625, which created the social problem of responsibility for those individuals orphaned by the battle. *"Thus,"* Maulana Maudoodi argues, *"this verse did not indicate any new permission; it urged that a particular current practice, which was permissible, should be resorted to for the solution of a social problem."* [52]

So far as such matters as women wearing the veil and the payment of interest are concerned, Maudoodi's position is the same. It is not the Islamic concept that has changed, but the mentality of certain Muslims. The dynamics of Islam do

[52] Khursheed Ahmad, ed., *Studies in the Family Law of Islam* (Karachi, 1961), p. 24. This quotation is from Maulana Maudoodi's reply to a questionnaire distributed early in 1956 by a government-appointed Commission on Marriage and Family Laws. Italics are in the original.

not lie in reinterpretation and conscious adaptation to changing conditions, but rather in the simple affirmation that the Qur'an is God's own Word—His last Word, giving to man the information necessary to enable him to live a moral life and so to gain salvation; in the simple fact that Muhammad, of all men, was chosen by God to carry His last message to mankind because he was already an exemplar among men.

To claim any other dynamics is blasphemy. If Islamic religious experience is dynamic in the way many modernists assert, then one must ask what the relationship of the prophetic stage to the post-prophetic stage of Islam is? Was the Persian mystic Rumi, for example, more advanced than Muhammad? So far as Maulana Maudoodi is concerned, such an idea is preposterous. Muhammad was the last and the greatest of the Prophets—the only one whose revelation remains, the only one whose revelation was in itself complete, and the only man who had been raised not for a single nation, but for all the world.[53] Man's dynamics can only be toward closer and closer obedience to the sayings and actions of the Prophet.

Unfortunately, Maulana Maudoodi maintains, Muslims have been straying from the path. On the one hand western civilization has so affected men's minds that it is becoming increasingly more difficult to adopt an Islamic viewpoint. On the other hand, Islam has failed to produce the thinkers and scholars who can adequately criticize the foundations of western civilization from the standpoint of their faith.[54] Maudoodi's purpose has been to bring all Muslims back to the path, ultraconservative as well as ultramodernist. But he

[53] Maududi, *Towards Understanding Islam*, pp. 69–70.
[54] This and the following two paragraphs are largely based upon a translation of Maudoodi's article, "Our Mental Enslavement and Its Causes," prepared by Mazheruddin Siddiqui.

finds it a hard struggle, for genuine Islam is scarcely to be found; he believes that the West has never met Islam—only its corruptions. If the West had ever had to face true Islam, the westerners rather than the Muslims would have been conquered. Maudoodi's position resembles very much that old standby among sermons delivered by preachers of a different faith: "How do you know Christianity won't work? It has never been tried!"

Maudoodi wanted to have Islam, as he understood it, tried again; he was sure it would work, because he believed it had actually been tried in the glorious days of the early caliphate. He castigated the traditionalist theologians for never having studied western society firsthand, and for not having utilized western techniques to further Muslim ends.[55] They had, he said, "become accustomed to the worship of the past, and to an uncritical reliance on their predecessors." He castigated the West, "a purely materialistic civilization whose system of life is entirely devoid of piety, truthfulness, virtue, chastity, modesty—all those values on which Islamic civilization is built," and he castigated those Muslims who were attracted by western ideas.[56] His insistence that one had to go back to the time of the Companions of the Prophet to find pure Islam removed him from the ranks of the traditionalist theologians, who had built their doctrine on the decisions and interpreta-

[55] It is interesting to note that of the approximately 1,000 members of the Maulana's party in 1954, no more than two had ever been to Europe, and none had ever been to America. Many, of course, had taken the pilgrimage to Arabia. Information is from Mian Tufail Muhammad.

[56] Maudoodi wrote this some years before partition, in his article "Our Mental Enslavement and Its Causes." From my own personal acquaintance with him, I would say he may have somewhat modified the views expressed here, at least to the extent of admitting a less extreme position.

tions of medieval jurists. Maulana Maudoodi removed himself from the ranks of the modernists because he insisted, unlike Sir Syed Ahmad Khan, that the Qur'an can be interpreted only against a background of Muslim philosophy, that western philosophy has no place in it.[57] When, for instance, a British scholar advocated a synthesis of scientific and religious spirit, Maudoodi argued that no such synthesis could ever be effected because religion is "the soul and the guiding spirit behind science." Here is another example of the western habit of dual thinking meeting the sternly unitarian intellectual approach of Islam.

Maulana Maudoodi opposed nationalism because it is un-Islamic; he refused to support the movement for the separation of Pakistan from India because he believed the Muslim leadership cared little about Islam or Islamic principles. With the establishment of Pakistan as an independent nation, however, he began to work toward molding the new Muslim state to fit his idea of an Islamic state. In this endeavor he failed. During the early years of Pakistan, when the country in its initial enthusiasm was trying to be more Islamic than anywhere else, Maulana Maudoodi attracted a great deal of attention through his lectures, his writing, and his party; so much that the Pakistan government saw fit to jail, or otherwise inhibit, him periodically.

One of the statements most often reiterated by Muslims is that Islam is more than a religion, it is a complete code of life: a political system, an economic system, it is everything. Islam is a great practical religion because it is complete. Maulana Maudoodi made precise and emphasized just what he conceived this to mean.

A Muslim, he said, is one who has surrendered himself to

[57] Binder gives a précis of a Jama'at publication in which this point is made, although not by Maudoodi, p. 83.

God and to God's laws, and who has formed a society with other Muslims. The society itself is governed by the law prescribed by the Qur'an and the Prophet Muhammad—the shari'a. Only by following literally the precepts of the Qur'an, as amplified by the sunna, the practices of the first four caliphs, and guided by the rulings of great jurists, could an Islamic state be built up—a process he thought might require ten years.[58] So long as the shari'a is obeyed completely, in all of its parts, the society will prosper; if even one of its stipulations is ignored, the whole structure will be weakened. He believed that one must observe Islamic forms implicitly, for while form without spirit is meaningless, it is also true that the existence of form is the only evidence that the proper spirit might also be present. The creation of an Islamic state required the translation into practice of "the entire programme of life and not merely a fragment of it," [59] and in large part the enforcement of that program by the coercive power of the state, that is, the society.

One of the difficulties facing the adoption of Maudoodi's concept of an Islamic state was that it involved isolation from the world community. To the leaders of the new state of Pakistan, dependent upon the world community for survival, Maudoodi's concepts were impossible.

[58] Syed Abul 'Ala Maudoodi, *Islamic Law and Constitution*, ed. by Khurshid Ahmad (Karachi, 1955), p. 56.

[59] *Ibid.*, p. 37.

Chapter Six

Muslim Modernism
in Pakistan

"Pakistan was founded," Prime Minister Liaquat 'Ali Khan told the Constituent Assembly of Pakistan in March, 1949, "because the Muslims of this sub-Continent wanted to build up their lives in accordance with the teachings and traditions of Islam." With these words Liaquat 'Ali summed up the sincere feeling of many Muslims; there was no unanimity of feeling, however, either before the creation of Pakistan or after, as to what "in accordance with the teachings and traditions of Islam" might mean.[1] There was not, in fact, even political unification among Muslims in the drive to establish Pakistan.

Those traditionalists, led by the scholars of Deoband, who had actively campaigned for the departure of the British had many reservations about the proposed state of Pakistan. For one thing, they distrusted the leadership of the westernized Muslims, who to them often seemed to have no real under-

[1] *Constituent Assembly of Pakistan Debates*, Vol. V, no. 1, March 7, 1949, p. 2.

183

standing of Islam. Some Muslim legislators, the Khilafat
leader Maulana Mohamed Ali once complained, "no doubt
born in Muslim families, but certainly not believing in Islam
as a perfect and complete faith needing no reform . . . can
be found seeking to improve upon Islam by their own crazy
handiwork. . . ." [2] Many of the Muslim League proponents
of Pakistan fell within this criticism. Maulana Maudoodi,
whose position was similar to that of Deoband, refused, too,
to support the Pakistan movement, because he did not believe
a nationalist movement could be Islamic, and because he did
not trust the movement's leadership. [3]

There were other Indian Muslims, such as Abul Kalam
Azad, the first education minister of the Republic of India,
who did not support Pakistan because they believed in an
undivided India. They did not accept the theory promoted
by Mohamed Ali Jinnah (and first tentatively suggested by
Sir Syed Ahmad Khan) that the "difference between Hindus
and the Muslims is deep-rooted and ineradicable. We are a
nation with our own distinctive culture and civilization . . .
we have our own distinctive outlook on life and of life. By
all canons of International Law we are a nation." [4]

[2] Afzal Iqbal, ed., *Select Writings and Speeches of Maulana Mohamed Ali* (Lahore, 1944), p. 452. The quotation is from a statement
to the Viceroy in opposition to the Sarda Act, defending Muslim
personal law, 9 November 1929. The Maulana, it should be pointed
out, was a graduate of Aligarh and not Deoband.

[3] Freeland Abbott, "The Jama'at-i-Islami of Pakistan," *The Middle
East Journal*, XI, 1 (Winter, 1957), 40.

[4] Jamil-ud-din Ahmad, ed., *Some Recent Speeches and Writings of
Mr. Jinnah* (2 vols.; Lahore, 1952), I, 427. The two-nation theory
seems to have been first suggested at a Provincial Muslim League
Conference held in Karachi in October, 1938. See A. H. Albiruni,
Makers of Pakistan and Modern Muslim India (Lahore, 1950), p. 218.
The idea had been suggested, although not seriously entertained, by
the London *Times* in commenting on the 1935 India Act (*Recent
Speeches and Writings*, I, 176).

Abul Kalam Azad had no patience with Jinnah's theory of the two nations. "As a Muslim," he wrote, "I for one am not prepared for a moment to give up my right to treat the whole of India as my domain and to share in the shaping of its political and economic life. To me it seems a sure sign of cowardice to give up what is my patrimony and content myself with a mere fragment of it." [5]

The Ahmadiyas were another group that did not support the Pakistan movement. The entire Indian independence movement was somewhat embarrassing to them, for they looked upon the British as protectors—a point upon which their critics loved to dwell. With the partition of India, however, the town of Qadian fell on the Indian side of the line, and the Qadianis moved to Rabwah in the Punjab and established a new center. Similarly, Maulana Maudoodi moved from Pathankot, which was also on the Indian side of the line, to Ichhra, a suburb of Lahore. If there was to be an Islamic state, he reasoned, it would more likely be created by a community of Muslims, and as a Muslim it was his duty to promote it as much as he was able.

The motive force for Pakistan came largely from the middle-class Muslims, many of whom had been educated at Aligarh, and many of whom accepted the spirit—they were often hazy about the ideas—of Syed Ahmad Khan and Muhammad Iqbal. These leaders of the Muslim League tended to look askance at the traditionalist leaders of Muslim India; in their minds the movement for Pakistan meant a reorientation of Islam in India, not a re-establishment of the Wahabis. It is questionable whether the leaders of the Muslim League even viewed the problem as fundamentally religious, however willing they may have been to appeal to religious senti-

[5] Abul Kalam Azad, *India Wins Freedom* (New York, 1960), p. 168.

ments. Mohamed Ali Jinnah, while explaining the 1940 Resolution of the Muslim League (which had moved beyond
Iqbal's 1930 plea for a Muslim state in the northwest to include a state in the east of India as well), remarked, "It is
extremely difficult to understand why our Hindu friends fail
to understand the real nature of Islam and Hinduism. They
are not religions in the strict sense of the word, but are, in
fact, different and distinct social orders. . . ." [6]

Jinnah, Iqbal, and Liaquat 'Ali Khan were clearly concerned primarily with a social approach to Islam; in addition,
their interests determined a *direct* approach. Social justice
was to them something to be built up by action resulting in
social justice—however we define the term; it was not something to be built up as a result of actions following from a
particular ritualistic approach. On this simple distinction the
modernists and traditionalists met at loggerheads. Jinnah seems
to have either underestimated the influence of the mullahs,
the largely rural-based leaders, or to have felt that they represented a risk he had to take. Whether the strength of the
mullahs was underestimated or not, the governmental leaders
had no desire to become involved in any protracted disputes
with them. It was a risk, however, that became intensified
when many mullahs migrated to Pakistan upon the partition
of the subcontinent. This risk explains in part the delay of
eighteen months before a resolution expressing even the general principles to be incorporated in the constitution was submitted to the Constituent Assembly of Pakistan.

As a practicing politician, the leader of the Muslim League,
and advocate of partition, Mohamed Ali Jinnah was forced

[6] *Recent Speeches and Writings*, I, 177–178. This quotation is from
Jinnah's Presidential Address at the 1940 session; the particular comment refers to a London *Times* comment on the India Act of 1935
which dismisses the two-nation idea as superstition.

to handle the question of religion. He was a nonsectarian who might attend either Shi'a or Sunni services; he had earlier been an apostle of Hindu-Muslim unity, an attitude he abandoned only after it had become apparent that the Congress (and to Jinnah that meant the Hindus) would offer no special safeguards to the Muslim minority. As the accepted leader of the Muslim League it became necessary for him to acquire something of the quality of attraction that came so naturally to Gandhi, or that seemed to encompass Abdul Ghaffar Khan, "the frontier Gandhi," a Muslim leader whose loyalty lay with the Congress. Jinnah's success in this respect is borne out by the numbers of Muslims who flocked to Pakistan following partition, although it must not be assumed that they were all motivated by religious fervor, or, indeed, that they could separate Mr. Jinnah from the Mr. Pakistan to whom many of them in their fear and ignorance fled—or think of either as other than some kind of vague refuge to which they were forced to turn.

With the establishment of Pakistan in 1947, Jinnah found himself with a national state on his hands, a state determined to be Islamic and filled with conflict as to what "Islamic" really meant. In the early days of Pakistan traditionalist leaders insisted that women should not be seen in public, even Jinnah's sister, Fatimah, or Liaquat 'Ali Khan's wife, Raana. And where, they asked, was the Islamic state Pakistan was meant to be? Jinnah kept quiet; he was too busy ensuring the existence of the state to devote much time to describing the nature of a particular kind of state. Eventually he did speak out, but in general terms that satisfied no one. "Islamic principles have no parallel," he is reported to have once said. "Today they are as applicable in actual life as they were 1,300 years ago. Islam and its idealism have taught democracy. They have taught equality of man, justice and fairplay to everybody." Later, he expressed himself more clearly, although not without inconsistency, when he said, "Islam is not only a set of rituals, traditions and spiritual doctrines, Islam is a code for every Muslim, which regulates his life and his conduct in all aspects, social, political, economic, etc. It is based on the highest principles of honour, integrity, fairplay and justice for all. One God, equality, and unity are the fundamental principles of Islam." [7] However one might choose to interpret this statement, it is obvious that its approach is a social one.

The new government assumed a particular interpretation of Islam without trying to spell it out in any detail; the government could not, in fact, do anything else, even if it had not been thoroughly convinced of its wisdom in this course. It was necessary to establish a viable government to serve seventy or eighty million people: to operate railroads and post offices, to promote commerce, to provide for millions of refugees still flooding into the country—to create, in short, an entire government and a total economy. This could not be done without help; the new Islamic state of Pakistan had to become involved in international affairs. Consequently, the complete acceptance of traditional forms involving the acceptance of slavery, the mutilation of thieves, or the execution of prisoners of war, seemed out of the question on practicable grounds alone. Pakistan, governmental leaders asserted, should not attempt to follow these medieval practices or it would become a pariah among nations.

The traditionalist leaders long objected to this state of affairs. They were not impressed by the argument that a nation had to live with its neighbors and to observe accepted standards of international conduct; after all, some of them

[7] The quotations are from Fareed S. Jafri, "Pakistan: Growth of an Ideology—VII," Pakistan *Standard*, January 30, 1955.

pointed out, Russia frequently did not observe these standards, yet there was no question that Russia was fully accepted as a member of the international community. The glory of being an Islamic state in a very real sense was sufficient for them.

Most secular leaders believed the ulama were confusing religion with religiosity.[8] The leaders agreed that Islam provided a complete code of life, but they did not believe that the details of that code were forever fixed and irrevocable. The general attitude is well expressed by the university student who wrote that Islamic principles "are dynamic not static. Why should we not adopt and adapt when it fits our present-day society?"[9] Zahid Hussain, president of the Pakistan Economic Association and chairman of the Government Planning Board, expressed this view in an address before the Economic Association. He felt that the belief, which he shared, that Islam provided a complete code of conduct "must rest on our ability to distinguish clearly between beliefs, traditions and institutions which are of abiding value from age to age and those that serve only ephemeral purposes and must change to meet changing conditions. . . . Islamic institutions and traditions of abiding value must be preserved."[10]

Such attitudes as these, of course, merely underlined the traditionalist's objections. How does one determine an abiding value of Islam? Who determines which are abiding values? Should it be individuals who are little learned in the Qur'an and hadith, or individuals who all their lives have been

[8] Khalifa 'Abdul Hakim, *Islamic Ideology* (Lahore, 1953), p. 14.

[9] Nur Ahmad Perhar, "Model Constitution of Pakistan and Its Basic Principles" (unpublished Master's thesis, University of the Punjab, 1951).

[10] Speech at Association meeting in Peshawar, January 11, 1955; Pakistan *Standard*, January 16, 1955.

studying nothing else? These were questions the traditionalists had long asked, and for which they had long found definite and precise answers.

The position of the traditionalist scholars was seriously weakened as a result of the Punjab disturbances of 1953. These riots, so serious that the city of Lahore was placed under martial law, were both political and religious in nature; they centered around traditionalist objections to the acceptance of the Ahmadiyas, particularly Qadianis (although in the popular mind little distinction was made between the two branches), as full-fledged citizens of an Islamic state, and to their employment in governmental positions. (Sir Muhammad Zafrulla Khan, Foreign Minister at the time, was a member of the Qadiani branch of the Ahmadiya.) The rioting was finally put down by the central government and a court of inquiry established to study its causes. The inquiry attracted a great deal of attention, and its report was widely read; the government clearly extracted every possible advantage from the situation. The mullahs and the ulama, after promoting riots and bloodshed against the Ahmadiyas for not being Muslims, proved unable to agree among themselves as to what actually made a man a Muslim.[11] The inability of the traditionalist Muslim scholars to agree on a single definition is not astonishing, for a sampling of Christian clergy might very well produce as great a variety of definitions of a Christian—if it were possible to agree on just who is a Christian clergyman. It did serve, however, somewhat to discredit the traditionalist scholars in the eyes of many educated Pakistanis, and to emphasize that Islam could be just as divisive a force as a uniting one. The blow was especially telling at

[11] *Report of The Court of Inquiry Constituted under Punjab Act II of 1954 to Enquire into the Punjab Disturbances of 1953* (Lahore, Government Printing, 1954), pp. 214–218.

the time: it had only recently been proposed, as one of the basic principles of the Constitution, that every parliamentary bill to which any single assembly member should object on the grounds that it violated the Qur'an or the sunna be submitted to a board "of five members learned in Islamic law for opinion." [12]

The report, commonly referred to as the Munir Report after the chairman of the inquiry, represented a negative attack by the government on those legal interpretations of Islam with which the government could not agree. The Constituent Assembly had agreed in its Objectives Resolutions that fundamental rights should be guaranteed, including "freedom of thought, expression, belief, faith, worship and association, subject to law and public morality." [13] The sponsors of the Punjab disturbances, on the other hand, would have maintained that in an Islamic state a Muslim could not renounce Islam without being guilty of treason, and so subject to the death penalty. This same concept, incidentally, is one of the issues that aroused Europe to over a hundred years of religious wars, during which it was generally believed that if the citizen did not accept the religious view of the head of the state he could not faithfully support the state. It is a concept that has not been completely lost even to this day.[14] The question of apostasy in the case of Pakistan, according to some of the traditionalist scholars, was academic, for this punishment could not be applied until the state itself was thoroughly "Islamic."

The principle expressed in the Objectives Resolution, and

[12] Leonard Binder, *Religion and Politics in Pakistan* (Berkeley, 1961), p. 257.

[13] *Constituent Assembly of Pakistan Debates*, Vol. V, no. 5, March 12, 1949, p. 100.

[14] See Francis L. Broderick, "But Constitutions Can Be Changed," *The Catholic Historical Review*, XLIX, 3 (October, 1963), 390–393.

incorporated into the preambles of both the 1956 and 1962
constitutions, was always put into practice with great regard
for its qualifying clause, "subject to law and public morality."
The government moved prudently to avoid tipping an un-
steady boat. Censorship, for instance, was imposed on a
biography of Aisha because it was objectionable to the
Sunni, although there was nothing in the book to which a
Shi'a would object. Similarly, when *Life* magazine, in reply
to a letter from a reader, published a small reproduction of
a Shi'a painting of Muhammad, the offending picture was
removed from every copy sold in Pakistan. The Shi'as were
the minority and, where public order seemed to be threatened,
were treated like a minority.

There were many attempts made to bring Shi'as and Sunnis
together. In July, 1958, a meeting of one hundred ulama
from both Sunni and Shi'a sects was convened under the
presidency of the Prime Minister of West Pakistan. The
meeting passed a resolution of cordiality, but Sunni-Shi'a
quarrels and riots continued. Indeed, there seemed no immediate way to end them, for to rely on the traditional
Muslim reference to *ijma*—the consensus of the community
—would likely place the Shi'as at a disadvantage. In one
study in Lahore, 94 per cent of the Sunni questioned did
favor a resort to *ijma*, but only 7 per cent of the Shi'as favored
it.[15]

The communal bickering of Sunnis and Shi'as posed only
one problem for the government. Political problems had to
be considered as well. Were the country to adopt universal
suffrage the likelihood that a religious party, such as Maulana

[15] Shams-ur-Rahman Chaudhry, "Shia Sunni Tension with Special
Reference to Social Distance Scale" (unpublished Ph.D. dissertation,
University of the Punjab, 1959), pp. 5–6, 8. This study involved a
sample of 68 Sunnis and 43 Shi'as.

Maudoodi's Community of Islam (Jama'at-i-Islami), would be successful at the polls was very real. In the view of government leaders a viable Pakistan could not develop under the political leadership of the mullahs; on the other hand, a strong Pakistan was not likely to develop without their help. The central government both wooed the mullahs and ridiculed them. The "Basic Principles" on which the Constitution was to be built were introduced in the Constituent Assembly more than forty months after the Objectives Resolutions had been introduced. Their secular nature aroused opposition from the traditionalists, and the modernists objected because they had been drawn up in consultation with the traditionalist scholars.[16] The postponement of elections was in part an admission of fear that the religious groups might well prove to control a large proportion of the votes. "Surely," wrote one commentator, "no democracy in history has been as innocent of elections as that of Pakistan." [17]

Governmental policy was simply to tone down the religious issue in internal affairs. In external affairs attempts were made to woo other Muslim nations—a pan-Islamic tinge, so to speak—but nothing came of it. India's gambits, in fact, proved more attractive to Egypt than did those of Pakistan, and Turkey requested that the Pakistan ambassador be recalled: his approach was too religious. For the most part the government chose to ride the religious problem out, and to trust that eventually, once the first flood of enthusiasm over the creation of a new Muslim state had receded, the religious problem might appear in a simplified manner. It was not, of course, a matter that could be ignored. References to the social structure of Islam were frequent; the anniversary of

[16] See Binder for a discussion of the framing of these Principles.
[17] W. A. Wilcox, *Pakistan, The Consolidation of a Nation* (New York, 1963), p. 195.

Muhammad Iqbal's death, April 21, became a national holiday and the occasion for country-wide speeches and newspaper articles remarking on the poet's vision.

"There is nothing against which Iqbal battled so vigorously and persistently as against the lack of faith which saps the will to action," said Chaudry Muhammad 'Ali, the Finance Minister, in one such speech. "Faith is the pre-requisite of all endeavour; and it is by our endeavour that we shall be judged." Chaudry Muhammad 'Ali was deeply and sincerely religious. His address noted that both Russia and the United States were powerful, not because of what they *believed*—their philosophies and values were different—but because each was industrialized. Pakistan, he concluded, can industrialize and maintain its Islamic conception; "centuries of decadence and un-Islamic ways of thought and conduct" have caused Muslim society to deteriorate, and a "tremendous effort will be required to reconstruct the foundations of our life on an Islamic basis." [18] The effect of such lectures as this, widely publicized by the government, was to strengthen the views of those whose concept of Islam was already "modernized" and to promote broader concepts on the part of those who still pictured Islam as bound by the habits of a society thirteen centuries old.

This speech by Chaudry Muhammad 'Ali, who later became Prime Minister of Pakistan, portrays an attitude that could be acceptable to almost everyone except what might be called the hard-core traditionalist. While it advances an argument every modernist would accept, it is not necessarily one that, for example, a follower of Maulana Maudoodi would

[18] Chaudry Muhammad 'Ali, *The Task Before Us*, Iqbal Day Address by The Honorable Mr. Mohamed 'Ali, April 21, 1952, Karachi, pp. 41, 39.

reject; Chaudry Muhammad 'Ali, in fact, was an admirer of Maulana Maudoodi.

It is difficult to estimate the effectiveness of such speeches. The speeches themselves rarely reached the villager directly, but the spirit that prompted them was developed in the Village Aid Program and so carried to the villager. A comparative study was once made of two Punjab villages, only three miles apart: Dost Pura, which had been a recipient of Village Aid, and Qutba, which had not. Only 13 per cent of Dost Pura considered the traditions of their forefathers important; almost 94 per cent of Qutba valued these traditions highly. Five per cent of the people of Dost Pura and 80 per cent of the people of Qutba believed in the efficacy of charms. As one might expect, more people were fatalists in Qutba (about two-thirds) than in Dost Pura (about 13 per cent). The acceptance of fatalism is not necessarily an indication of reaction, however: the exponent of free will may believe he can achieve constructive reform—and do it; the fatalist may believe he is fated to achieve constructive reform—and do it. Or either may resign himself to the power of those around him.

In the case of Qutba, 78 per cent argued that crop diseases or pests represented the will of God and should not be checked—an attitude shared by only about 8 per cent of the village of Dost Pura. Over 58 per cent of Qutba favored giving a western-type education to children, including over 18 per cent who favored such education for both male and female; in Dost Pura over 83 per cent of the people favored western education for both boys and girls, and everyone favored such education for boys.[19]

[19] Abdul Hamid, "A Comparative Study of Two Rural Communities: Dost Pura and Qutba in Kasur Development Area of Lahore

Other examples of changing attitudes developing among the villagers of Pakistan can be found, for pressures are being exerted upon them from all sides. In the Bahawalpur area villages chose to maintain the textbooks used in their mosque schools rather than abandon the illustrations which clarified those texts, even though the provincial Ecclesiastical Office had spoken against them. Illustrations of humans are not usually permitted in mosques. The villagers did not think the pictures were being used for idolatrous reasons, and chose to ignore the edict of the ulama. The teaching of the Muslim modernists, however, very seldom reaches into the villages, perhaps when a village son returns from the army, or the city, for a visit. The teaching of new agricultural techniques, or new handicraft methods, is more commonly to be found, but many villages have not yet been affected even in this way, although more are steadily being reached. The villager frequently puts more faith in his Pir, his "religious guide," than his local mullah, although the Pir may have little actual knowledge of Islam, however great his leadership ability.

In themselves these examples do not specifically pertain to the heart of the religious problem in Pakistan, the disparate views of modernists and traditionalists. The government has consistently tried to keep that problem in the background, and has largely been successful. But it will have to be faced some day. Ayub Khan has broached the question more forcefully than most Pakistan leaders, although Iskander Mirza, as Governor-General, once echoed the thoughts of the Delhi sultan, Muhammad ibn Tughluq, when he pointedly remarked that

---

District—regarding the Differential Rates of Progress of V-Aid Programme" (unpublished Master's thesis, University of the Punjab, 1959). The population of Dost Pura was 480, that of Qutba, 510; this study was computed from a sample of 60 from Dost Pura and 55 from Qutba.

religion and politics do not mix. But it was Ayub Khan who, when asked at a public gathering in Chittagong whether he believed religious sanction should be obtained from the ulama for popularizing family planning among the masses, said, "Religion is for man and not man for religion. My religion is to do good to mankind." To these words, so reminiscent of Syed Ahmad Khan, he added that those religious leaders who had feeling for the people would come to the same conclusion when they realized the benefits of family planning toward solving the pressing food problem.[20]

"An Islamic constitution, however," he said on another occasion, "did not mean that the Pakistani nation should revert to backwardness. Islam is a progressive religion and a religion for all times and people." [21] On another occasion he remarked that if being a Muslim meant going back to the world of 1,300 years ago, then he was not for being a Muslim.

With these words, in fact, Ayub was pinpointing the basic difference between the modernist and the traditionalist. Essential to the modernist position, the assumption without which modernism in Islam in Pakistan is meaningless, is the idea that Islam is a universal religion. The traditionalists accept this, too; but whereas the traditionalist assumes the world must adjust to Islam or the faith will become adulterated with an abominable innovation, the modernist assumes that much of the better things of the world are Islamic in themselves. If Islam is a universal religion, then local customs and local habits are nonessential. In this the modernists hark back to Shah Waliullah. But the problem that faced the eighteenth-century theologian remains today: how does one separate local customs and local habits and remain true to the Qur'an and sunna? Does one reject most of the hadith,

[20] Pakistan *Observer*, January 25, 1960.
[21] Pakistan *Observer*, January 26, 1960.

and call only those one accepts "sunna"? Does one read the Qur'an in terms of broad principles instead of particular injunctions?

One legal measure passed in Pakistan definitely reflects a modernist approach. On August 4, 1955, a seven-member commission was appointed to study the existing laws of marriage, divorce, and family maintenance to determine whether those laws needed modification "in order to give women their proper place in society according to the fundamentals of Islam." The commission was composed of six laymen, three of whom were women, and one religious scholar. Almost eleven months later the commission published its report; a note of dissent was later received from the traditionalist scholar and separately published.[22]

The complexities of both modernism and traditionalism are evident in the activities of the commission. Among other things, the commission recommended that the laws of divorce be changed to make it impossible for a man to divorce his wife by saying rapidly, "I divorce thee, I divorce thee, I divorce thee." The traditionalist member had announced that on this point the commission could make no recommendation: the four imams had supported as valid the practice of pronouncing the divorce formula three times at one sitting, and the commission could not recommend something with which the imams disagreed—could not, in short, ignore tradition.

The modernist members of the commission—all the rest—thought otherwise. Because "Islam inculcates happiness and security in family life," they reported, then "easy divorces

[22] *Gazette of Pakistan Extraordinary*, June 20, 1956, Report of the Commission on Marriage and Family Laws; the note of dissent by Maulana Ihtisham-ul-Haq appeared in the *Gazette* on August 30, 1956. (Hereafter referred to as *Marriage Report* and *Marriage Commission Dissent.*)

should be prevented." [23] In this instance the majority members were able to adduce strong qur'anic support. Muhammad had tried first to prevent all divorce, and then to prevent capricious divorce; the Qur'an acknowledges that incompatible people are not happy together and might better be divorced, but the divorce procedure prescribed in the Qur'an requires a minimum of three months to effect. The custom of quick divorce began after Muhammad's death, apparently introduced by 'Umar, the second caliph. Quick divorce was described by all the four imams as an "undesirable innovation," but they all acquiesced to its legitimacy, bowing, like 'Umar, to the force of custom. The position of the traditionalist scholars is, on this point, represented by Maulana Maudoodi, who held that the imams were right, but "it is an admitted fact that, although legally valid, it is still a sin as it goes contrary to the method of divorce taught by God and his Prophet (peace be on him)." [24]

Nothing more clearly illustrates the nature of the gap between the modernists and the traditionalists than this question of divorce. But the issues are not always so clear, although the assumption that Islam promotes happiness and security in family life (and any rule which does not do this, the modernist would argue, cannot be Islamic) is consistently followed. The question of polygamy is more complicated, for it involves several problems of qur'anic interpretation. The majority members of the commission maintained that the qur'anic reference to polygamy relates only to the protection of the rights of orphans,[25] and that the qur'anic injunction grant-

[23] *Marriage Report*, p. 1212.

[24] Khursheed Ahmad, ed., *Studies in the Family Law of Islam* (Karachi, 1961), p. 21.

[25] *Marriage Report*, p. 1216. The passage in question, 4:3, reads: "If ye fear that ye shall not be able to deal justly with the orphans,

ing permission to marry more than one wife was designed to assure social justice. It stated that in an emergency a man might marry more than one woman, provided he married orphan girls and widows who might otherwise be exploited. Furthermore, the majority report maintained, "a proviso was attached to this permission that if this way of solving the problem leads to injustice in family relations then the Muslims are advised to practise monogamy only."[26] Because this only conditional permission for monogamy has been so frequently abused, it becomes necessary for the state to see that polygamy is properly supervised. The commission recommended that a man desiring a second wife be made to establish before a Matrimonial and Family Laws Court valid reason for so doing: a wife who is insane, or suffering from some incurable disease, or some other such circumstance. He must also satisfy the Court that he can afford to maintain two families; indeed, it is the responsibility of the Court to determine the amount to be reserved for his first wife.

This is a modernist view, predicated upon the belief that the Qur'an must be read with the requirements of social justice ever in mind. The majority members of the commission went farther. Citing Iqbal as their authority they insisted that ijtihad—independent judgment in legal matters exercised by learned scholars—was necessary for jurists and judges, for "life can improve only by freedom of judgment."[27] The laws and injunctions of Islam, they maintained, were not inflexible and unchangeable, and distinctions might be drawn between them "on the basis of their universality or applica-

---

marry women of your choice, two, or three or four; but if ye fear that ye shall not be able to deal justly [with them], then only one, or [a captive] that your right hands possess. That will be more suitable, to prevent you from doing injustice."

[26] *Marriage Report*, p. 1216.
[27] *Marriage Report*, p. 1201.

bility to a particular structure of society in a particular epoch and in a particular region." This position was not, of course, accepted by traditionalist scholars.

Maulana Maudoodi argued that the commission's interpretation of this qur'anic verse relating to polygamy was in error. Polygamy, he said, had existed in Arabia before Muhammad, yet the Prophet did not try to end it. The verse in question, consequently, is not concerned with the permissibility of the institution; its purpose is only to point out a solution to the problem of unattached orphans and widows created by the deaths of many Muslims at the battle of 'Uhud.[28] That solution is polygamy. Something new was added, however, for where restriction had previously not existed, the revelation now limited the number of one's wives to four.[29]

The dissent of Maulana Ihtisham-ul-Haq, the traditionalist scholar on the commission, provided still another interpretation of this verse. He believed that the mention of orphan girls in the verse in question was made only to emphasize their conjugal rights.[30] The verse prohibits guardians of orphans from marrying them only for their property and then, in effect, abandoning them. He cited the example of Muhammad and his Companions, all of whom married more than one wife, and whose additional wives were not orphans. When 'Ali, married to Muhammad's daughter Fatimah, announced his intention of taking a second wife, Muhammad (although he did not like the idea) did not insist that 'Ali marry an orphan. The weight of hadith seems to be strongly on the side of the Maulana.

[28] The battle of 'Uhud, March 23, 625, represented a defeat of Muhammad's community by a strong Meccan force; approximately 75 Muslims were killed, a substantial percentage of the adult male members of his small community.

[29] Khursheed Ahmad, pp. 23–24.

[30] *Marriage Commission Dissent*, p. 1595.

"There is," he wrote, "no restriction or restraint on marriages up to the limit of four. This being the position, it would be an interference in the revealed religion, if the plurality of marriages is declared to be unlawful or any restriction is imposed on it." [31] The abuse of family relationships, he observed, is not in the law of Islam, but in the lack of understanding of that law. What is needed is the education of society to make it "mentally prepared to act in the spirit of the law." [32]

Whatever the meaning of the verse in question, it is obvious that each interpretation has its own specific emphasis. The commission, strongly asserting the right of independent judgment, is concerned, under its terms of reference, to determine whether Muslim women under existing laws "achieve their proper place in society according to the fundamentals of Islam." Their emphasis is on the individual woman: Is quick divorce fair to the woman? How does one stop the abuses of polygamy? This primary stress on the individual perhaps represents some absorption of eighteenth-century humanitarian ideas.

Both Maulana Maudoodi and Maulana Ihtisham-ul-Haq regret the abuses that have crept into Muslim marriage and divorce practices. Neither would consider capricious divorce to be Islamic; but each puts primary emphasis on the preservation of tradition over the interests of the individual. Maulana Maudoodi has above all been concerned to preserve the shari'a as traditionally interpreted, and to prevent any conflict between it and the law of the land. Thus, while acknowledging the legal validity of the traditional interpretation of quick divorce, he regards it as a sin and, in fact, suggested means by which it might be discouraged. Maulana Maudoodi reflects

---

[31] *Marriage Commission Dissent*, pp. 1597–1598.
[32] *Marriage Commission Dissent*, p. 1566.

both modernist and traditionalist views, for he does acknowledge the pitfalls of the traditionalist view.

Maulana Ihtisham-ul-Haq, on the other hand, has no misgivings about the decision of the four imams. It is not only legal, it is in keeping with practice subscribed to by Muhammad. He cites hadith indicating (the matter pivots upon the particular meaning of an Arabic word) that Muhammad had himself believed three successive pronouncements of the divorce formula to be irrevocable—in this instance apparently placing the sunna above the Qur'an. If the story of 'Umar allowing quick divorce is true, he asks, why did not any of the Companions object? Did not Muhammad say, "My community can never agree over an error"? It is obvious to the Maulana that to effect a divorce by reciting the divorce formula three times at a single sitting cannot be considered un-Islamic, however much the practice may be abused.

To Maulana Ihtisham-ul-Haq the majority members were compounding errors in the name of independent judgment. They were bound by their own words to conform "to the details" of the Holy Qur'an and sunna, yet failed to realize that where there is a clear injunction the question of independent judgment does not arise at all. The Maulana apparently did not realize that the majority members of the commission did not see the injunction as clearly as he did: they asked one set of questions as they read the passage, while he read it asking an entirely different set.

In addition, asserted the Maulana, "only that '*Ijtihad*' is reliable which is exercised in the light of the Holy Quran and the Sunnah, and not that '*Ijtihad*' which ignores the Holy Quran and the Sunnah and relies on human reason. The Holy Quran and the Sunnah show light to reason but reason is no guidance for the Holy Quran and the Sunnah." [33]

[33] *Marriage Commission Dissent*, p. 1566.

The Maulana was attacking a point basic to all modernists: the right of the learned scholar (which the majority members considered themselves to be) to exercise independent judgment in legal matters—ijtihad. It was almost a travesty to the traditionalist Muslims that the majority members of the commission should choose to exercise their own judgment against the unanimous judgment of the four great imams,[34] when not one of them had produced any work comparable to that of any one of the imams.

Much of Maulana Ihtisham-ul-Haq's dissent was aimed at the secretary of the commission, Dr. Khalifa 'Abdul Hakim, who wrote the introduction to the report (the rest of which was written by the president of the commission, a former chief justice of Pakistan, Mian Abdul Rashid). Khalifa 'Abdul Hakim died early in 1959, two years before the government of Pakistan passed the Muslim Family Laws Ordinance, embracing many of the commission's recommendations.[35]

Khalifa 'Abdul Hakim had been the director of the Institute of Islamic Culture in Lahore, a research organization supported by government funds, which published books in both English and Urdu that expressed modernist views of Islam. Its purpose seems to have been to counter conservative influences in general, and perhaps that of Maulana Maudoodi's party in particular. Khalifa 'Abdul Hakim had gathered around him a capable group of research workers, including Mohammed Mazheruddin Siddiqui and B. A. Dar. His own

[34] It should be understood that there has always been some divergence of opinions among Muslims on these matters. Both ibn Taimya (1263–1328) and ibn Kaiyim (1292–1350), for instance, opposed quick divorce. Orthodox ulamas have said of them that "their intellect was not equal to their knowledge . . . ," *Dissent*, p. 1583.

[35] Freeland Abbott, "Pakistan's New Marriage Law: A Reflection of Qur'anic Interpretation," *Asian Survey*, I, 11 (January, 1962), 26–32.

chief work was *Islamic Ideology*, described by one critic as "unoriginal, and much indebted to Iqbal," and by another as "the greatest Islamic book since the Qur'an." *Islamic Ideology*, in fact, remains one of the best statements in English of a reasoned, liberal expression of Islam; it is a philosophical synthesis of the ideas of Syed Ahmad Khan and Muhammad Iqbal, designed to persuade the Muslim agnostic of the validity of Islamic religious experience. 'Abdul Hakim developed some of Iqbal's ideas beyond the point to which Iqbal was willing to carry them, but perhaps the essential difference between the two was that Khalifa 'Abdul Hakim was almost thirty years younger than Muhammad Iqbal. Otherwise, each was a philosopher by training, and each had made a deep study of Persian mysticism. 'Abdul Hakim was an acknowledged authority on Iqbal and his thought.

It being the aim of 'Abdul Hakim to avoid politics, he never established any organization. His influence was undoubtedly weakened because his institute was supported by the government, but he was content to direct it (and the Iqbal Academy associated with it) and shun attention. At least twice he stepped out of this retiring role—once, during the period of the Punjab disturbances, to write, at the request of the Punjab government, a pamphlet on Iqbal and the mullahs, and again when he accepted the position as secretary to the Family Laws Commission.

'Abdul Hakim's traditionalist critics accuse him of reading into the Qur'an whatever he chose; the same criticism was made of Syed Ahmad Khan, and for much the same reason. Khalifa 'Abdul Hakim asserted:

Islam is not the name of any static mode or pattern of life; it is spirit and not body; it is an aspiration and not any temporal or rigid fulfillment. The essence of life is constituted of Perma-

nence and Change. The ideal only is permanent; the changes or
the regulations that deal with particular situations of a particular
epoch can never assume the status of the Ideal. Land and Capital
mean different things in different epochs; the mode of handling
them too must change accordingly.[36]

The trouble with the traditionalists, in 'Abdul Hakim's view,
was that they had confused the permanent Ideal with the temporary regulations.

'Abdul Hakim was essentially a transcendentalist—a rare
thing among modernists, who tend to deny (or at least to ignore) the transcendental idea. He saw in Nature a graded existence: matter, life, animal mind, human mind, each of which
seems supernatural to that below it. The laws of the lower
grades do not apply to the higher, but the higher incorporates
the lower within it.

This is our realm of common experience and there is nothing
irrational in the religious belief which extends the gradations of
being still further and asks us to believe that Nature is not exhausted in our experience gradations; it extends from matter to
God. And if the lower is taken up, transformed and transcended
by the higher and not superseded and annihilated by the emergence of the higher, then entire Nature must be somehow absorbed in the Nature of God who is immanent in it and also
transcends it.[37]

Few traditionalists, incidentally, would find much to criticize
in Khalifa 'Abdul Hakim's philosophical arguments for religion, provided they were not pushed into pantheism, as
Jalal al-din Rumi did with similar thoughts.

[36] Dr. Khalifa 'Abdul Hakim, *Fundamental Human Rights* (Lahore,
1952), p. 24.
[37] Hakim, *Islamic Ideology*, p. 19.

'Abdul Hakim believed that religious truth, like scientific truth, progresses from error to error. Both the study of science and the study of religion express fundamental human needs, but the only value with which science is concerned is that of phenomenal truth; when science begins to speculate on absolute beginnings and endings, it enters the domain of religion. On the other hand, the end of scientific inquiry is not reached when science does frame its ultimate postulates, but rather a stable basis is thus created from which further advance can continue. The case of religion is similar: once its fundamental postulate has been achieved, spiritual progress will remain indefinitely open to mankind. It is the teaching of Islam, Khalifa 'Abdul Hakim maintained, "that religion reached its ultimate postulate when it taught humanity to worship one Good God and man has to assimilate His attributes of goodness within human limitations." [38]

The ultimate religious postulate is that one God, a creative, sustaining, and loving God, exists; from this is derived the necessary corollary of human morality. All Reality is one, and it is governed by an order which is at once rational, moral, and the preserver of all real values. This is the fundamental postulate of the Qur'an as it is the fundamental postulate of all true religion. The real meaning of the expression "Muhammad is the Seal of the Prophets" is that Muhammad had expressed this ultimate religious postulate—no one who followed him could possibly add to it. 'Abdul Hakim emphasized, too, that the essential point is belief in the One God. This is the meaning to him of the qur'anic passage, "Whoever directs his whole being towards God and does good to man, he is saved. For him there shall be no fear or grief." [39]

[38] *Ibid.*, pp. 9–10.
[39] 2:112.

The traditionalist would dispute the meaning of the phrase "directs his whole being towards God," maintaining that the only evidence of such wholehearted direction would be the proper observation of ritual. Not so to Khalifa 'Abdul Hakim. He was fond of quoting the story of the great mystic, Jalal al-din Rumi, who spoke of the external forms of religion as bare bones—the flesh and the blood and the soul lay elsewhere.

It was the dully literal, unimaginative approach of the mullahs as a class that as much as anything ensured the decline of Islam, 'Abdul Hakim believed. A literal approach had been deliberately adopted as a security measure in those dark days when the Muslim community was being weakened by internal troubles and by invasions from without, and when the activities of second-rate commentators could only add to the cultural confusion. To save the structure of Muslim law such inept commentators had to be stopped. But that which was expedient became permanent, and as a result Islam practically lithified. Now, Khalifa 'Abdul Hakim maintained, Islam lies buried beneath "heaps of retrograde legalism and life-thwarting practices," its spirit smothered by centuries of clericalism and despotism—centuries during which the West adapted itself to new knowledge and began to describe Islam as an "outworn creed incapable of adaptation to changing circumstances." [40] Such a statement as this, of course, could not fail to elicit a response from the traditionalists, who maintained that modernist Muslims had sacrificed their faith "on the altar of blind imitation of the West" and in the name of elasticity wanted to change every Islamic value which did not accord with western life. The traditionalists, in short, accused the modernists of "blind following" in much the same way as the

[40] *Marriage Commission Report,* p. 1200.

modernists had accused the traditionalists.[41] The traditionalists viewed this as anti-Islamic. Many individuals with modernist tendencies who could find no uniquely Islamic value
in their society, or who tended to identify religion with
ethics, did become thoroughly agnostic.[42] The slogan, "Islam,
Qur'an, Iqbal," one university professor said, is approved by
many individuals who do not know what Islam is, what the
Qur'an means, or what Iqbal said. The professor himself believed that in the modern world religious feeling was dead.

Khalifa 'Abdul Hakim wanted to show, above all, that
there was a place in the modern world for genuine religious
feeling. The early centuries of Islam, he argued, were dynamic, creative, and formative. They produced eminent jurists who, faced with problems unforeseen by the Prophet,
did not hesitate to develop new rulings based on "liberal interpretations, analogy, equity, and commonweal." [43] But mo-
narchical and "feudal" influences, and the resulting apathy of
the custodians of the law, sapped Muslim society. It grew
dormant and stagnant; the natural process that served to rejuvenate Muslim society was thus smothered, and undue rev-
erence for the past became an article of faith. Independent
judgment in legal matters was prohibited, and the Muslim
peoples retreated farther into reaction, because they were unwilling to appreciate the significance of changing realities and
the introduction of new factors. "Islam," Khalifa 'Abdul Ha-

[41] See *Marriage Commission Dissent,* p. 1572.

[42] A strictly social definition of religion, for instance, appeared in
an article by Jagadish Chaudra Dhali, "Teachers' role in preaching
religions," *Education: The Official Organ of the East Pakistan
Teachers' Association,* IX (no. 12), p. 3. "Religion is that which
uplifts mankind. To be honest in word and deeds is the sign of a
religious man. Nay, to devote oneself to the service of humanity and
to sacrifice self-interest for the good of common people are religious."

[43] *Marriage Commission Report,* p. 1201.

kim wrote, "does not insist on belief in any dogma which is to be believed without evidence or against the dictates of reason, observation and experience."[44]

'Abdul Hakim provided a philosophical basis on which Islamic modernism in Pakistan might build, although his influence in this respect seems to have been slight. He was too philosophical to attract a wide audience (he had been head of the department of philosophy, as well as Dean, at Osmania University, Hyderabad, Deccan). This was unfortunate, for 'Abdul Hakim was trying to do something most religious liberals in Pakistan were not. He was trying to express his rationale of Islam in positive terms. He was not an apologist, but neither was he a great crusader; he was a strategist who, while indicating lines of defense and attack, chose to keep as far as possible from the battle. Many more people must have read his ideas as they were expressed in the introduction to the Family Laws Commission report than ever read his *Islamic Ideology*. But 'Abdul Hakim built on Syed Ahmad Khan and Muhammad Iqbal, and the spirit of these men, if not their actual ideas, had become general throughout much of the educated classes in Pakistan. Consequently, the approach of Khalifa 'Abdul Hakim was much like that of every other modernist; it had become almost unconsciously accepted throughout Pakistan—East and West—by those Muslims with modern leanings.[45]

Modernism, of course, contained many variations. Khalifa 'Abdul Hakim represented something close to a rational sufism; Ghulam Ahmad Parwez seems not to have been touched

[44] Hakim, *Islamic Ideology*, p. xiii.

[45] Such expressions may be found, for example, in Abul Hashim, *The Creed of Islam* (Dacca, 1950); Syed Abdul Latif, *The Mind Al-Quran Builds* (Hyderabad-Deccan, 1952); Ghulam Jilani Burque, *The Religion of Humanity* (Lahore, 1956); or in *The Jamia Educational Quarterly*, III, 1 (January, 1962).

with mysticism. Parwez, a civil service officer who resigned in 1959 to devote his full time to religious studies, is the only modernist leader—if we except Maulana Maudoodi and the Ahmadiya—who has developed an organization. The Movement for the Establishment of a Quranic Social Order has a monthly publication, *Tolu-e-Islam,* founded in 1938, with a distribution apparently stabilized at about 3,000 copies.

Parwez no longer claims to be a follower of Iqbal, but except for one or two variations he seems to be in considerable agreement with the other modernist groups. He rejects Khalifa 'Abdul Hakim outright as primarily a philosopher and not a theologian. Like those of other modernists Parwez' points of variance with the traditionalists are actually not extensive. The principal difficulty, interestingly enough, is the same as that which estranged Mirza Ghulam Ahmad. The latter's new revelation—and the claims of prophethood which it involved—had ranged Muslim religious scholars against Mirza Ghulam Ahmad. It is Parwez' concept of revelation, too, that the traditionalists find most disturbing. Muhammad, Parwez says, was just the carrier of God's revelation; once he voiced it he was the same as any other man. Consequently, his governmental schemes, or his prayer forms, are no better than those of anyone else. As head of the state Muhammad had the power to determine how *zakat,* the alms tax, would be collected; every subsequent head of the state has the same power. Muhammad, except for his qur'anic message, is thus stripped of all power. He remains an individual whose social and individual behavior might well be copied, but no more than that of any other exemplary man. There is no real connection between Parwez in this respect and the Ahl-i-Qur'an; his rejection of hadith is a direct result of his concept of revelation, not because the hadith are in themselves unreliable.

Islam, Parwez asserts, is not a religion in the ordinary sense of the word. The Qur'an uses the expression *din* (pronounced *deen*), which means a way of life, something more than just the worship of the Almighty and the attempt to placate him with sacrifices, gifts, and ceremony. Din is a body of social law that must be followed in its entirety; it is the body of law that God has designed for man's development, and that has been preserved in the Qur'an.

The qur'anic concept of life, as distinct from the materialistic concept, views the development of Personality as the purpose of man's life. This is not, Parwez insists, mere spiritual advancement in the sense that other religions have expressed it, because the Qur'an says that in order to further the development of human Personality man must gain control of the physical world, have all that is required to maintain life, and lead a corporate life in a social order designed to develop his Personality. All this leads to his contention that the state must "make itself *responsible* for the development of every citizen, his Personality as well as his body." [46] This is an extremely interesting concept, for Parwez appears to be caught up in eighteenth-century humanitarianism, nineteenth-century science, and the twentieth-century welfare state. If so, he would not be unduly disturbed, because he believes something like this combination is what Islam is.

The secret of the qur'anic social order as expounded by Parwez lies in what he calls the two-sided relationship between the individual and the state: "The individual . . . in offering obedience to the laws of God surrenders, without any compensation, his life and property to the Islamic State, and in return the State assumes full responsibility for providing

[46] Ghulam Parwez, *Islamic Ideology* (Lahore, [c. 1959]) p. 13. This is a 30-page pamphlet by the Movement for the Establishment of a Qur'anic Social Order.

him the basic necessities of physical life and all the means required for the development of his Personality." [47]

The society that is formed from this total reliance on din
is that which will best promote the development of Personality. Islamic law at any period will be qur'anic law, plus
whatever may be required by the evolving conditions of the
particular time. A distinction is thus made between the permanent values—those parts of the law eternally fixed—and
those for which only general principles have been laid down.
These permanent values, or inviolable principles, form the
basic theme of the entire Qur'an. As enumerated by Parwez,
they include man's respect for man; his belief in the oneness
of humanity and in human freedom; cooperation in matters
that promote man's development; justice, that is, the right of
every citizen to be provided with work, the basic necessities
of life, and the means of development of his Personality; res-
toration of disturbed proportions, for example, by old age
pensions, or illness and accident insurance; public consultation
at all levels; the pooling of individual surpluses for the good of
all; and as capstone, the existence of a state that will, subject
to the inviolable laws of the Qur'an, champion the freedom
of individual will, enforce respect for the law, and stop with
a stern hand all unlawful activity.[48]

Parwez reached these principles by a zealous study of the
Qur'an, although some of his critics maintain that he has been
guilty of mistranslation. Certainly his reading of the Qur'an
supports his picture of Islamic ideology. The phrase, for instance, "and pay the zakat" is interpreted to mean "and develop the creative personalities of others as much as possible."

[47] *Ibid.*, p. 16.
[48] *Ibid.*, pp. 20–27. I am indebted for some of this material on Parwez
to Dr. Raymond Gastil of the Hudson Institute.

Such phrases as "praise God" and "pray to God" mean "develop the creative possibilities of your own personality as much as possible." The qur'anic injunction that seems to say "strike off the hand of the thief" should properly be read, Parwez maintains, as "prevent the hand from doing further damage"—in practice this might merely mean to place the hand, and its owner, in jail.

Parwez has attracted attention mostly because he advocates the abolition of private property, and because he has so completely discarded the hadith. Quite likely these two positions —the only basic differences from Khalifa 'Abdul Hakim— have determined the relatively small size of his organization. The question of the authenticity of hadith has proved disturbing to Muslims for centuries. Khalifa 'Abdul Hakim believed that the test of a hadith was the Qur'an—if the particular story agreed with the Qur'an, in particular or in spirit, it could be accepted; if it did not, it should be rejected. In fact, this is little different from Parwez' radical position, although its expression is more modest. Both men place ultimate authority in the Qur'an; Khalifa 'Abdul Hakim is pleased to find supporting hadiths, while Parwez does not particularly care. The application of such a test as this, of course, is dependent upon one's reading of the Qur'an, and nothing like unanimity of opinion concerning the body of hadith could ever be realized.

A similar problem was faced by Protestants after the Reformation, when, having abandoned all religious authority except the Bible, they were forced to find the substance for their beliefs in the Scripture. The result was a wide variety of sects, one emphasizing the importance of baptism by immersion, another emphasizing the importance of congregational organization, and so on, but the essential religious doctrines among these various sects do not seem to have varied widely.

Even Maulana Maudoodi's position on the hadith was not, at least at one time, so very different. The sunna, Maudoodi held, meant the conduct Muhammad was commissioned to teach and propagate. His personal habits, reflecting him as an individual in a given age and a given society, should be excluded. Social and cultural habits, he believed, fell under two categories, those containing moral principles Muhammad was trying to teach, and those practical forms which were, in part, the outcome of the Prophet's personal tastes, likes, and dislikes—forms that in themselves were dependent upon the customs and traditions of the Arabs of Muhammad's time. "It was not the Prophet's purpose to declare as his *Sunnat* all these forms of practical behaviour without regard to persons, nations, and socio-economic conditions." [49]

The specific subject that excited the most attention in the new State of Pakistan, and around which contention swirled boisterously, was the question of the nature of an Islamic state and of Islamic laws. In part this argument reflected a crude bid for political power, by modernists and traditionalists alike, but it also reflected genuine religious concern. One could practically sum up the difference between the two positions by noting that the modernists looked for general, and the latter for specific, guidance from the Qur'an and the sunna. An extended argument thus raged over the nature of the regulations that would make Pakistan an "Islamic state."

Nevertheless, the whole idea of an "Islamic state" seems to be comparatively recent; there never existed within Islam a political state following definite "Islamic regulations," and the modern idea of such a state cannot avoid including nationalistic elements that in themselves are comparatively recent. Some observers in Pakistan maintain that Muhammad himself

[49] Maudoodi, *Tafhimat* (Part I); translated by Mazher-ud-din Siddiqui.

shrank from specific, ironclad regulations. Aisha reported that whenever two alternatives faced the Prophet, he always took the easier: to do so is one of the undoubtedly valid principles of Islamic legislation that may be drawn from the Qur'an. Similar to it, in spirit, is the often-repeated qur'anic injunction that religion is not meant to add to man's burdens, but to lighten them, indicating that laws, too, should be designed in this light. A third principle, that of gradual development, or reform, may also be found, illustrated by Muhammad's stage-by-stage prohibition of intoxicating beverages, or his slow steps that seemed to be leading to the complete abandonment of slavery.

To go beyond these principles in developing what could be called a specifically "Islamic" political science seemed questionable; nevertheless, many words have been written purporting to detail highly intricate and specifically Islamic political systems. The application of all these systems, and their enforcement, turned on the legislature. Every Muslim agreed that Pakistan would be an Islamic state, although it meant different things to different Muslims. But whatever an Islamic state was, it would not pass laws repugnant to the Qur'an and the sunna. But who should decide whether or not specific legislation *was* so repugnant? On that point the government temporized; it was willing to grant concessions to the traditionalists, but not to surrender to them.[50]

Whether or not a law was repugnant depended upon one's concept of Islam. Who, then, should decide among rival interpretations? President Ayub Khan, hoping to find a simple, understandable statement of Islamic ideology that would serve to unite Pakistanis rather than divide them, urged scholars to define "in simple, brief but catchy language which will also

[50] See the discussion in Binder, pp. 315–344.

appeal to reason" the ideology of Islam.[51] The first response, from the son of Muhammad Iqbal, reflects an even more extreme modernist position than that taken by any of the individuals so far mentioned. Javid Iqbal, a Lahore barrister, and advocate in the High Court of West Pakistan, seems to represent the logical extension of the Muslim modernist movement in Pakistan. Syed Ahmad Khan, Mirza Ghulam Ahmad, and Ameer Ali all represent the first stage of the Muslim response to the West, the stage of apologia; the second stage, that of a serious re-evaluation of Islam in terms of a new age, is best represented by Sir Muhammad Iqbal; the third stage, marked by a critical evaluation of the Muslim past—to end the escapist methods that have marked many Muslim scholars —may be indicated in Javid Iqbal. Muslims, he feels, have developed a penchant for a piecemeal approach to history; why, he asks, do they not recognize that they have been wrong? In India Muslims like to ignore all Mughuls but Aurangzeb, or all caliphs except Abu Bakr and 'Umar. Mahmud of Ghazni, Javid Iqbal notes, is cited by Muslims for his raids against the Hindus, but his raids into central Asia may have helped open the way for the Mongol invasions that proved so disastrous to the Islamic world. Unless Muslims are willing to approach their history critically, he believes, they will be subject to increasing forces of disruption.

Modern youth is revolting against the discipline of medieval Islam which, among other things, insists upon escapist analyses of history, according to Javid Iqbal, who sees the entire modernist movement in Islam in these terms. In a sense, he says, Sir Syed Ahmad Khan is a reaction from the Wahabis (de-

[51] Javid Iqbal, *The Ideology of Pakistan and Its Implementation* (Lahore, 1959), p. xii. The quotation is from the foreword by President Ayub Khan.

spite the influence Sayyid Ahmad Shahid seems to have had on him), just as Deoband is a reaction from Sir Syed. The romantic idea of Islam, marked by medieval discipline, is no longer valid, he maintains, and he cites the Khilafat movement following World War I in his support: when it failed the Muslims didn't know what to do. The revolt against discipline continues.

Javid Iqbal's book, in response to Ayub Khan's request, is really a commentary on his father's writings, although it is written from a background of law and politics rather than from one of poetry and philosophy. It has been harshly criticized by the traditionalists, who point out that in the entire book he "does not quote any Arabic or Persian authority of which he has a first-hand knowledge." [52] "God knows," one reviewer wrote, "where our *Intelligentsia* learnt to dabble in subjects which they have never studied. . . . But our *Intelligentsia* are ever ready to speak out with authority on any and every subject. A writer on the Law of Islam should be fully conversant with the legal literature of Islam which, unfortunately for our *Intelligentsia*, is enshrined in books written in Arabic, Persian and Urdu while English is the only language our *Intelligentsia* are interested in." The revolt against discipline seems also to involve not so much a revolt against but a changed attitude toward some of the traditional languages in which Muslim religious literature has been expressed. In a world in which commercial and industrial activity becomes increasingly important, so, too, do the languages of that activity. In non-Arabic lands the Arabic language is going the way of medieval Latin because youth prefer a different second language and, except for the linguistically gifted, there is not enough time to master a third language.

This poses a problem on which the traditionalists and the

[52] *Al-Islam*, March 15, 1960, p. 41.

modernists can never meet, for if Islam cannot really be understood except by those who have mastered Arabic, then a
gulf will always exist between the rulers of the State and the
interpreters of the faith—a distinction that theoretically, at
least, is inconceivable in Islam. Maulana Maudoodi believes
that Islam can be saved from a priesthood by making the study
of Arabic compulsory—then everyone would be able to read
the Qur'an authoritatively. Javid Iqbal posed an out-and-out
modernist solution to this problem. "Since each generation is
to solve its own problems," he wrote, "there is no reason why
the power to interpret the law of Islam should not be given
to the National Assembly." Obviously, he continued, such a
modern-day Muslim assembly would have little knowledge
of the subtleties of Islamic law, but this would not matter if
their instincts were healthy, and if—he quotes his father—
they have "the courage to rush into sun-lit space and do, even
by force, what the new conditions of life demanded." This
is the spirit that marks the central government of Pakistan
and has, with few exceptions, since its beginning. Although
the traditionalist leaders have been treated carefully, and although some policies may have been slowed in deference to
them and others nebulously expressed, few government policies have been abandoned. Maulana Maudoodi has fought
hard to promote his own political organization, dedicated to
a traditionalist conception of an Islamic state, but his wings
have been clipped whenever he seemed likely to develop real
strength. The traditionalist has not, in fact, since partition,
and particularly since the Punjab disturbances, been in a position to exercise real political power, although he can still fo-
ment trouble.

Javid Iqbal also proposes that if possibilities of erroneous
interpretation seem still to exist, the study of Islamic law
should be reformed in the light of modern jurisprudence. This

would produce a group of lawyers trained to interpret Islamic law "in the light of modern experience and the changed conditions of modern life." [53] With such lawyers sitting in the Assembly the likelihood of erroneous interpretation, he feels, would be greatly reduced. Obviously he places little stock in the traditionalist argument that the longer one studies the religious books, and only the religious books, the more competent he is to interpret them.

Javid Iqbal seems to view Islam very much as a nationalized church. The government, through a Ministry of Religious Affairs, would own all the mosques in the country and appoint all the imams, leaders in the mosques, who would be considered civil servants and receive a fixed salary, in somewhat the same manner as control was exerted in Revolutionary France under the Civil Constitution of the Clergy. A governmental license would be required to lead congregational prayers or to preach in the mosques.[54] Javid Iqbal believes that no hesitation should prevent making religion a vital organ of the state, because religion and the state are one. His juxtaposition is interesting, for the traditionalist would have said that no hesitation should prevent the state from being a vital organ of the religion. In medieval Europe the disorganized Christian state eventually asserted itself over the organized Christian church; in Pakistan an organized Islamic state is faced with a disorganized Islam. The state is trying to inject some organization, not in the sense of a hierarchy, but in the sense of a common response broad enough to assure unity for the state. This may, indeed, be necessary, although it also poses serious problems. Historically, because of its own lack of organization, Islam has always tended to take the organiza-

[53] Iqbal, p. 19.
[54] *Ibid.*, p. 22.

tional form that existed: an aesthetic base in Iran, a militaristic base in Turkey. Undoubtedly in much of India and Pakistan the rural imams in the past have been little more than Hindu priests in new garb.

The nature of an Islamic education in the modern world is one of the really decisive problems in Pakistan today. Pakistani society is clearly divided between two groups: supporters of those technologically-oriented individuals who think in terms of the schooling necessary for the modern complex state, and those who support the assertion of the primary value of religious education. To resolve this situation Javid Iqbal proposes that all imams not only be licensed by the government, but also be required to have degrees in theology from state-recognized universities, and to be trained social workers as well.[55] In time, under conditions such as these, the traditionalist scholar, the mujtahid, would doubtless practically disappear. The question remains, however, of the nature of the instruction to replace the teaching of the traditionalists and to cross the gap between the several divergent sects of Islam. Except for outlining a compulsory introduction to Islamic theology for schoolchildren, Javid Iqbal is silent on this. (Such compulsory instruction exists in Pakistan today.)

His emphasis, like that of almost every contemporary reformer, is basically social rather than religious. The attitude, incidentally, is to be found among such liberal sects in America today as the Unitarian-Universalists. To expound on the nature of God, or to explain what God is thinking, is not as appealing a subject for discussion as it once was; if God is Inscrutable and Unknowable then such discussion seems futile. The modernist, consequently, is left with man, and his approach to religion is largely ethical. "Religions which stress

[55] *Ibid.*, p. 27.

too much theological and metaphysical differences," one young Muslim wrote, "and maintain an exclusive attitude, ignoring the universal human values and decencies, will not be able to do much good to a world which is urgently in need of international sanity and human fellowship. Men can never agree on the nature of the Godhead and the nature of the afterlife." [56] This is as true for the advocate of liberal religion in the West as it is for the Muslim modernist. It is the route opened in Islam by Muhammad Iqbal through his new emphasis on the individual and his exposition of the Ideal Man.

It is a route opened, too, by an emphasis on humanitarianism springing from more sources than Iqbal alone. If one turns from contemplation of the nature of God to the nature of man, humanitarianism may be the natural result; but there must be strong secular forces at work, too. The Christian religion existed for almost two millennia before a strong humanitarian movement appeared in parts of Christendom in the eighteenth century. Here, too, it was part of a broader movement that stressed the importance of the individual, and grew from eighteenth-century rationalism with its revolutionary conceptions of the nature of God and of man. The direction of the young Muslim modernist in Pakistan is frequently toward what might be called a liberal unitarian humanism. This is not necessarily dissimilar from what some less liberal Muslims desire, although the latter often fail to realize that Islam is not likely to be both world-wide and Arabic in nature.

Some modernists find this tendency disturbing, however. Fazlur Rahman, director of the Central Institute of Islamic Research in Karachi, an institution authorized by the 1962 constitution of the Islamic Republic of Pakistan, once warned an audience:

[56] J. W. Syed, "Religious Belief in the Atomic Age," *The Jamia Educational Quarterly*, III, 1 (January, 1962), 50.

In fact, modern humanistic relativism and its consequent sectionalism—a prey to a myriad of whims—is the same kind of *shirk* and *kufr* against which Islam had risen in the first place. Modern humanists, in effect, say: "Religion and morality are, surely, at the service of mankind, for they satisfy human needs." We admit this; but we emphasize further that religion and morality *cannot serve* mankind *unless* they *rule* mankind, and are placed above man as such. This is exactly what the Qur'anic concept of "*ibada*" or "service to God" means.[57]

It may not be to the advantage of the State to encourage any attitude, however common it may or may not be, which merely equates Islam with other great religions. Pakistan was created to be an Islamic state. Ayub Khan once told an audience, "There are other Muslim countries, if they leave Islam they can still exist, but if you leave Islam we cannot exist. Our foundation is Islam."[58] This may mean only a state in which a Muslim majority determines its own fate, or it may mean a state in which positive principles of Islam are expounded and practiced. Much of the discussion about Islam has been in negative terms, in denouncing what are considered medieval forms or practices. The positive search has just begun, and sometimes the reformer seems to make his search in a strikingly negative way. He abandons the fixed forms of the traditionalists, he acknowledges that life is dynamic and that change is its essence, and he upholds Islam because it offers a code of life, fixed and eternal. The Muslim modernist in Pakistan is trying to reconcile his need for change with his need for something stable and substantial to which to cling.

No Muslim, modernist or traditionalist, is likely to deny that Islam offers a fixed code. Khalifa 'Abdul Hakim may be

[57] Dr. Fazler Rahman, "Presidential Remarks," *The Jamia Educational Quarterly*, III, 1 (January, 1962), 109.
[58] Pakistan *Times*, October 23, 1964.

taken as representative. Islam, he said, "is a complete code of
life based on a definite outlook on life." [59] The traditionalist
has that code; the modernist searches for it. The traditionalist
argues that when that code was neglected, Islam declined; the
modernist believes that the growing rigidity of interpretation
denied the heart and soul of that code, and Islam declined,
"fossilized into various specimens of orthodoxy," so much so,
that "Muslims too have become monopolists of salvation." [60]

Al-Majlis—an organization of conservative religious scholars set up to reconcile the different sects of Islam and to ex-
plore the "futility of Greek philosophy and establish the superiority of Islamic scholastic theology"—reflects a cardinal
difference between the modernist and the traditionalist.[61]
Such an attitude, so far as it is meant to promote Islam by
undermining the bases of the western heritage, reflects an
unawareness of the nature of modern thought. Greek philosophy has been extended, assimilated, adapted, outgrown—all
of these—by the modern world. The question of the futility
of Greek thought had meaning in the early days of the
Mu'tazila controversy; today it is tilting at windmills. The
vitality of the West lies in large part in the fact that it is a
mixture of East and West; it may be argued that one reason
for the decline of Islam was that it was not such a mixture.
A force propelling the modernist in Pakistan today is the
effectuation of it.

The dynamics of Islam are unlikely to be found along the
course charted by Al-Majlis. The validity of religious experience, whatever the faith, has to be found in contemporary
experience, has to be presented in terms of answers to contemporary questions: perhaps this is the *raison d'être* of re-

[59] Hakim, *Islamic Ideology*, p. xi.
[60] *Ibid.*, pp. xii, xiv.
[61] *Dawn*, March 31, 1960.

ligious change, and in this sense all religious faiths sit in the same boat today. In Pakistan, among those who are trying to think out their faith, it is a small minority, growing smaller, that seeks to turn back. The idea that the gates of independent judgment are closed is held only by the most intransigent traditionalists. Maulana Aminul Ehsan, head of the traditionalist Madrassah-i-Alia in Dacca, for instance, believes that the doors of independent judgment have never been closed. New questions are always arising, he says, that must be tested, and the testing must utilize all past sources. *Taqlid*, the following of a particular jurist, he believes to have marked the last period of Islamic jurisprudence, but it was only a period. Nevertheless, Maulana Ehsan does not believe that Hanifi law needs to be rewritten, although the prospect does not fill him with horror. Shah Waliullah, the fountainhead of the movement for *ijtihad*, is today endorsed by both modernists and fundamentalists.

The idea that the religion practiced in its early days was perfection itself, and that a return to this period is all that is necessary, is not now so frequently found. The exponents of this view—besides looking backward for their utopias—maintain that the greatest error of the West has been to measure moral heights by material gains. Increasingly the reply is heard that neither are moral heights measured by disease, malnutrition, and poverty. The young Muslim looks forward to his future, and because this is so, and because the benefits of material gains are obvious and enticing, the old ways of thinking—the scholastic syllogism or the abstruse theological argument—do not hold any appeal. One young Muslim, for example, remarked that for God to end revelation suddenly after he had begun it, was inconsistent with Him, and thus not likely. He was perhaps reflecting the softening effect of sufism as well as confidence in his own rational powers. It will be a long time, however, before the nature of revelation is openly debated.

The young Muslim represents a revolt against intellectual monopoly—a revolt that also motivated the Renaissance and the Reformation in Europe. In Pakistan traditionalist scholars who had established themselves as religious authority have been challenged by the laity and have been forced to give ground. This has happened before in the history of Islam, and with a change of government traditionalism has re-established itself, as with the defeat of the Mu'tazila; but that was an isolated and medieval world, and such a reversal, even if it were politically possible, seems highly unlikely today. The result is not so much a new Islam, as a re-expression of some of the religious insights of Muhammad. The modernists' ideas are often geared to the modern age, but they can often be found among Islamic thinkers of the past.

President Ayub Khan has been outspoken in disapproving of the traditional approach to Islam. During the 1964 election campaign he declared that the people of Pakistan were traditionalists by nature; they wanted to hang back and rely on their forefathers. The last thing in the world, Ayub said, that the average man wants to utilize is his thinking power—and "that was why the people were traditionalists." [62] In a real sense Ayub is the first individual who has undertaken the practical application of Iqbal's philosophy.

This practical application is reflected in several ways. Pakistan's constitution describes the nation as an "Islamic Republic," not an "Islamic state." The distinction not only limits, but orientates. Such terms as "basic principles of Islam" or "the essence of Islam" seem to be replacing the phrase "Holy Qur'an and sunna." President Ayub Khan rarely uses the latter phrase, probably because it is so difficult to know just

[62] Pakistan *Times,* November 27, 1964.

what the sunna includes, and because it seems to place its emphasis on the past. During a speech at Dacca, Ayub remarked that he would be only too glad if the laws of the country were brought in line with the Holy Qur'an and the sunna, but when the introductory speaker noted that under an Islamic system an amir was elected for life, Ayub quickly brushed the suggestion aside as being neither constitutional nor in the best interests of the country.[63] "Fear of God, love of humanity, sympathy for the neighbor, help to the poor, and care of the orphans—these," Ayub Khan has said again and again, "are the basic principles of Islam which can never perish." [64]

The distinction between other political leaders of Pakistan —including Mohamed Ali Jinnah—and Ayub Khan is that Ayub has dealt with specifics. Every leader has expressed himself in generalities, and most never got much beyond them. But when during the election campaign Ayub was asked what he had done to promote an Islamic constitution, he could reply that religious education was required for the first eight years for Muslims, that the 1962 constitution he had prepared contained Islamic clauses, that the Advisory Council on Islamic Ideology was functioning, and that the Islamic Research Institute was a going concern.[65]

Even when Ayub speaks in generalities on the basic principles of Islam his emphasis is not new. It is as old as Muhammad. A hadith in the collection assembled by ibn Hanbal records that when Muhammad was asked, "What is Islam?" he replied, "Purity of speech and hospitality."

"And what is faith?"

[63] *Ibid.*, November 8, 1964.
[64] See, for instance, his remarks on February 25, March 6, and May 3, 1959, and September 4, 1960.
[65] Pakistan *Times*, December 17, 1964.

"Patience and beneficence."

"And what is the best part of faith?"

"A kindly disposition." [66]

In the 1964 election, when Ayub Khan defeated a rather disparate coalition headed by Miss Fatimah Jinnah, he identified Islam with democracy, with nationalism, and with progress. Maulana Maudoodi and his Jama'at-i-Islami, of the opposition coalition, were identified with dictatorship, with opportunistic interpretations of the Qur'an, and with failure to realize the truly Islamic character of the people of Pakistan. These were arguments the Maulana found it difficult to answer, especially because the government controlled the press.[67] Maudoodi was also ridiculed (but not by Ayub) for supporting Miss Jinnah when he had previously given the opinion that a woman could not be head of an Islamic state. This argument was used continually throughout the campaign, and although it was effective, there is no doubt that the president in permitting its widespread use was stooping rather low.

Maulana Maudoodi had opposed the concept of nationalism in the pre-partition days. Ayub placed great weight on what he called "Muslim nationalism," and Allama Alauddin Siddiqui, the chairman of the Advisory Council on Islamic Ideology, had given it his approval. "Nationalism has good points in it as well as bad," he said. "But when we say Islamic nationalism we eliminate all bad points from it. By Islamic nationalism is meant love for Islam and the country both,

[66] Mirza Abu'l-Fazl, ed., *Sayings of the Prophet Muhammad* (Allahabad, 1924), no. 217, pp. 53–54. Only part of this hadith, to be found in the collection of Ahmad b. Hanbal, is reproduced here. It is a fine example of the kind of hadith that would appeal to Khalifa 'Abdul Hakim, although it is not to be found in any of the six favored collections of hadith.

[67] Pakistan *Times*, October 27, 1964.

without any ill will or malice for any religion or any nation or country." [68] One can argue that this, too, represents an opportunistic interpretation of the Qur'an, but one should remember that the Qur'an was a revelation for the Arabs, even though its message was universal. Ayub's "Islamic nationalism" seems well-grounded in precedent, too.

A deliberate attempt is being made to preserve the Islamic heritage, but what is to be preserved is being carefully selected, and even the selection has some bearing on the interpretation of the Qur'an. Selection, too, and forced interpretations are to be found in every religion; Jesus' words about the inability of a rich man to enter heaven may serve as one illustration of this. Within Islam in Pakistan the concept of polygamy, the injunctions against interest, the education of women (and the status of women in general), the phrase "no compulsion in religion," are all being reworked, as well as many others. These changes are assimilated by repetition as much as by anything—in schools, in newspapers, and by other means. Everything is tied in with the development of literacy, a point recognized by the Pakistani newspaper editor who remarked that the country needed education, not theological schools. This point bears more weight when one considers that, according to the 1961 census, almost half of the inhabitants of Pakistan are less than twenty years old, and only 16 per cent are over 45! Indeed, those simple statistics may explain the fundamental reason for the eventual success of the government in trying to achieve an understanding of Islam removed from medieval social customs. The opposition can express itself vigorously—in the case of the marriage law controversy it is doing so—but the bulk of future citizens will likely be persuaded by the government's voice.

The question is no longer: "Is there an Islamic reforma-

[68] *Ibid.*, October 23, 1964.

tion?" The reformation may be almost over. Religious change —reformation—is only a matter of slight changes in emphasis; it is not an overnight revolution for something called modernism. In India and Pakistan the traditionalist champions have not been able to fight everywhere at once, partly because they have been fighting themselves, and partly because they remain essentially scholastic in a nonscholastic world. They have become preoccupied in attacking only one facet of opposition argument—the morality of the West—while they ignore the constructive aspects of the West. This strategy fails increasingly because a sense of self-confidence and individual initiative is developing within the country. President Ayub has recalled the words of Muhammad, "Take what is clean; abstain from that which is unclean," in encouraging selective borrowing from non-Islamic civilizations.[69] But the presence of traditionalism does not indicate the absence of a reformation; the absence of all criticism does. The presence of criticism, however, implies self-confidence, individual respect, and perhaps even orientation.

Undoubtedly there has been a great deal of change of this sort in Pakistan, as there has been in India. What remains is for a "higher criticism" to appear—the ability to examine dispassionately the tenets of one's own faith.

Nevertheless, one cannot look for "higher criticism" until the reformers themselves become a less disparate lot, until the present defensive attitude disappears (the fundamental urge sometimes strikes an observer as being not so much to establish one's identity as a Muslim as to create an identity of separation from something), and very likely not until a renewed interest in theological problems themselves develop. A reformation requires a lay mind; the "higher criticism" demands

[69] Message to Afro-Asian Islam Conference, Bandung, Pakistan *Times*, March 6, 1965.

the theological mind at work on the new concepts provided by the reformation. In Pakistan religious change has so far been essentially juridical, but it has been definite and effective, and it shows no sign of slackening. The assault on juridical precepts crosses more than merely legal boundaries, however. Christianity at an early date adopted theoretical ideas and social attitudes which in the course of time became neither applicable nor acceptable. Highly developed theological arguments supported the story of creation, or the condoning of social inequality, until the demands of a new society made such positions untenable—a society that was commercially and industrially, rather than agriculturally, based, and that reflected the increase in man's knowledge. The Christian commitment to such ideas and attitudes, however, was so close and strong that often the religion itself was identified with a lack of sense of reality and a lot of superstition. The agnostics of the western world and the agnostics of Islamic Pakistan represent similar responses to the same question— only the religion is different. The role of the theologian in each religion becomes the same: to find some synthesis between the new society and the old faith. This may be done by redefining the faith in terms acceptable to the new age, at the price of ignoring much that may have been prized in the past, or in developing new explanations—new insights—in relation to old passages, or in establishing new emphases among ideas that may have long been latent, but which have always been present.

Pakistan has thus far produced few theologians to take their places among the modernists, but their appearance must soon be expected, unless the process of religious change has little in common among religions, or unless the idea of religion itself has no place in the modern world.

Bibliographical Essay

The best volumes for the reader interested in pursuing this subject further are *The Muslim Community of the Indo-Pakistan Subcontinent* (The Hague, 1962), by I. H. Qureshi; and *Studies in Islamic Culture in the Indian Environment* (Oxford, 1964), by Aziz Ahmad. A. T. Embree has prepared an English edition of much of S. M. Ikram's three-volume Urdu study, *Āb-i-Kawthar* (Lahore, 1952), *Mawj-i-Kawthar* (Karachi, 1958), and *Rūd-i-Kawthar* (Karachi, n.d.), titled *Muslim Civilization in India* (New York, 1964). With Sir Percival Spear, Ikram has published a useful summary, *The Cultural Heritage of Pakistan* (Karachi, 1955). Also excellent is *Islamic Surveys: 3*, by Kenneth Cragg, *Counsels in Contemporary Islam* (Edinburgh, 1965). The Islamic Research Institute in Karachi is presently preparing a multivolume cultural history of Pakistan.

There is no single book that does justice to the political development of Pakistan. The Pakistan Historical Society is currently engaged in preparing a four-volume *History of the Freedom Movement* (Karachi, 1957–), three volumes of which have appeared. Although uneven in quality and, like all such works, filled with special pleading, they are indispensable. Wilfred Cantwell Smith, *Islam in Modern India* (London, 1946), is another indispensable work; a kind of sequel appears in the chapter on Pakistan in his *Islam in the Modern World* (Princeton, 1957). Among the books that have appeared on Pakistan one might cite *Moslem Nationalism in India and Pakistan* (Washington, D. C., 1963), by Hafeez Malik; and *Pakistan, The Formative Phase* (Karachi, 1960), by Khalid bin Sayeed. The study by Leonard Binder, *Religion and Politics in Pakistan* (Berkeley, 1961), is a detailed analysis of the attempts to frame a constitution with the assistance of traditionalist religious groups.

The commentary on the Qur'an by Maulana Abul Kalam Azad is being translated by Dr. Syed Abdul Latif of Hyderabad, India, *The Tarjumān al-Qur'ān* (New York, 1962); there is no better introduction to the Qur'an than this. A liberal exposition of Islam is in Khalifa 'Abdul Hakim, *Islamic Ideology* (Lahore, 1953). *Islam—The Straight Path* (New York, 1958), edited by Kenneth Morgan, contains a chapter on Islam in Pakistan by Mazheruddin Siddiqui, one of the country's leading liberal thinkers. Sir Muhammad Iqbal, *The Reconstruction of Religious Thought in Islam* (Lahore, 1951), remains the basic book.

The two most recent books on this general subject are *The Indian Muslims* (London, 1967), by M. Mujeeb; and *Islamic Modernism in India and Pakistan, 1852–1964* (London, 1967), by Aziz Ahmad.

Index